European Homeland Security

This book examines the processes and factors shaping the development of homeland security policies in the European Union (EU), within the wider context of European integration.

The EU functions in a complex security environment, with perceived security threats from Islamist terrorists, migration and border security issues, and environmental problems. In order to deal with these, the EU has undertaken a number of actions, including the adoption of the European Security Strategy in 2003, the Information Management Strategy of 2009 and the Internal Security Strategy of 2010. However, despite such efforts to achieve a more concerted European action in the field of security, there are still many questions to be answered about whether the European approach is really a strategic one.

European Homeland Security addresses two major debates in relation to the development of homeland security in Europe. First, it reflects on the absence of 'homeland security' from European political debates and its potential consequences. Second, it examines the significant policy developments in the EU that suggest the influence of homeland security ideas, notably through policy transfer from the United States.

The book will be of great interest to students of European security and EU politics, terrorism and counter-terrorism, security studies and international relations.

Christian Kaunert is Senior Lecturer in EU Politics & International Relations at the University of Salford, Marie Curie Senior Research Fellow at the European University Institute, Florence, and Editor of the Journal for Contemporary European Research (JCER). He has previously published *European Internal Security: Towards Supranational Governance in the Area of Freedom, Security and Justice* (2010).

Sarah Léonard is Lecturer in International Security at the University of Salford, and Marie Curie Research Fellow, Sciences Po Paris, France. She is also Editor of the Journal of Contemporary European Research (JCER).

Patryk Pawlak is Research Fellow at the European Union Institute for Security Studies in Paris. He holds a PhD in Political Science from the European University Institute in Florence (EUISS). Prior to joining the EUISS, Patryk was a visiting scholar at numerous research institutions, including the Center for Transatlantic Relations (Washington, DC).

Contemporary Security Studies
Series Editors: James Gow and Rachel Kerr
King's College London

This series focuses on new research across the spectrum of international peace and security, in an era where each year throws up multiple examples of conflicts that present new security challenges in the world around them.

NATO's Secret Armies
Operation Gladio and terrorism in Western Europe
Daniele Ganser

The US, NATO and Military Burden-sharing
Peter Kent Forster and Stephen J. Cimbala

Russian Governance in the Twenty-first Century
Geo-strategy, geopolitics and new governance
Irina Isakova

The Foreign Office and Finland 1938–1940
Diplomatic sideshow
Craig Gerrard

Rethinking the Nature of War
Edited by Isabelle Duyvesteyn and Jan Angstrom

Perception and Reality in the Modern Yugoslav Conflict
Myth, falsehood and deceit 1991–1995
Brendan O'Shea

The Political Economy of Peacebuilding in Post-Dayton Bosnia
Tim Donais

The Distracted Eagle
The rift between America and old Europe
Peter H. Merkl

The Iraq War
European perspectives on politics, strategy and operations
Edited by Jan Hallenberg and Håkan Karlsson

Strategic Contest
Weapons proliferation and war in the greater Middle East
Richard L. Russell

Propaganda, the Press and Conflict
The Gulf War and Kosovo
David R. Willcox

Missile Defence
International, regional and national implications
Edited by Bertel Heurlin and Sten Rynning

European Homeland Security

A European strategy in the making?

**Edited by Christian Kaunert,
Sarah Léonard and Patryk Pawlak**

Routledge
Taylor & Francis Group

LONDON AND NEW YORK

First published 2012
by Routledge
2 Park Square, Milton Park, Abingdon, Oxon OX14 4RN

Simultaneously published in the USA and Canada
by Routledge
711 Third Avenue, New York, NY 10017

Routledge is an imprint of the Taylor & Francis Group, an informa business

British Library Cataloguing in Publication Data
A catalogue record for this book is available from the British Library

Library of Congress Cataloging-in-Publication Data
Library of Congress Cataloging-in-Publication Data
European homeland security : a European strategy in the making? /
edited by Christian Kaunert, Sarah Léonard and Patryk Pawlak.
   p. cm. – (Contemporary security studies ; 94)
   Includes bibliographical references and index.
   1. Security, International–Europe. 2. National security–Europe. 3.
Internal security–Europe. 4. Terrorism–Europe–Prevention. I.
Kaunert, Christian. II. Léonard, Sarah, 1978- III. Pawlak, Patryk.
JZ6009.E85.E88 2012
355'.03354–dc23

                                                            2011041479

ISBN: 978-0-415-67794-3 (hbk)
ISBN: 978-0-203-12245-7 (ebk)

Typeset in Baskerville
by Wearset Ltd, Boldon, Tyne and Wear

1006665876

Printed and bound in Great Britain by
TJ International Ltd, Padstow, Cornwall

Contents

Figures and tables

Figure

Tables

Contributors

Javier Argomaniz joined the St Andrews Centre for the Study of Terrorism and Political Violence (CSTPV) in 2009. His general research interests include international cooperation in counter-terrorism and the European Union (EU) security policies. He completed his PhD in International Relations at the University of Nottingham (United Kingdom). He has undertaken research in a variety of national and international projects, including a UK Home Office-funded national evaluation scheme, and has published in the areas of European Studies, Criminology and International Security.

Raphael Bossong is a Research Fellow at the Institute for Peace Research and Security Policy at the University of Hamburg (IFSH) (Germany), and was previously Research Associate at the Global Public Policy Institute, Berlin. His research interests include international security, European integration and crisis decision-making. Raphael Bossong holds a PhD from the London School of Economics and Political Science. In 2006–2008, he was a research assistant for the CHALLENGE international research project on EU security policy.

Christian Kaunert is Senior Lecturer in EU Politics and International Relations, University of Salford (United Kingdom) and Marie Curie Senior Research Fellow, Robert Schuman Centre for Advanced Studies, European University Institute, Florence (Italy). He holds a PhD from the University of Wales, Aberystwyth (United Kingdom). In 2010, he was a Visiting Research Fellow at the *Institut Barcelona d'Estudis Internacionals* (IBEI). His first monograph entitled *European Internal Security: Towards Supranational Governance in the Area of Freedom, Security and Justice* was published by Manchester University Press in 2010. He is editor of the *Journal of Contemporary European Research* (JCER), as well as a member of the executive committee of UACES.

Xymena Kurowska is Assistant Professor at the Central European University, Budapest (Hungary). She is an International Relations (IR) theorist interested in interpretive policy analysis and ethnographic methods as applied in IR and European studies research. She received her doctoral degree from the European University Institute, Florence (Italy). Her research focuses on interdisciplinary approaches to security studies and European foreign policy, including state-building. She has published her research in journals such as *Perspectives on European Politics and Society* and *European Foreign Affairs Review.*

Sarah Léonard is Lecturer in International Security at the University of Salford (United Kingdom) and Marie Curie Research Fellow at the Centre for European Studies of Sciences Po, Paris (France). She received her PhD from the University of Wales, Aberystwyth (United Kingdom). She was a Visiting Research Fellow at the *Institut Barcelona d'Estudis Internacionals* (IBEI) in 2010. She is also editor of the *Journal of Contemporary European Research* (JCER).

Alex MacKenzie is a PhD candidate at the Centre for European Security of the University of Salford (United Kingdom). He holds an MA in Intelligence and Security Studies from the University of Salford. His research interests include counter-terrorism, the external relations of counter-terrorism, and homeland security in Europe and in the United States. His first article was published in the *Journal of Contemporary European Research* (2010).

Patryk Pawlak is a Research Fellow at the European Union Institute for Security Studies (EUISS), Paris (France). He holds a PhD in Political Science from the European University Institute, Florence (Italy). At the EUISS, Patryk deals with EU–US relations, US domestic and foreign policies, and EU Justice and Home Affairs (in particular, its external dimension, border management and data protection). He has published articles in numerous peer-reviewed journals and contributed to several collective research and publication projects.

Ursula C. Schroeder is Lecturer in International Relations at the Free University Berlin (Germany). Previously, she pursued post-doctoral research at the German Institute for International and Security Affairs (SWP), Berlin and held a temporary lectureship at Humboldt University, Berlin. Ursula holds a PhD in Political and Social Sciences from the European University Institute, Florence (Italy). Ursula's current research focuses on the changing nature of international security assistance policies.

Cécile Wendling is a Research Fellow at the Institute for Strategic Research (IRSEM) of the French Ministry of Defence and teaches crisis management at Sciences Po, Paris (France). Her research areas include civilian and military crisis management, the comprehensive approach, the global commons, new threats and risks (cyber-attacks, pandemics). She holds a PhD in Political Science from the European University Institute, Florence (Italy). She worked for the European Commission Crisis Centre for civil protection (Monitoring and Information Centre) in 2007.

Preface

This book is about European homeland security, both conceptually and empirically. It highlights an interesting paradox. The term 'homeland security' is conspicuously absent from European political debates, most likely due to its controversial association with George W. Bush. Yet, significant EU policy developments suggest an influence of homeland security ideas, despite the lack of usage of this label. Thus, although 'homeland security' is not part of the EU's security rhetoric, we argue in this book that it is both appropriate and beneficial for researchers to use this concept to analyse various developments in EU security in recent years.

European Homeland Security is based on many discussions that the editors and the contributors to this book have shared. From exchanges over a glass of wine at various conferences to panels organised at the Annual Conference of the University Association for Contemporary European Studies (UACES), this book has taken shape through vivid intellectual exchanges. It is fair to say that the idea of using the concept of 'homeland security' to analyse European security policy developments was originally not warmly welcomed by all audiences. Some of the people attending our research panels rejected it out of hand due to its association with George W. Bush and accused us of promoting a neo-conservative political agenda. This is emphatically not the case. In this book, we argue that using the concept of 'homeland security' is beneficial because it highlights certain policy trends, which may not be identified otherwise. Furthermore, we show in this book that, despite the increasing prevalence of homeland security ideas, this process has not led to the adoption of any overarching strategy for European homeland security, not even under a different label. In contrast, we have witnessed the adoption of partially overlapping security strategies, including the European Security Strategy (ESS) and the Internal Security Strategy (ISS).

We are grateful to a great number of people – family members, friends and colleagues – who have helped through the various stages of writing this book. Without these very special people, writing this book would have been impossible. In addition, Sarah Léonard and Christian Kaunert wish to thank the University of Salford for its support, as well as the European

Commission for funding their Marie Curie Intra-European Fellowships (within the 7th European Community Framework Programme) at Sciences Po, Paris and the European University Institute in Florence, respectively, while Patryk Pawlak wishes to thank the European Union Institute for Security Studies in Paris. All these institutions have supported us in this research project. While writing this book, we also benefited enormously from the comments and insights of numerous experts in the field. We would like to thank in particular John Occhipinti, Mark Rhinard, Thierry Balzacq and Oldřich Bureš. The support and expertise of UACES has also been outstanding. Furthermore, Sarah Léonard and Christian Kaunert are also very grateful for the constant support and the critical questioning of their ideas by their doctoral students Kamil Zwolski, Alex MacKenzie, Sergei Mudrov, Viviana Merendino, Briony Callander, Stephen Rozée and Ulrike Hoffmann. Sarah Léonard and Christian Kaunert would also like to thank IBEI, the *Institut Barcelona d'Estudis Internacionals*, for its support during their respective research fellowships while they had the good fortune to be on sabbatical from the University of Salford in 2010. Moreover, throughout the entire publication process, Andrew Humphreys at Routledge provided extremely useful comments and suggestions. The support by Annabelle Harris at Routledge was also exceptional and very much appreciated. Finally, we thank three anonymous reviewers for their helpful comments and suggestions.

Christian Kaunert, Sarah Léonard and Patryk Pawlak

Florence/Paris

1 Introduction

European homeland security – a European strategy in the making?

Christian Kaunert, Sarah Léonard and Patryk Pawlak

On 7 July 2005, four young Islamist suicide-bombers attacked London's transport system, killing 52 members of the public and injuring several hundreds more. The London bombings were the first attacks on British soil to be carried out as part of the global *jihad*, but had been preceded by other major terrorist attacks on the United States (US) on 11 September 2001 and on Spain on 11 March 2004. Despite setbacks, militants have continued to plan attacks, as evidenced by the 2007 suicide attack on Glasgow airport. In October 2010, warnings against terrorist attacks were issued in France, Germany and other European countries. Subsequently, a package sent from Yemen and containing a bomb device, which had been designed to go off on a US-bound aircraft, was intercepted at East Midlands Airport in the United Kingdom (UK) (BBC News 2010). As highlighted by Europol's (2011) 'EU Terrorism Situation and Trend Report' (TE-SAT 2011), Islamist terrorism remains a 'high and diverse' threat to European Union (EU) Member States (Europol 2011: 6).

In November 2010, Greece saw the arrival of a large number of irregular migrants and asylum-seekers at the Greek–Turkish border and requested EU support to strengthen its border controls. In response, Frontex, the EU External Borders Agency, coordinated the deployment of more than 150 armed border guards from a large number of EU Member States. Those border guards, who were part of so-called Rapid Border Intervention Teams (RABITs), conducted 24-hour joint surveillance with their Greek colleagues at the land border with Turkey (Frontex 2010b). Italy also requested EU support in February 2011 following the arrival of about 3,000 irregular migrants and asylum-seekers on the Italian coast in the space of a few days, most of whom were heading from Tunisia. EU support mainly took the form of a joint patrolling operation in the Central Mediterranean area, called 'Joint Operation Hermes 2011' and coordinated by Frontex, which was designed to enhance border surveillance (Frontex 2011). Those are only two recent examples of the numerous tasks conducted by Frontex, which has proved to be one of the most dynamic of all EU agencies.

In 1999, the tanker *Erika* had sunk off the coast of France causing one of the greatest environmental disasters in the world (BBC News 2000).

Three years later, another massive oil spill affected the coastlines of several EU Member States following the sinking of the *Prestige* (BBC News 2002). In 2006, heavy rain and melting snow caused significant floods in Serbia, Bulgaria and Romania (BBC News 2006), while severe fires in Greece forced thousands of people to abandon their home in 2009 (BBC News 2009). In October 2010, the Hungarian government had to declare a state of emergency after toxic sludge had leaked from an alumina factory (*Guardian* 2010). Thus, various natural and man-made disasters hit Europe every year calling for a concerted and effective European response.

These examples underline the complexity of the security environment in which the EU operates. In order to tackle these challenges, the EU Member States have undertaken a number of actions, including, among others, the adoption of the European Security Strategy (ESS) in 2003 (which was updated in 2008), the Information Management Strategy (IMS) for EU internal security of 2009 and the Internal Security Strategy (ISS) of 2010. However, despite these efforts aiming to achieve more concerted European action in the field of security, it is not clear to what extent the EU's approach to these security challenges can be considered to be strategic. Indeed, can it be seen as strategic if several security aspects are addressed separately, rather than in the framework of a more general 'homeland security' policy? What would be the potential benefits of examining and conceptualising the EU's security policies as part of 'homeland security', rather than fragmented 'internal security' policies? These are some of the major questions that this edited book addresses. Previous studies have tended to examine empirical developments in specific policy areas (see, for example, Kurowska and Pawlak 2009a; Wolff *et al.* 2009a; Kaunert and Léonard 2010), while conceptual debates have tended to focus on the nexus between internal and external security (Bigo 2000; Eriksson and Rhinard 2009; Balzacq 2009). However, it is also necessary to ask broader questions, notably about the political community that is being secured by security policies and the overall direction of the European integration process. This book puts forward the idea that using the concept of 'homeland security' can illuminate various EU policy developments in interesting ways, despite its cultural and political connotations, which are fully acknowledged and will be explored later.

This book puts forward three main arguments. First, it shows that, although 'homeland security' as a term has been largely absent from European political debates, there have been significant policy developments in the EU in recent years that suggest the influence of homeland security ideas, notably through policy transfer from the US to the EU. This also means, and this is the second argument put forward by the book, that 'homeland security' is an appropriate concept for analysing various policy developments in EU security in recent years, although it is not part of the EU's security rhetoric. This book also argues that using this concept has the advantage of highlighting certain trends, which could not be identified otherwise. Finally, the third argument developed in this book is that, although homeland security ideas have implicitly underpinned EU policy developments to a significant extent in recent years, the EU Member States have not adopted any overarching strategy for European homeland security yet. On the contrary, European homeland security has seen a plethora of policy initiatives, which have led to the adoption of partially overlapping security strategies, including the European Security Strategy (ESS) and the ISS.

The emergence of 'homeland security' on the US political agenda

Crenshaw (2005) has argued that US policy-makers have long recognised the dangers of terrorism. After the Iran hostage crisis, President Reagan entered office with terrorism being at the top of the political agenda. President Clinton was also concerned about terrorism after the attacks on the World Trade Center in 1993 and on Oklahoma City. Thus, there was general awareness of the terrorist threat in the US, but not of the threat posed by Al-Qaeda in particular (Crenshaw 2005). It all changed on 11 September 2001, which saw the worst event of modern international terrorism, with nearly 3,000 people being killed (Martin 2006; Hoffman 2006). Many commentators instantly drew a parallel with the Japanese attack on Pearl Harbor on 7 December 1941. As a result, 'homeland security' gained an increasingly significant place as both a rhetorical tool and an important policy area in the US and beyond (Cameron 2007).

Its significance is confirmed by its high profile at all levels of the governmental and societal agendas. Both the private and public sectors now devote a lot of attention, as well as human and material resources, to 'homeland security'. The Patriot Act virtually abandoned post-Cold War-era barriers between foreign intelligence and domestic law enforcement. Major structural and institutional changes have been undertaken at the state and local levels. In particular, the decision of President George W. Bush to create the Department of Homeland Security (DHS) in 2002 was seen as 'the most ambitious effort to recognise and expand the federal government in the area of foreign policy since 1947' (Rosati 2004: 211). Pennsylvania Governor Tom Ridge was named as the first office holder. His mission was defined, in George W. Bush's words, as to 'lead, oversee, and coordinate a comprehensive national strategy to safeguard our country against terrorism and respond to any attacks that may come' (Relyea 2002a: 400).

According to several scholars, the idea of 'homeland security' is rooted in historical efforts of civil defence (Relyea 2002a, 2002b; Seiple 2002; Bullock *et al.* 2006). US President Bush recognised this in his address on homeland security on 8 November 2001 (cited in Relyea 2002b: 218): 'We will ask state and local officials to create a new modern civil defense service, similar to local volunteer fire departments, to respond to local emergencies when the manpower of governments is stretching thin'. Civil defence began during the First World War, but due to the lack of a real threat of air attacks on the US, it did not develop in the US until May 1941 (Bullock *et al.* 2006). As the war ended, the US Administration examined the successes of British, German and Japanese civil defence. The new Office for Civil Defense Planning adopted a document entitled 'Civil Defense for National Security' (Relyea 2002b: 218), which served as a programme for the Cold War era. However, with the end of the Soviet Union, civil defence as a concept also became a relic in the US.

In light of these developments, Relyea (2002a: 397) critically observes that 'homeland security' may be a substitute for the Cold War-weary 'national security' concept, 'devoid of its intellectual development, but prone to the same use as a justification for the exercise of prerogative powers in ways harmful to constitutional arrangements of government and guaranteed citizens' rights'. He suggests that some might regard this concept as being unpleasantly linked to past nationalist invocations of the 'fatherland' or the 'motherland', and therefore possibly reminiscent of national leaders pursuing cultural or racial purity, such as Hitler or Stalin. This is emphatically not the understanding of 'homeland security' underpinning this book, which emphasises that importing 'homeland security' into political and academic debates in Europe has both advantages and drawbacks. It is therefore necessary to critically reflect on the concept of 'homeland'.

Smith (1981) refers to the concept of 'homeland' in a triangular relationship between culture, state and territory. He identifies four dimensions to the homeland: boundaries, culture, self-sustainability and nation-building. In the US, after 9/11, homeland security also included a 'concerted national effort', implying that the former is not only the task of governmental agencies, but actually of the entire society, including the federal government, state and local authorities, the private sector and the American people. Why was a mere reference to the territory not enough to mobilise society? Why was it seen as necessary to frame the policy problem as a 'national' one, which includes a discussion about homeland, territory and ethnicity? While a 'territory' is the underlying feature of autonomous and abstract institutions within a modern state, a 'homeland' constitutes a space on the basis of which a sense of given historic community emerges as a modern nation (Smith 1981: 187). Therefore, speaking in terms of 'homeland security' has the advantage of capturing the important symbolic dimension of the 'homeland' with regard to political cohesion and nation-building.

'Homeland security' in Europe

One of the major characteristics of the European approach to homeland security rests on the fact that there has been hardly any effort on the part of EU policy-makers to mobilise society towards the protection of a 'homeland'. In contrast, there have been more sustained efforts towards the definition of an EU territory through the deployment of a wide range of border control practices, as discussed by Pawlak and Kurowska later in this book, and the establishment of the External Borders Agency Frontex, which is the object of Léonard's chapter. Thus, while the EU does not have a clearly defined territory in principle because of repeated enlargements and the lack of statehood, it is undergoing a process of territorial construction, which occurs against security threats, both external and internal.

There is no clear indication of what a European homeland might mean for Europeans, other than the treaty provision stating that '[the] Union shall offer its citizens an area of freedom, security and justice without internal frontiers, in which the free movement of persons is ensured in conjunction with appropriate measures with respect to external border controls, asylum, immigration and the prevention and combating of crime (Article 3 of the Treaty on European Union (TEU)). Therefore, rather than aiming to create a big platform of support for the European homeland, the EU sees itself as the one responsible for the provision of security – the 'guardian of the people' (Mitsilegas *et al.* 2003).

The complexity of this situation is compounded by the fact that the EU does not squarely fit within accepted categories of political organisation: less than a 'federation', but more than a mere 'regime'. Most modern states sought and achieved national political communities out of diverse groups living within their borders (Linklater 1998). While this political community-building process is at the heart of the European integration process, it is still rather under construction. The EU has already made concerted efforts to prevent war and violence by building a new form of international political community, which erodes many of the traditional monopoly powers of the nation-state. However, attempts to define the territory through the twin processes of integration and enlargement have also created instances of 'variable geometry'. Through various opt-outs, opt-ins (concerning the UK, Ireland and Denmark) and intergovernmental agreements, such as the Schengen and Prüm Conventions, attempts at defining the EU territory have been accompanied by trends obscuring this very definition.

It can be argued that a 'European Homeland Security Area' is emerging, which has a broader thematic and institutional scope than the Area of Freedom, Security and Justice (AFSJ). The new security environment that appeared in the aftermath of the 9/11 terrorist attacks has led to the development of a security dimension in a growing number of policy areas, such as asylum and migration, transport, critical infrastructure protection and civilian crisis management among others. The official EU terminology, however, imposes borders that are unnecessary from an analytical point of view, as a term such as the 'AFSJ' leaves aside issues such as transport or customs policy, which constitute important functional elements of homeland security. As the concept of 'homeland security' has not been very well received in Europe (Dubois 2002), the more traditional terms of 'Justice and Home Affairs', 'Justice, Liberty and Security' or 'Area of Freedom, Security and Justice' are still predominant. However, although it is slightly different from the term 'homeland', it is interesting to note that 'European Home Affairs' is increasingly used. This was notably the case in the final report of the so-called 'Future Group' (2008). Also, the 'Justice, Liberty, and Security' Directorate-General (DG) in the Commission has recently been split into two new DGs (Justice (JUST) and Home Affairs (HOME)).

Moreover, the scholarly investigation of these developments has generally contributed to preserving the image of European homeland security as a highly disintegrated area, politically, functionally and academically. Most scholars tend to focus on only one of the aforementioned elements, such as asylum and migration or civil crisis management. Policies that cut across a large range of policy sectors such as counter-terrorism are also frequently disaggregated to allow for a fine-grained analysis of one of its dimensions (for exceptions, see Bures 2011 and Argomaniz 2011). This is understandable given the fast pace at which each of these policies has been growing and the level of expertise required for analysing them. However, such a disaggregated approach has the drawback of not addressing questions regarding the 'big picture', such as the development of European integration.

Neofunctionalism (Haas 1958) defines European integration as 'the process whereby political actors in several distinct national settings are persuaded to shift their loyalties, expectations and political activities towards a new center, whose institutions possess or demand jurisdiction over pre-existing national states' (Haas 1958: 16). The 'loyalty' of the citizens of a community can shift towards a new political entity, notably supranational organisations such as the European Commission. Yet, opponents, on the other side of the conceptual debate, portray this differently. Moravcsik (1998, 1999) has portrayed the EU as largely intergovernmental and dominated by national interests. In his view, national leaders make choices in response to constraints and opportunities derived from economic interests of powerful domestic constituents and the relative power of each state in the international system. International institutions are merely there to bolster the credibility of interstate commitments (Moravcsik 1998). Thus, from this viewpoint, the EU strengthens the nation-state, rather than weakens it. This classic debate over the nature of EU integration can usefully inform the analysis of the development of European homeland security.

Towards European homeland security?

This book starts from the premise that the integration process in European internal security could progress towards the idea of homeland security as set out above, i.e. as security for a new kind of political community. Cooperation on various security matters was already taking place on the basis of bilateral contacts and within multilateral organisations even prior to the adoption of the Maastricht Treaty in 1992 (Kaunert 2005). Several international conventions have been adopted in the frameworks of the United Nations (UN)[1] and the Council of Europe,[2] while cooperation has also developed in the framework of Interpol[3] and the Organization for Economic Cooperation and Development (OECD) Financial Action Task Force (FATF).[4] The increased international activity in these multilateral forums coincides with the development of intergovernmental security cooperation between EU Member States. In 1976, 12 twelve countries agreed to establish a group composed of their Home Affairs ministers, tasked with coordinating police cooperation and counter-terrorism efforts, which was known as the TREVI Group. The intergovernmental nature of this group meant that European institutions were not significantly engaged in its works. The adoption of the Single European Act, and the framing of the free movement of persons as one of the key elements of the Single Market, was a breakthrough. It began to shift the aforementioned cooperation towards the Community institutions. Consequently, new working groups established in the area of immigration, drugs and customs included representatives of the European Commission. The abolition of internal borders stimulated a discussion about giving more powers to the European Community, but it was not until the Maastricht Treaty that concrete decisions were taken. Until then, EU cooperation progressed largely outside the EU structures through the adoption of classic international legal instruments, such as conventions, resolutions and recommendations.

The Maastricht Treaty brought about some changes, with the creation of 'Justice and Home Affairs' (JHA) as a new policy area (Kaunert 2005). JHA was defined as encompassing 'matters of common interest' such as asylum and immigration, the external borders of the EU, judicial cooperation in civil and penal matters, customs cooperation, police cooperation for fighting and preventing terrorism, drug trafficking and other serious forms of international crime, as well as combating drug addiction and international fraud. However, JHA was created as the third 'pillar' of the EU (alongside the second 'pillar' devoted to foreign and security policy), which was governed by different decision-making rules. According to the Maastricht Treaty, the JHA institutional arrangements were largely intergovernmental, with significant powers left to the EU Member States, and only a limited role for the EU institutions. The European Commission had to share the power of legislative initiative with the Member States, and was only to be 'associated' with the work in this policy area. The European

Parliament was to be regularly informed and in particular cases consulted on JHA policy developments. The fact that most decisions needed to be taken in the Council of Ministers by unanimity considerably slowed down policy developments in JHA under the Maastricht Treaty.

The adoption of the Amsterdam Treaty is of much larger significance (Kaunert 2005), as this treaty notably contained the new major objective of developing the EU as 'an area of freedom, security and justice' (AFSJ). Some policy areas shifted to the European Community pillar, such as the protection of external borders, asylum and the visa policy. Others remained in pillar III – namely the provisions on police and judicial cooperation on criminal matters, including closer cooperation between police forces, judicial authorities, customs authorities and other competent authorities in the Member States as well as the approximation of rules on criminal matters. On the basis of the Amsterdam Treaty, the EU also acquired competences to conclude agreements with third parties on behalf of its Member States.

These new institutional arrangements needed to be given a more precise policy purpose. The Tampere European Council in October 1999 gave the EU a policy direction to what had been hitherto a somewhat incoherent approach. Until then, debates had mainly focused on whether national sovereignty should be preserved or, in contrast, could also be pooled at the EU level with respect to these policy matters. The Tampere Council marked the beginning of increasingly in-depth debates on the exact aims and purposes of European cooperation in internal security. Here, opinions ranged from considering the AFSJ as an 'add-on' to the Single Market to envisaging it as a free-standing policy area (Kaunert 2005). The terrorist attacks on 11 September 2001 had an important impact on the development of the AFSJ. The European Commission played a significant part in the construction of a role for the EU with regard to internal security matters by acting as a 'supranational policy entrepreneur' (Kaunert 2007, 2009, 2010a, 2010c; Kaunert and Della Giovanna 2010).

The Lisbon Treaty further increases the potential for the development of this policy area, which could see tremendous growth in the years to come (Kaunert 2010b, 2010c) given the instruments that it has granted the EU. It is important, again, to underline the role of the European Commission in this process of constructing an AFSJ. Kaunert (2010c) has argued that the Commission, through alliances with other institutional actors, has managed to incrementally contribute to a shift in political norms towards an acceptance of EU pooling of national sovereignty, which manifested itself specifically during the negotiations of the Constitutional Treaty and the subsequent renegotiation of the Lisbon Treaty, resulting in these important developments.

Thus, following on from these institutional developments, one can note that the normative debate in this policy area has been structured between those wishing to preserve national sovereignty and those wishing to pool sovereignty at the EU level. Before the Maastricht Treaty in 1992, national sovereignty was safeguarded very closely. Internal security and the police were widely perceived to be vital and, indeed, core areas of the state. However, cooperation was increasingly perceived as an important counter-measure to the dismantling of internal borders at the heart of the Single Market. The Maastricht Treaty confirmed the preservation of national sovereignty and the purpose of cooperation as a flanking measure of the internal market. The Amsterdam Treaty in 1997 established for the first time the grand objective of an 'Area of Freedom, Security and Justice', but did not supranationalise the policy area. The main normative change was a shift away from a full preservation of national sovereignty towards a partial pooling of national sovereignty with limited mandates and weak institutional instruments and structures. This indicates some normative movement, albeit limited in nature. In addition, there was also some development on the axis of what the aims and the purpose of such legislation should be. Here, the evolution ranged from a flanking measure of the Single Market to a free-standing 'Area of Freedom, Justice and Security', separate from the Single Market. This trend was further reinforced by the Lisbon Treaty, which entered into force on 1 December 2009. This, however, may only be the first step towards a more significant shift towards a 'European Homeland Security Area', as illustrated by Figure 1.1 below.

In recent years, several key documents have also been adopted to guide the development of EU homeland security policies. Those include the Stockholm Programme of December 2009 (European Council 2010a), which is a multi-annual programme for the AFSJ that succeeds the Tampere Programme of 1999 (European Council 1999a) and the Hague

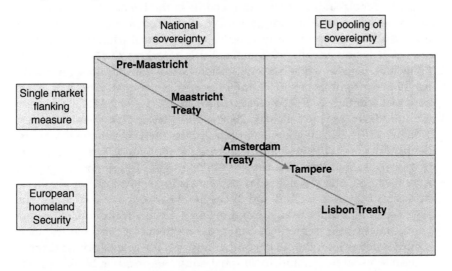

Figure 1.1 The norm matrix for the AFSJ.

Programme of 2004 (European Council 2004b). The EU Member States have also added new security strategies to the European Security Strategy of 2003 (European Council 2003b), in particular the Information Management Strategy (IMS) of 2009 (Council of the European Union 2009d) and the Internal Security Strategy of 2010 (European Council 2010b). The IMS aims 'to support, streamline and facilitate the management of information necessary to the competent authorities to ensure the EU internal security' (Council of the European Union 2009d: 3), while the ISS defines internal security as 'a wide and comprehensive concept which straddles multiple sectors in order to address these major threats and others which have a direct impact on the lives, safety, and well-being of citizens, including natural and man-made disasters such as forest fires, earthquakes, floods and storms' (European Council 2010b: 8). The major objective of the ISS is to 'to help drive Europe forward, bringing together existing activities and setting out the principles and guidelines for future action. It is designed to prevent crimes and increase the capacity to provide a timely and appropriate response to natural and man-made disasters through the effective development and management of adequate instruments' (European Council 2010b: 9). These key programmatic documents are examined in the various contributions gathered in this book and will also feature prominently in the concluding chapter. In that regard, the book l also examines the key question of whether the adoption of these various documents actually amounts to the development a coherent security strategy for the EU.

About this book

While the scholarship on homeland security in the US has developed at an extraordinary pace, as shown by Pawlak in the next chapter, scholarship devoted to homeland security in Europe still remains limited. Where it does exist – and usually without explicitly referring to the concept of 'homeland security' – it consists of a patchwork of contributions representing different approaches to counter-terrorism, emergency management, or, broadly defined, 'JHA' policies (now known as the 'AFSJ') (see, for example, Kurowska and Pawlak 2009a; Wolff *et al.* 2009a; Kaunert and Léonard 2010). This book aims to look across these specific policy areas, identify horizontal themes and investigate the 'politics of European security' (Kurowska and Pawlak 2009b). It offers insights into the processes and factors shaping the development of homeland security in the EU. The various contributions identify and discuss both endogenous and exogenous factors shaping European homeland security, i.e. the institutional arrangements, the interests of Member States, the influence of third parties, such as third states or international organisations, and the role of private actors.

Despite its strengths and its original contributions, this book also has some limitations, which it is important to acknowledge. In particular, this book is only a first step towards the development of a more systematic research agenda on European homeland security. In particular, due to space constraints, it has not been possible to include in this book some policy issues that would also fall under the umbrella of 'homeland security', such as pandemics and threats to critical infrastructures and transportation systems. In addition, while this book underlines the analytical value of using the concept 'homeland security' for the purpose of analysing EU policy, it needs to be acknowledged that this approach carries some political risks. Due to its prominence under the Bush Administration in the US, 'homeland security' is often perceived to be closely connected with a 'neo-conservative' terminology. Actually, this is historically inaccurate, as the concept finds its origins in the two World Wars (Relyea 2002a, 2002b; Seiple 2002; Bullock *et al.* 2006). In addition, it is important to emphasise that this book does not use this concept to suggest that connections with nationalist rhetoric is desirable. In fact, all contributors reject any linkages with possible misinterpretations of 'homeland security'. In this book, the concept is used as an analytical device, and not a political rhetorical tool. It is argued that it is an analytical device particularly well-suited to analysing inter-linking policy areas, which, as a whole, all contribute to the creation of a post-sovereign political community in Europe.

This book addresses three major themes. First, it examines the concept of 'homeland security' in general and in relation to the various security strategies that have been adopted by the EU. The first chapter by Pawlak underlines the benefits of conceptualising EU internal security policies under the umbrella term of 'homeland security'. Intentionally or unintentionally, the introduction of 'homeland security' into a political debate raises important questions about our societies. As a consequence, conceptual debates about homeland security have shaken fundamental concepts, such as sovereignty and borders. At the same time, one has seen a rise in the acceptance by society of internal security policy measures, such as increased surveillance and the erosion of civil liberties, which, under different circumstances, would have been difficult to implement. Nevertheless, while the Bush Administration in the US managed to implement far-reaching homeland security measures, this was more difficult in Europe, which sometimes led to transatlantic tensions. Pawlak's contribution emphasise the importance of analysing how similar threat scenarios have given rise to different policy responses on both sides of the Atlantic.

The conceptual introduction in this book continues in the following chapter by Schroeder. She argues that the development of various EU security strategies has differed considerably from the comprehensive top-down overhaul of US security thinking after the 9/11 attacks. In contrast with the situation in the US, the EU did not radically depart from established security concepts and procedures. Instead, her chapter shows that EU security strategies developed by stealth, rather than by design. As a mostly bottom-up, service-level process that culminated in the publication of several sectoral security strategies in recent years, the process of strategy development in the EU has remained largely capability-driven. Enabled by this strategic void at the heart of the European security project, actors in the EU's internal and external security institutions have developed ever broader and more encompassing security strategies with sometimes overlapping or conflicting strategic aims, including, among others, counter-terrorism, human security, common defence, crime-fighting and stability. This incremental and sometimes accidental strategy-building process has resulted in a strategic landscape made up of diverging security ends and objectives.

After this conceptual discussion, the book moves on to its second theme, as it investigates what is arguably the major factor driving the development of homeland security policies in Europe, namely counter-terrorism. Chapter 4 by Bossong analyses the starting point of the development of European homeland security. He outlines how counter-terrorism became a focal issue for the EU, as each serious attack was also seen as an opportunity for expanding security integration on a wide front. However, he also unveils shortcomings in the EU's fight against international terrorism in the light of its own four-pronged counter-terrorism strategy. As the policy agenda becomes increasingly mature, one can raise both normative and functionalist criticisms of the EU's role in this policy area.

Chapter 5 by Argomaniz shows how this key element in European homeland security, namely counter-terrorism, has been profoundly affected by the proliferation of bureaucratic actors with competing competences, a process that has led to severe coordination demands. These needs, which have only been partially addressed to date, have the potential to undermine the EU's effectiveness as a counter-terrorism actor. The chapter argues that, although the EU has traditionally been unable to provide a satisfactory response to the substantial obstacles to institutional coherence that exist in this area, the reforms introduced by the Lisbon Treaty have strengthened the EU's capacity to better address these weaknesses in the near future. This has important implications for the future development of European homeland security given the symbolic and political relevance of counter-terrorism as one of its key components.

Chapter 6 by MacKenzie demonstrates how developments in EU counter-terrorism have expanded the boundaries of this policy area and have served as a reason to expand the EU's external involvement, creating yet another level of homeland security. EU activity outside Europe has developed very quickly since 2001. In the aftermath of 9/11, EU Member States have rapidly recognised that international terrorism could not be combated by a single state, which led to efforts being made to cooperate at the European level. Furthermore, the EU had to act externally in order to provide homeland security for Europe due to the threats emanating from other regions of the world. EU cooperation with third states now includes a number of key agreements with the US – the EU's main partner – as well as Passenger Name Record (PNR) Agreements with Canada and Australia. The chapter argues that such developments indicate that the EU is becoming an increasingly significant counter-terrorism actor, which is recognised as such by a growing number of third states.

Chapters 7, 8 and 9 address the third theme of our book, as they focus on other aspects of European homeland security than counter-terrorism, namely the EU emergency and crisis management and border protection policies. Chapter 7 by Wendling analyses the EU's response to crises as part of its crisis management policy, as the EU has witnessed a large number of major emergencies and crises over the last decade. Thus, the chapter examines how the EU has developed a Community mechanism in the field of civil protection, which is managed by the European Commission under the label of 'Community Civil Protection Mechanism' (CCPM). Moreover, in 2005, the EU adopted the so-called Emergency and Crisis Coordination Arrangements (CCA), which are to be activated in cases where EU interests are at stake both inside and outside EU borders. Both EU tools were adopted to enhance cooperation among Member States in cases of crises and emergencies. Analysing the CCPM and then the CCA, this chapter identifies the elements of constraint, opportunity and repositioning that have influenced the implementation of these tools by the EU.

In Chapter 8, Kurowska and Pawlak provide an overview of the EU border protection policies and instruments. The last few years have seen a substantial growth in the EU's border activities, which not only include rules for the internal movement of persons and goods, but also concern third countries under the paradigm of 'integrated border management'. As a consequence, the EU border protection policies have grown to include border assistance missions in third countries, as well as technologically advanced instruments, including the Schengen Information System, the Visa Information System and passenger name records. This chapter addresses the governance challenges that all these instruments entail.

Chapter 9 by Léonard continues the discussion about European borders policies. It focuses on the creation of the Agency for the management of operational coordination at the external borders of the Member States of the European Union (Frontex) as a new, and at times controversial, actor in the area of European homeland security. The aim of this chapter is to examine the political dynamics that have led to the establishment of this new institution in the AFSJ and that affect the current debates on its development. In particular, it examines the role played by the EU institutions and by some key Member States in the definition of the tasks of the Agency, its relations with other EU institutions, and the debates on its future missions.

Finally, Chapter 10 by Léonard, Kaunert and Pawlak reflects on the development of European homeland security in the post-Lisbon and post-Stockholm context. This volume demonstrates that, to date, the EU has lacked a strategic vision for the development of its homeland security policies, which it still considers to be distinct and separate, rather than forming one single and cohesive policy area. The development of homeland security policies in the EU has generally resulted from uncoordinated decisions. In turn, this absence of an overarching strategy has posed several challenges to the governance of European homeland security. This final chapter sheds light on the conditions that should be fulfilled to see the development of a more cohesive European homeland security policy and the challenges of intra- and inter-policy coordination. It highlights that a shift towards thinking more in terms of 'European homeland security' would have the advantages of both increasing coordination among policies and emphasising the issue of 'whom' exactly is being secured through the deployment of security policies in the EU.

Notes

1 For example, the International Convention against the Taking of Hostages of 1979; the Convention on the Physical Protection of Nuclear Material of 1979; the Convention for the Suppression of Unlawful Acts Against the Safety of Civil Aviation of 1971; the International Convention for the Suppression of Acts of Nuclear Terrorism of 2001; the International Convention for the Suppression of the Financing of Terrorism of 1999; the International Convention for the Suppression of Terrorist Bombings of 1997; and the Protocol for the Suppression of Unlawful Acts of Violence at Airports Serving International Civil Aviation, Supplementary to the Convention for the Suppression of Unlawful Acts against the Safety of Civil Aviation of 1998.

2 For example, the European Convention on the Suppression of Terrorism of 1977 and Amending Protocol of 2003; the European Convention on Extradition of 1957 and first and second Additional Protocols of 1975 and 1978, respectively; the European Convention on Mutual Assistance in Criminal Matters of 1959 and first and second Additional Protocols of 1978 and 2001, respectively; the European Convention on the Transfer of Proceedings in Criminal Matters of 1972; the European Convention on the Compensation of Victims of Violent Crimes of 1983; the Convention on Laundering, Search, Seizure and Confiscation of the Proceeds from Crime of 1990; the Convention on Cybercrime of 2001 and the Additional Protocol concerning the criminalisation of acts of a racist and xenophobic nature committed through computer systems of 2003; the Council of Europe Convention on the Prevention of Terrorism of 2005; and the Council of Europe Convention on laundering, search, seizure and confiscation of the proceeds from crime and on the financing of terrorism of 2005.

3 Created in 1923, it is one of the oldest organisations of this type. Its main objective is to facilitate police cooperation in fields such as drugs, criminal organisations, public safety and terrorism, corruption and trafficking in human beings.

4 The FATF was created in 1989 as an intergovernmental policy-making body, which develops and promotes national and international policies to combat terrorism financing and money-laundering.

2   Homeland security in the making

American and European patterns of transformation

Patryk Pawlak

The idea of securing the homeland is more politically loaded than generally believed. The introduction of 'homeland' into a political debate raises
several questions about our societies, many of which have their origins in
discussions about ethnicity and nationalism. As this chapter demonstrates,
a better understanding of certain assumptions and concepts related to the
idea of homeland is necessary in order to gain a grasp of current developments in the realm of homeland security, both in Europe and the United
States (US). For instance, a well-crafted rhetoric of homeland security has
not only shaken such fundamental concepts as territory, sovereignty or
borders, but has also increased societal acceptance for policy measures
that under different circumstances would have been extensively criticised
for their intrusion into civil liberties. Furthermore, gaining an insight into
complementarities (or trade-offs) between security and other fundamental
values is a prerequisite for a more complete understanding of 'homeland
security'.

This chapter argues that patterns of homeland security-making in
Europe and the US are very similar and reminiscent of what Smith (1981)
calls an 'ethnic homeland'. The idea of an ethnic homeland in Smith's
writing is based on four elements: boundary, history, self-sufficiency[1] and
nation-building, which emerge from the relationship between culture,
state and territory. It is important however to investigate how these concepts work in context and take into account their dynamic nature,
meaning that it is necessary to 'investigate the semantic field in which they
are embedded and see which practices are thereby enjoyed, permitted and
demanded' (Kratochwil 2011). Consequently, as a social construct, 'homeland' is no longer linked to territory only, but becomes an element of
nationalist constructs, constitutes a space on the basis of which a sense of
given historic community emerges as a modern notion (Smith 1981). Territory, on the other hand, is viewed as 'material for a political construct, as
an element that goes to make up a satisfactory "homeland", one that can
preferably furnish the basis of a successful nation-state' (Smith 1981: 187).
However, territory itself is no longer the underlying feature of 'autonomous and abstract institutions within a modern state' (Smith 1981),

because the image of 'international system as consisting of sovereign units that all claim an exclusive space [...] is incomplete and thus misleading' (Kratochwil 2011: 12). This also means that the concept of borders needs to be re-examined. Although a cartographic, spatially ascribed understanding of borders as geographical lines remains unchanged, their meaning needs to be complemented by political, legal and societal processes which shift the meaning of borders. The 'smart borders' doctrine introduced into the homeland security lexicon after the 9/11 terrorist attacks serves as an excellent example.

Boundaries and borders

Boundaries relate to the discussion about the spatiality of the homeland – they cannot be just any boundaries, but need to be drawn according to natural or historical criteria. As Smith (1981: 191–92) argues:

> the creation of political geography has been used to fence in the nation's homeland, to make it impregnable to enemies and impermeable to members. For the nationalist, this is not just a question of security. Much more important is the idea that a nation's boundaries reveal its true identity [...].

In that sense, 'drawing' borders is not only a cartographic exercise, but rather a political process during which basic concepts such as 'enemy' or 'identity' are defined.

The US government defined homeland security as a 'concerted national effort to prevent terrorist attacks within the US, reduce America's vulnerability to terrorism, and minimise the damage and recover from attacks that do occur' (The White House 2002a).[2] The omnipresent terrorist threat provided a major stimulus for the US as 'a Nation at war'. Understanding terrorism and terrorists as strategic actors dominated homeland security efforts. Especially since agents of terror were groups operating globally, 'lurking in the shadows' with one important tactical advantage: '[t]hey are able to choose the time, place, and method of their attacks. As we [the US] reduce our vulnerabilities in one area, they can alter their plans and pursue more exposed targets' (The White House 2002a). Therefore, it became crucial to uncover the identity of the enemies. The major objective has been to differentiate potential terrorists or dangerous elements from the group of legitimate travellers (i.e. tourists, businessmen, students); in other words, to separate 'bad apples from good apples'.[3] A closer analysis of major US legislative acts in the field of homeland security (Congress of the United States of America 2001a, 2001b; 2002, 2004; The White House 2002a, 2002f; US Homeland Security Council 2007) provides a better overview of who constitutes a potential threat. At the forefront come violent Islamic extremists trained in certain Arab countries operating outside and within the US borders. This is why addressing radicalisation and terrorist recruitment became an important policy objective (US Homeland Security Council 2007: 9). Another group are the so-called 'single-issue' domestic terrorist groups including white supremacists, animal rights extremists, and eco-terrorist groups among others (US Homeland Security Council 2007: 9). Foreign employees and students also constitute a potential threat and need to be monitored through either worksite enforcement programmes and electronic employment eligibility verification systems or the Student and Exchange Visitor Information System (US Homeland Security Council 2007: 16).

Such an approach had several implications. A 'smart borders' doctrine became a prevailing approach guiding the government in both domestic and international politics. In light of such definition of a potential threat it does not come as a surprise that improving borders protection was a primary objective of the Bush Administration, whereby clear boundaries were drawn between terrorists and those who harbour them on one side and Americans with their allies on the other side. This was an underlying feature of the US border protection policy since 9/11: 'deny entry into the United States of aliens associated with, suspected of being engaged in, or supporting terrorist activity; [...] and to locate, detain, prosecute, or deport any such aliens present in the United States' (The White House 2001b). The strategy of 'smart borders' presented by the White House also assumed that:

> [t]he border of the future must integrate actions abroad to screen goods and people prior to their arrival in sovereign U.S. territory, and inspections at the border and measures within the United States to ensure compliance with entry and import permits [...].
>
> (The White House 2002b)

Geography has always played an important role in the US approach to security, and homeland security is not an exception. With two oceans protecting its shores in West and East and friendly neighbours in North and South, the US considered their location as a huge strategic advantage. The 9/11 terrorist attacks have eroded such thinking (Pawlak 2010b). The new philosophy was very well summarised by a former Homeland Security Secretary Chertoff:

> [t]he fact is that homeland security does not simply begin at the water line. That is the last place you want to stop problems, not the first place. Much of what we do in homeland security begins even before a person sets foot on an airplane in Europe or a container is loaded on a cargo ship in Asia.
>
> (US Department of Homeland Security 2007)

When geographical borders do not offer protection anymore the US needed to learn reading maps in a completely new way whereby borders were established by a level of threat coming from a particular area, rather than political borders determined by national sovereignty.

Consequently, the place of the citizen in society and the concept of authority have changed. Boundaries between a 'governor' and those 'governed' – previously based on clear-cut territorial approach to authority of a sovereign over his subjects – became even more blurred with the concept of extra-territorial instruments expanding the authority beyond one's borders (Pawlak 2010c). The new conception of territoriality has also reshaped the tasks assigned to the Department of Defence whose primary mission was to defend the country's territory and fight wars (Hsu 2009). Subsequently, military was also charged with the mission of homeland defence which in most basic terms can be understood as protection of the homeland overseas by military means. This was the primary reason for waging the war in Afghanistan.

The use of the Passenger Name Records (PNR) for security purposes offers a good example. Collected by airlines, the PNR was originally conceived as a means to exchange reservation information between airlines responsible for a passenger's travel arrangements. However, the 9/11 terrorist attacks have increased the value of this tool for the security practitioners as a potentially useful tool in identifying suspicious individuals and finding connections between potential perpetrators. The new security scheme introduced by the Bush Administration extended the obligation on the airlines to transfer their PNR data to the US authorities – a move that was controversial for several reasons. First, any such transfer from the European (EU)-based operators constituted a breach of the EU data protection laws which requires that any transborder data flaw from the EU can be authorised only if the third party has been established to provide 'an adequate level of data protection'. No such decision was issues concerning the US data protection system. Second, the security use of data collected for purely commercial activity was problematic since the consent provided by data subjects (i.e. passengers) did not initially include counter-terrorism. Third, and resulting from the previous two, was the question of citizens' rights. The PNR mechanism has automatically moved the citizens of the EU away from the jurisdiction of the EU law and under the umbrella of the US legislation on data protection, which raised justified questions about the access to data, judicial redress and remedies. The issue was of particular importance to the European Parliament which described this new approach as a form of 'creeping extraterritoriality' (Guild and Brouwer 2006; Pawlak 2007, 2009a, 2010a).

History, ideology and homeland

Another important aspect in the discussion about homelands is history, whereby a 'historic right' becomes a criterion that validates the creation of homelands as the basis of Nation States (Smith 1981: 193). However, history and historical 'truth' are usually based on a limited knowledge of facts and defined by experiences and interpretations of particular groups. Consequently, what constitutes or will constitute a historical event may become a matter of an a priori attribution rather than a posteriori evidence. Even though there is no doubt that the 9/11 terrorist attacks was unprecedented in US history – which finds confirmation in both the scope of this event and its subsequent domestic and international policy developments – there were many a priori attributions about the significance of this event without a thorough investigation and putting this event in a broader historical context. Consequently, the 9/11 was often interpreted as a new beginning ('ever since') or a significant breakthrough ('in the aftermath of').

In the post-9/11 official discourse, the notion of history was substituted with the one of ideology, values and a 'way of life'. Even though the claims of Al-Qaeda were partly grounded in the history of the US presence in the Arab peninsula and against the 'alliance of Jews, Christians, and their agents', much of this confrontation was ideological due to competing visions of social order (i.e. freedom, democracy). As President Bush put it, 'America was targeted for attack because we're the brightest beacon for freedom and opportunity in the world'. This idea was further developed in the US National Homeland Security Strategy of 2002:

> [t]errorism directly threatens the foundations of our Nation – our people, our democratic way of life, and our economic prosperity [...]. American people and way of life are the primary targets of our enemy, and our highest protective priority. Our population and way of life are the source of our Nation's great strength, but also a source of inherent vulnerability.
>
> (The White House 2002a: 7)

The strategy explains further that the US 'way of life' is based on five pillars: democracy (i.e. the rule of law, system of checks and balances, rights and freedoms of individuals), liberties (i.e. freedom of expression, religion, movement; property rights; freedom from unlawful discrimination), security (both externally through strong global political, economic, military and cultural engagement; and internally through justice system and law enforcement), economy (i.e. free market system) and culture (i.e. engagement in dialogue rather than the dogmatic enforcement of any set of values or ideas). Thus, values and way of life rather than history became one of the defining aspects of homeland and community (i.e. 'our way of life, our very freedom came under attack'). This opinion has been expressed by President Bush on several occasions and served to build his policies right in the aftermath of the attack and has been regularly repeating since then in his State of the Union addresses. Therefore, the fight nowadays takes place not between states invoking history to validate their claims, but between states and other groups invoking values and ideologies in order to support their rival interpretations of social order.

Nation-building and a sacrifice

The nation-building dimension helps to understand how the reference to a 'concentrated nation effort' can be used in creation of a homeland defined as 'an arena for practical construction and a reservoir of men power' (Smith 1981: 194). Traditionally, the nation-building programmes relied on work on land as their essential aspect that was supposed to bring people together and transform their mentality. But for this to happen, as Smith puts it,

> the population at large must be mobilised. They must be catapulted out of their daily lives and routines and made to feel part of a project and a community and a destiny larger than themselves, one in which they can find personal meaning for their lives and where they can come to feel a sense of likeness and belonging with fellow-toilers [...]. Practical work on the land, therefore, serves the double purpose of providing the homeland with an infrastructure, and of imbuing its manpower with the necessary zeal to make the sacrifices to modernisation.
>
> (Smith 1981: 194)

Such interpretation resembles a contemporary discourse about homeland in the post-9/11 environment. The rhetoric of war used by the Bush Administration has accelerated the momentum and strengthened the force with which US society has been 'catapulted' from their daily routine.[4] The opinion polls conducted in the aftermath of 9/11 clearly demonstrate that such a manoeuvre has been successful. Americans viewed the 'war on terror' as a primary policy issue while the President's approval rates amounted to 90 per cent.[5]

President Bush also indicated that the US:

> will direct every resource at [its] command – every means of diplomacy, every tool of intelligence, every instrument of law enforcement, every financial influence, and every necessary weapon of war – to the disruption and to the defeat of the global terror network.
>
> (The White House 2001a)

This promise was later translated in the National Strategy for Homeland Security which established the principle of shared responsibility between various levels of government, private sector and the society at large. A revised version of the National Homeland Security Strategy of 2007 is even more specific in calling for a nation-wide mobilisation:

> [t]his Strategy also calls on each of you. Every one of us should develop our own personal and family readiness plans to help protect us in the event of a natural or man-made disaster, enabling emergency responders and resources to be focused on those in greatest need.
>
> (US Homeland Security Council 2007)

It states furthermore that '[f]ederal, State, local, and Tribal governments, the private and non-profit sectors, communities, and individual citizens all share common goals and responsibilities – as well as accountability – for protecting and defending the Homeland' (US Homeland Security Council 2007: 4). Private sector was implicated given that it owns or operates almost 85 per cent of the US critical infrastructure and plays a key role in supply chains, research and development or technology. Therefore, a close partnership between government and private actors was necessary. Also non-governmental organisations and think tanks have claimed their role in the process – not so much on the basis of a governmental mandate as on the mandate derived from their missions. Last, but not least, the society at large was asked to sacrifice some of its habits or privileges in order to comply and support the endeavour of homeland protection. This has been most visible across various surveillance and screening programmes such as the REAL ID Act[6] or The United States Visitor and Immigrant Status Indicator Technology (US-VISIT) program.[7]

However, the idea of a sacrifice to be made is also inherent to the idea of homeland. In the aftermath of 9/11 a number of potential costs emerged. First, the wave of new legislation (i.e. the PATRIOT Act) increased the powers of government and law enforcement authorities while at the same time substantially encroaching into many civil liberties (see Congress of the United States of America 2001b). Since the 'nation' was 'at war' and a military response was part of a strategy of fighting the 'enemy' potential human sacrifices could not be excluded. Furthermore, the costs of increased security of customs, transportation or protection of the critical infrastructure had to be paid by businesses. Because of their divergent approach, in comparison to the official government line, many think-tanks or civil rights organisations were not taken seriously or rather treated by the Bush Administration as an unwelcome participant. And finally, the price needed to be paid by individual members of society. The increased security controls at airports or more intrusion into personal life and privacy are only some of the costs that a regular person was faced with. There is no doubt that the US homeland security measures have imposed on the US another important cost and that is a loss of global support and sympathy that the US enjoyed right after 9/11. The unilateralist and inconsiderate way of US homeland security measures in combination with their far-reaching consequences have rendered the world very sceptical. The support for the US has declined even among its traditional allies, most notably in Europe. The assumption that everyone can pose a threat undermined the foundations of our societies based on mutual trust. While terrorism may constitute a threat to 'way of life', so can the response to terrorism. While the objective of homeland security is to protect the liberties and democracy, sometimes the response may undermine the very values it aims to protect. Therefore, the balancing needs to be carefully conducted in order to avoid situations when solutions might be more expensive than the problem itself.

One illustration of this approach is the invasion into the privacy of individuals. In an emerging post-9/11 border regime individuals and foreigners in particular became in the eyes of policy-makers 'a prima-facie face of terrorism' (Guild 2003: 336). The reliance on personal information and an increasing use of new technologies – like biometrics, profiling – were perceived to constitute justified tools for a redefined security policy. Most of these solutions came initially at a price of civil liberties and data protection. A subsequent balancing exercise has gradually departed from the antagonising language towards a more sensible reference to 'privacy by design' whereby security and privacy are mutually enhancing.

A European homeland

An obvious question that follows is if and to what extent similar patterns of transformations have taken place in the EU. There is little indication what a European homeland might mean for Europeans other than the Treaty provisions and recently adopted policy documents like the Stockholm Programme and the EU's Internal Security Strategy. Article 3 of the Treaty on European Union (TEU) states that:

> the Union shall offer its citizens an area of freedom, security and justice without internal frontiers, in which the free movement of persons is ensured in conjunction with appropriate measures with respect to external border controls, asylum, immigration and the prevention and combating of crime.

Furthermore, Article 67 of the Treaty on the Functioning of the European Union (TFEU) states that:

> the Union shall endeavour to ensure a high level of security through measures to prevent and combat crime, racism and xenophobia, and through measures for coordination and cooperation between police and judicial authorities and other competent authorities, as well as through the mutual recognition of judgments in criminal matters and, if necessary, through the approximation of criminal laws.

In order to further advance the area of freedom, security and justice and to demonstrate its commitment to a 'European security model' the EU adopted the Internal Security Strategy in February 2010. The EU internal security means 'protecting people and the values of freedom and democracy, so that everyone can enjoy their daily lives without fear' (European Council 2010b: 4). At the same time, it is understood as 'a wide and comprehensive concept which straddles multiple sectors' in order to address major threats 'which have a direct impact on the lives, safety, and well-being of citizens, including natural and man-made disasters [...]' (p. 2). The Strategy was further complemented by an Action Plan adopted by the EU Council in November 2010. Therefore, the EU as a 'guardian of the people' (Mitsilegas *et al.* 2003) becomes responsible for the provision of security. Having said that, the European road towards achieving the Area of Freedom, Security and Justice (AFSJ) carries many similarities with the US reference to 'homeland'.

From 'fortress Europe' to 'pushing the borders out'

Smith views territory as

> material for a political construct, as an element that goes to make up a satisfactory 'homeland', one that can preferably furnish the basis of a successful nation-state and that goes beyond the territorial aspect of homeland [...]. A 'homeland' constitutes a space on the basis of which a sense of given historic community emerges as a modern nation.
>
> (Smith 1981: 187)

The European reference to an 'area' seems to have much clearer territorial attachment, which stems from the fact that the EU is still a group of several Member States with different integrationist dynamics. Given the differences in legal systems and constitutional orders of its members, the 'area' was still to be constructed rather than prescribed in purely geographical space.

Rather than based on geographical criteria, the AFSJ was determined by the distribution of certain norms and laws, which EU Member States decided to comply with. This consequently resulted in a complicated cartographic exercise, whereas some countries participated in certain regulatory solutions but not others. For instance, whereas UK, Ireland and Denmark decided to opt out from the Schengen Conventions, countries like Norway, Iceland and Switzerland have joined.[8] Another example is the Prüm Agreement concluded initially between seven EU Member States with the objective to strengthen cooperation between law enforcement authorities.[9] This varied dynamics required a certain shift in looking at and reading a map of Europe. It was no longer an assembly of geographically located European nation states but a community of countries bound by various sets of common rules and norms which not always correspond with geographical borders. It does not mean, however, that a strictly territorial approach was absent in the European construction.

Recalling Smith's argument, 'the creation of political geography has been used to fence in the nation's homeland, to make it impregnable to enemies and impermeable to members. For the nationalist, this is not just a question of security. Much more important is the idea that a nation's boundaries reveal its true identity' (Smith 1981: 191–92). The process of 'fencing' in order to protect some sort of 'Europeanness' can be traced through the EU's history. European integration has been increasingly subjected to discussions about the borders of Europe. The application of Morocco was rejected in 1987 on the grounds that it is not a European country, whereas the accession of central and eastern European countries in 2004 was perceived as 'a unique, historic accomplishment' (European Commission 2008a). At the same time, an increasing reluctance to welcome new countries translated in a number of regionally oriented initiatives – 'rings of friends' – offering 'sharing everything but institutions' (European Commission 2002a). Consequently, as further discussed in the chapter by Pawlak and Kurowska in this book, while the expansion of the geographical borders of the EU is subjected to territorial qualification, its regulatory borders become increasingly 'pushed out' through approximation of laws or regulatory expansionism to other countries and regions that are subjected – in one way or the other – to the European *acquis*.[10]

In comparison to the US to homeland security, the European equivalent was defined in much broader terms than just the fight against terrorism. The report of the Informal High Level Advisory Group on the Future of European Home Affairs Policy identified three major challenges 'essential to safeguard and complete the area of justice, freedom and security in the light of continuously changing framework conditions': the growing interdependence between internal and external security; balancing mobility, security and privacy; and improving flow of data within European-wide information networks (The Future Group 2008). The first one was particularly important since, as the report claims, 'a responsible policy needs to follow the principle "prevention is better than a cure"' (The Future Group 2008). Consequently, the EU engaged in a number of policy initiatives aimed at developing politically shaped strategies vis-à-vis third countries with a particular focus on border management. The 2005 EU Strategy on the External Dimension of the Area of Freedom, Security and Justice made it clear that:

> [t]he projection of the values underpinning the area of freedom, security and justice is essential in order to safeguard the internal security of the EU. Menaces such as terrorism, organised crime and drug trafficking also originate outside the EU. It is thus crucial that the EU develop a strategy to engage with third countries worldwide.
>
> (European Commission 2005b: 3)

In terms of border protection, the Stockholm Programme prescribes that the

> access to Europe for businessmen, tourists, students, scientists, workers, persons in need of international protection and others having a legitimate interest to access EU territory has to be made more effective and efficient. At the same time, the Union and its Member States have to guarantee security for its citizens. Integrated border management and visa policies should be construed to serve these goals.
>
> (European Council 2010a: 5)

Therefore, the external border is being designed in the framework of several political developments: the enlargement of the EU (where being 'a European state' and the adoption of the *acquis communautaire* constitute a primary condition for membership); the emergence of various initiatives such as the European Neighbourhood Policy (ENP) or the Union for the Mediterranean or the Eastern Partnership (which de facto determine the geographical border of Europe along natural and historical criteria whereas at the same time expanding regulatory borders of the EU); migration and border management policies adopted by the Union (i.e. readmission agreements with third countries, setting up the Agency for External Border Protection – Frontex); and through a number of EU missions throughout the world which aim at improving the security environment by providing military, police, civil protection, development aid and rule of law devices.

While gradually removing its internal borders, the EU focused on security of its territory from external threats such as illegal immigration, transnational organised crime and fraud resulting in the creation of a 'fortress Europe' or as it has been more recently called 'a cyber fortress Europe' (Guild *et al.* 2008). The transformation of borders in the EU from physical to amorphous or even virtual can be best explored on the example of the so-called 'border package' presented by the European Commission in February 2008. The aim of this set of proposals is to develop the integrated Border Management Strategy of the EU in a comprehensive way, taking into account the possibilities offered by new technology, in particular the use of biometrics (European Commission 2008a). An important aspect of these initiatives is their reliance on biometric and other personal information as a way to pre-screen travellers before they arrive in the EU. This is in particular the case of registered traveller programmes, the Electronic System for Travel Authorisation or the EU PNR system. The development of the European Border Surveillance System (Eurosur) is also significant in this context. It is designed as a 'system of systems' with a task to detect, identify, track and intercept persons attempting to enter the EU illegally outside border crossing points. The 'system of systems' approach relies on the use of existing systems (i.e. national systems, SafeSeaNet) and common surveillance tools (e.g. satellites or unmanned air vehicles – UAVs) while at the same time enabling the secure exchange of information and intelligence. It is supposed to be implemented in three phases and eight separate but interlinked steps as outlined in the Eurosur roadmap (European Commission 2008c). In addition, there has been a number of multilateral initiatives whose objective was to prevent a threat by close cooperation with third countries, in particular in the filed of illegal migration. For instance, the 'Seahorse' projects – which were initially conducted between 2006 and 2008 and then followed upon with the 'Seahorse Network' in 2007–2008 and 'Seahorse cooperation centres' in 2009–2010 – aimed at the 'reinforcement of African countries cooperation and improvement of their capacities to fight against illegal immigration' (Serrano 2010a). At the operational level it included reinforcing a joint patrols system between Morocco and Spain (to be enlarged to other countries) as well as establishing a network of liaison officers in order to facilitate the exchange of information with the African countries. Until May 2010, Cooperation Centres have been established in Spain, Portugal, Morocco, Mauritania, Senegal and Cape Verde. New contact points were established in Morocco, Gambia and Guinea Bissau. The establishment of Seahorse Mediterranean that would include other countries like France, Italy, Malta, Libya, Tunisia and Algeria is currently under discussion. Interestingly, cooperation with those countries is not only taking place at an operational level but aims at instigating a certain 'border protection culture' by providing coastal and maritime surveillance courses or providing other training and capacity-building activities.

History and ideology

Another dimension of homeland identified by Smith is the importance of historical linkages. And although history has played a limited role in the US transformation of homeland, it has been a very important element in European debates, together with other issues like common values and culture. The experience of two world wars and other tragic events in the history of the European continent lie at the origins of the European integration process. 'Never again' was the objective that the founders of the EU kept in mind when establishing the European Coal and Steel Community aimed at the reconciliation between former enemies: France and Germany. After over 50 years of European integration and six enlargements, common European history and identity are still vividly discussed, partly because the very same concepts have undergone expansions as well as embracing more diversity.

Terrorist attacks in Europe have been interpreted in exactly the same way as in the US – as acts 'against humanity itself and the values and freedoms we all share' (Council of the European Union 2001). More specific conceptualisation was provided in the aftermath of terrorist attacks on European soil whereby the EU:

> considers that the attacks are an affront to universal values on which the EU is based. Central to those values is a commitment to democratic and open institutions and societies governed by the rule of law within which people of all faiths and backgrounds can live, work and prosper together. The terrorists who reject that commitment and seek to use violence to impose their ideas will be defeated.
>
> (Council of the European Union 2005f)

As a consequence, the European values and 'way of life' became the subject of security. Other than democracy or rule of law, the European way of life is defined by several fundamental freedoms and the biggest challenge was to ensure that in the 'age of terrorism' citizens can still enjoy them. The search for appropriate tools has begun and has been mostly satisfied by enhanced cooperation between police officers and exchange of information.

Naturally, terrorism is mentioned in European treaties as one of the serious forms of crime to be prevented and combated through closer cooperation between police, justice and customs authorities of Member States. However, it was perceived more as an internal rather than an external problem, especially in the aftermath of Madrid and London bombings. Therefore, the focus was on 'violent radicalisation' defined as 'the phenomenon of people embracing opinions, views and ideas which could lead to acts of terrorism' (European Commission 2005a). The Commission proposal further explained why addressing radicalisation was so important:

> Fighting terrorism, in all its forms and irrespective of the aims or 'ideals' it purports to advance, is also an ideological struggle because terrorism has the potential to subvert the very founding principles of the EU. Although Europe has experienced different types of terrorism in its history, the main threat currently comes from terrorism that is underlined by an abusive interpretation of Islam. Nevertheless, many of the motivational factors for violent radicalisation and the remedies dealt with by this Communication are equally valid for all violent radicalisation, whether of a nationalistic, anarchic, separatist, extreme left or extreme right kind.
>
> (European Commission 2005a)

Thus, terrorism constitutes a threat to the 'way of life' and ideals.

The linkage between Islam and terrorism which emerged in the post 9/11 debates brought religion to the forefront of discussions about homeland and security. Although a role of religion in political life of the Union was in the past a vivid ideological issue,[11] it has recently surfaced at several different levels. In the context of the EU-Turkey accession negotiations the image of Turkey as a Muslim country with its distinctive set of customs and beliefs has substantially shaped the attitudes among Europeans. This perception was strengthened following the publication of the European Commission Progress reports in which Turkey has been constantly criticised for its record on fundamental rights and freedoms (European Commission 2010c). The image of clashing values was enhanced following the publication of cartoons portraying Prophet Muhammad which caused the outrage of Muslim population not only in Europe but particularly in other parts of the world. The conflict was further fuelled by the wave of legislation in France and Italy concerning the presence of conspicuous religious symbols in public spaces. These developments need to be interpreted in a broader demographic context whereby the European Muslim population is growing at a much higher rate than other groups and in a quite unfavourable political context whereas the Muslim population at large is still seen as being connected to global terrorist networks personified by Al-Qaeda.

The absent community-building dimension

The nation-building or rather 'community-building' as a dimension in European homeland may be perceived from two perspectives depending on the time frame that one takes as a reference. Taking the last 50 years of European integration as a point of reference, there have been certain efforts towards creating the feeling of a community. Although most recently the European project seems to be more distant from its citizens as exemplified by the result of referenda on the Treaty of Lisbon in Ireland, Europeans indeed:

> feel part of a project and a community and a destiny larger than themselves, one in which they can find personal meaning for their lives and where they can come to feel a sense of likeness and belonging with fellow-toilers.

> (Smith 1981: 194)

The creation of European citizenship[12] or principle of solidarity,[13] although often thought of as symbolic, have brought an important input to the emergence of a European homeland.

On the other hand, following the post-9/11 developments and later terrorist attacks in Madrid and London, there were not many efforts towards 'community-building' similar to those in the US. Although, indeed, those events have provided impetus for more integration at the European level and therefore the emergence of the idea of homeland security among European policy-makers, there were very limited efforts towards mobilising societies among the same ideals. This was partially due to the fact that the threat of terrorism and the necessity to address it have been present on European political agendas for decades. Many European states had dealt with terrorist groups operating on their territory like the IRA in the United Kingdom (UK), the ETA in Spain or the FLNC in France. Many countries have already had anti-terrorist legislation in place so there was a basis to work on.[14] Other countries have judged terrorist offences on the basis of common criminal offences. Also, Europeans have worked closely on counter-terrorism in the framework of the Council of Europe and intergovernmental cooperation developed through the establishment of TREVI Group in 1976.

In recent years, most of the work has shifted towards interagency cooperation as well as public–private partnerships. Most of the policy documents have adequately concluded that

> to reach an adequate level of internal security in a complex global environment requires the involvement of law enforcement and border management authorities, with the support of judicial cooperation, civil protection agencies and also of the political, economic, financial, social and private sectors, including non-governmental organisations.
> (Council of the European Union 2010b: 10)

The role of other institutions such as the European Parliament, the Court of Justice or national parliaments has substantially increased after the entry in force of the Lisbon Treaty and strengthened the policy-making process by enhancing its legitimacy and accountability of actors. The role of non-governmental actors and citizens is particularly important in the context of prevention which according to the Internal Security Strategy (ISS) should rely on strengthened cooperation with educational and financial institutions as well as civil society. However, while cooperation between those bodies has been taking place independently on additional stimuli, a more problematic issue remained a detachment between the citizens and political institutions and society at large. As British Prime Minister David Cameron put it at the Munich Security Conference in February 2011, '[w]e have failed to provide a vision of society to which they [young Muslim men] feel they want to belong' and described the activities of numerous community and spiritual leaders as engendering 'a sense of community' and a 'substitute for what the wider society has failed to supply'. Consequently, there is a need for the European construction of homeland to increasingly focus on the community-building dimension as a response to radicalisation and Islamic extremism. It does not come as surprise that the same speech by Cameron states clearly that 'governments cannot do this alone' and that 'we must build stronger societies and stronger identities at home' (Number 10 2011).

The price of security

The Stockholm Programme outlining the EU's agenda regarding the AFSJ until 2014 makes 'serving the citizen' one of its primary objectives. The AFSJ is an area which 'shapes the citizens circumstances of life, in particular the private space of their own responsibility and of political and social security, which is protected by the fundamental rights' (Bundesverfassungsgericht 2009) and therefore a part of this 'service' is finding an appropriate balance between security and justice. The need for finding a new middle ground is mostly a response to a growing legislative activity of several Member States, which, following the example of the PATRIOT Act in the US, have substantially broadened the scope of counter-terrorism measures and increased the competences of law enforcement agencies and judicial authorities without providing additional safeguards for their citizens. For instance, the object of Regulation 881/2002 of 27 May 2002 imposing specific restrictive measures directed against certain people and entities associated with Osama bin Laden, the Al-Qaeda network and the Taliban was to freeze the funds and prohibit any funding of those groups connected with Osama bin Laden, the Al-Qaeda and the Taliban. It covered all funds and economic resources belonging to these natural and legal people, group or entities which had been designed by the UN Sanctions Committee and listed by the EU under Regulation 881/2002 as terrorists. The Regulation was challenged before the Court of Justice of the EU as not respecting the fundamental right of defence and in particular on the right to be heard.[15] In the Yusuf Case, the Court of First Instance found that 'any opportunity for the applicants effectively to make known their views on the correctness and relevance of the facts in consideration of which their funds have been frozen and on the evidence adduced against them appears to be definitively excluded' (Court of First Instance 2005: paras. 319–20). Another good illustration comes from the Kadi II Case concerned with freezing assets of individuals supposedly sponsoring terrorism, where the General Court described such measures as 'draconian' and explained that:

> [...]. All the applicant's funds and other assets have been indefinitely frozen for nearly 10 years now and he cannot gain access to them without first obtaining an exemption from the Sanctions Committee [...] the UK Supreme Court took the view that it was no exaggeration to say that persons designated in this way are effectively 'prisoners' of the State: their freedom of movement is severely restricted without access to their funds and the effect of the freeze on both them and their families can be devastating.
>
> (General Court 2010: para. 149)

This trend was accompanied by the evolution of the concept of security itself which helped to extend the scope of measures which otherwise might not have been considered in the specific context of terrorism. In addition, the use of new technologies, many of which bear significant implications for privacy and data protection, has further shifted the equilibrium towards the security side of the equation (De Hert *et al.* 2008; Guild and Geyer 2008; Brouwer 2009; De Hert and Bellanova 2009). The use of new technologies such as biometrics and increasing capacities to store and exchange large amounts of personal information (e.g. development of large-scale IT systems such as EURODAC II, the SIS II, the Customs Information System or the VIS) while offering new tools in the areas of migration, border management and the fight against organised crime and terrorism have also undermined a number of basic principles on which the European system of data protection has been established (e.g. specificity, proportionality, purpose). Of course, an 'enhanced use of technological developments can provide satisfactory solutions to the important issue of how to ensure more security for citizens and at the same time greater protection of their right to privacy' (The Future Group 2008), but it also implies that such developments need to be carefully scrutinized.

Some indication of developing a balanced approach is provided in the European Convention on Human Rights (ECHR) with strict safeguards for the right to life and the right to liberty and security of persons (Articles 2 and 5) and by the jurisprudence of the European Court of Human Rights (ECtHR). Whereas the ECHR recognises the primary obligation of Member States to protect their citizens against serious threats and recognises that sometimes this 'may require certain limitations on the exercise of other fundamental rights and freedoms, such as those provided for in relation to the respect for private life' (Article 8.2), it also states that:

> any restriction of the privacy should be based on a clear legal basis, and only take place for specific legitimate purposes, to the extent necessary and proportionate for a pressing social need, with adequate safeguards to avoid any possible abuse.

The ECtHR has delivered in recent years some important judgements on the matter. The ECtHR case law accepts that a balance may need to be struck between security and privacy but only under the terms and within the limits of the Convention. Two cases are particularly interesting. The case of *Liberty and Others* v. *the United Kingdom* concerned a secret surveillance program of national and international public communications, operated by an Electronic Test Facility in the UK. It involved a sensitive issue of recourse to data mining and profiling. In the case of *S. and Marper* v. *the United Kingdom,* the ECtHR addressed the issue of data retention, in particular biometrics' samples and profiles (DNA and fingerprints) after criminal proceedings against individuals have ended in acquittal or have been discontinued. Retention and processing of biometrics are crucial issues in current development of the European security model and in the transatlantic context. Based on the ECtHR judgments in these two cases one can conclude that if the Court finds that a measure interferes with the right to the respect of private life under the Article 8, it can be justified only if it is 'in accordance with the law' (i.e. it needs an adequate basis in national law, must be precise and predictable for affected parties) (European Court of Human Rights 2008a) and 'necessary in a democratic society for a legitimate purpose' (i.e. it needs to respond to a pressing social need and be in line with the principle of proportionality) (European Court of Human Rights 2008b).

On 26 June 2009, the Czech Presidency submitted a proposal to the Ad hoc Working Group on Information Exchange for an Information Management Strategy (IMS) which is supposed to provide new tools and guidelines for law enforcement, border management and judicial authorities dealing with criminal matters. The primary objective of the IMS is to 'support, streamline and facilitate the management of information necessary to the competent authorities to ensure the EU internal security'. However, it is also supposed to provide the basis for a strong data protection regime and promote a 'European model' in the area of home affairs that guarantees 'a robust and comprehensive legal framework for data protection' (European Council 2010a) and in which security is 'one basis for freedom while at the same time offering strong standards of privacy' (The Future Group 2008).

Conclusion

Although this chapter may disappoint those who expect a clear answer about the European homeland and its territorial demarcation, it offers a number of ideas that should shape our thinking about the homeland and how the idea is carefully implemented without being explicitly mentioned.

First, given the history of Europe and the impressive development of the European integration project, there has been a lot of potential for the emergence of the ideal of 'homeland' as it has taken place in the US. However, European policy-makers have neglected the most important dimension of homeland; that is, 'community-building'. Although Europeans do feel part of a bigger project, very often they are neglected as a part of this process. The increasing activity at the policy-making level and the 'mushrooming' of new security projects and initiatives are unfortunately not accompanied by actions of similar strength that would aim to mobilise the populations and explain to them the objectives of those policies. The major problem here is that while policy-makers address the external source of a problem, they tend to forget that a large part of the problem is European society itself. This is, for instance, the case of religious groups and migrants – most of the integration or engagement efforts are targeting those groups, while at the same time completely neglecting working with host communities. This gap has been quickly filled in on one side by nationalist arguments that build on people's fears (e.g. increasing immigration) and by the feeling of disconnection on the other side (e.g. radicalisation of young Muslims).

Second, new dimensions of territoriality have resulted in the erosion of state authority and sovereignty. The process itself is very similar to a snowball effect whereby an initiative in one country quickly results in the adoption of similar measures in other countries, as illustrated by the case of the US and EU initiatives on border management. A solution could be a global approach, but this is difficult in light of the historical, ideological elements that a homeland security approach has generated among the domestic audience. Therefore, a successive redefinition would be necessary.

Third, the European idea of homeland also has a strong normative component, which is mostly defined by balancing justice, liberty and security. A major problem lies in the fact that these concepts are gaining new meanings as compared to the European Convention on Human Rights and the EU treaties. The jurisprudence of various bodies in recent years has made it crystal clear that the dynamic changes that our societies undergo also have an impact on how we make and execute laws.

Notes

1 The creation of homeland also has a power dimension, which is usually expressed by the self-sufficiency of a community in terms of manpower and material goods, especially land. This aspect will not be examined in this chapter because there is hardly any evidence that self-sufficiency was an important element from the US perspective. Still it needs to be said that it was undoubtedly one of the elements in the ideology built by fundamentalist terrorist organisations. For them, the US is an aggressor who not only uses other countries (i.e. in order to use their natural resources like oil), but even more importantly provides the support for other states who occupy territories of their brothers. Here the Middle East conflict serves as the best example of a pure nationalistic struggle for homeland.

2 The updated version of the National Homeland Security Strategy was adopted in 2007 and broadened the focus to real-world catastrophes such as Hurricane Katrina.

3 Interview with a former US official, Department of Homeland Security, Washington, DC, May 2007.

4 They have already been partially 'catapulted' by the terrorist attacks, but Bush's rhetoric has further enhanced this trend.

5 According to ABC News and the *Washington Post* opinion polls, the support for President Bush has changed from 55 per cent right before the 9/11 attacks to 86 per cent on 13 September in order to reach 92 per cent in October 2001 (the beginning of the war in Afghanistan). It remained above 50 per cent until April 2004.

6 The REAL ID Act establishes federal standards for state-issued driver's licenses and non-driver's identification cards.

7 It creates an entry and exit system, which uses biometrics to screen applicants

for admission to the US, on the basis of foreign travellers' arrival and departure records.

8　The Schengen area includes all EU Member States (with the exception of the UK, Ireland, Cyprus, Bulgaria and Romania) and non-EU states Switzerland, Norway and Iceland.

9　Belgium, Germany, Spain, France, Luxembourg, Netherlands and Austria.

10　For a more empirical discussion of the EU's border policies, see the two chapters by Pawlak and Kurowska and Léonard, respectively, in this book.

11　For instance, the case of the preamble to the Treaty establishing the constitution for Europe, where one of the controversies concerned the reference to God and the Judeo-Christian roots of the European civilisation.

12　It was introduced by the Maastricht Treaty and exists alongside national citizenship. According to Article 9 of the Treaty on European Union: 'Every national of a Member State shall be a citizen of the Union. Citizenship of the Union shall be additional to national citizenship and shall not replace it'. Articles 21 and 22 of the Treaty on the Functioning of the European Union further specify the rights and obligations attached to EU citizenship.

13　Article 222 of the Treaty on the Functioning of the European Union states:

> The Union and its Member States shall act jointly in a spirit of solidarity if a Member State is the object of a terrorist attack or the victim of a natural or man-made disaster. The Union shall mobilise all the instruments at its disposal, including the military resources made available by the Member States [...].

14　These were France, Italy, Germany, Portugal, Greece, Spain and the UK.

15　See Case T-306/01 and Case T-315/01, *Ahmed Ali Yusuf and Al Barakaat International Foundation and Yassin Abdullah Kadi* v. *Council of the European Union and Commission of the European Communities.*

3 Strategic patchwork or comprehensive framework?

Upside down security strategy development in the European Union

Ursula C. Schroeder

The 9/11 attacks fundamentally transformed the security landscape in the United States (US). Harshly criticised for its bureaucratic rivalries, lack of comprehensive intelligence and outmoded structures (e.g. US 9/11 Commission 2004), the US internal security architecture was overhauled swiftly and decisively during the past decade. Reviving earlier proposals by the Hart–Rudman Commission on institutional changes in the US national security architecture,[1] the Bush Administration appointed the first 'Homeland Security Tsar', published a National Homeland Security Strategy and created a Department of Homeland Security. Designed to overcome the fragmentation of homeland security competences into more than 40 federal agencies (see US Department of Homeland Security 2008: 3), the new Department became operational in early 2003.[2] Its creation was hailed as the 'most significant transformation of the US government in over a half-century' (The White House 2002e: 2).

In contrast, the reaction of the European Union (EU) to the terror attacks in New York, Madrid and London has been markedly different. Whereas the US government forged a new homeland security strategy and reorganised the established security system in line with it, the EU primarily built on existing capabilities. Unlike the US, the EU has not made use of the comprehensive 'homeland security' terminology in the development of its post-9/11 security strategies. In a bottom-up process, EU actors have instead focused on expanding established forms of internal security cooperation in Europe without paying much attention to larger strategic questions. Clearly, differences in the political systems of the US and the EU played a role here, as did the fact that counter-terrorism policies in the EU remain based on intergovernmental cooperation mechanisms. However, the chapter does not seek to explain the differential process of strategy development in the US and Europe. Instead, it focuses on the atypical process of strategy development in the EU. The analysis traces how and to what ends the EU has developed its internal and external security arms. In what scenarios is the EU willing to use its internal and external security capabilities?

In brief, the chapter argues that unlike in the US, the terror attacks of the past decade did not mark a strategic turning point for the EU. Instead, the EU has pursued a solution-driven approach to security strategy development, in which the evolution of strategy followed the availability of capabilities. The chapter outlines this upside-down process of strategy development in the EU and shows that its strategic priorities emerged primarily 'by stealth', instead of 'by design'. Addressing this book's interest in the evolution of a European homeland security policy area, the chapter shows that at least at the level of security strategies, this process has been incremental and not strategic. Diverging from traditionally hierarchical and top-down processes of national strategy development – as for example in the case of the US – security strategies in the EU have emerged both incrementally and belatedly.

The chapter first outlines the unusual process of creating the EU's security capabilities and strategic concepts. It shows that in contrast to traditional expectations of policy design (e.g. DeLeon 1999), EU internal and external security capabilities were constructed *before* EU Member States had come to a conclusion about the ends these capabilities and institutions should serve. In its second part, the chapter discusses the effects of bottom-up strategy-building on the development of EU internal and external security policies. Counter-intuitively, the chapter finds that this strategy-building process by stealth instead of by design had both enabling and constraining effects. As a result of the strategic void at the heart of the European security project, actors in several policy arenas within the complex EU architecture were able to develop different and sometimes conflicting strategic ends: human security, crime-fighting, common defence and stabilisation. Bypassing highly contentious political debates about the larger aims of European security policies, the incremental development of EU security goals made the emergence of a broad range of EU security strategies possible. At the same time, the phenomenon that several sectoral strategies developed in a parallel and fragmented process has led to fault lines in the EU's security policies and to a patchwork of strategic thinking.

The convergence of internal and external security strategies

National security strategies or 'grand strategies' have traditionally been military in nature. Outlining the political purposes of warfare, military strategy has been defined as 'the art of distributing and applying military means to fulfil the ends of policy' (Liddell Hart 1991: 321). In an alternative conception, it has been defined as the 'bridge that relates military power to political purpose' and as '*the use that is made of force and the threat of force for the ends of policy*' (Gray 1999: 17, italics in original; see also Strachan 2005). These adaptations of Clausewitzian thinking understand military strategy as an organizing principle for the larger political objectives of the use of force in warfare. Drawing on these definitions, but using them in a wider sense outside the exclusively military sphere, the article understands grand strategy as a plan of action that applies specific means to larger objectives. In relation to foreign and security policy, strategy links the use of economic, military or diplomatic power to specific political ends and foreign policy objectives (see further Kennedy 1991).

In brief, security strategies specify the security interests of a state and the means through which it aims to uphold these interests. They encapsulate a state's understanding of what security is and who the main addressees of security policies are. A contested concept *par excellence*, the specific understanding of security employed in a national security strategy is the outcome of political struggles over the allocation of state resources and capabilities for a set of security objectives. Security strategies thus serve as political frameworks that legitimise policy choices in the security field. For this reason strategy development is an eminently political and often contentious process.

National security strategies are usually structured in similar ways. Setting out a state's understanding of its specific security and threat environment first, most strategies follow this up with an outline of its vital political, military and economic interests. After first defining the longer-term purposes and larger aims of security policies, strategies outline specific policies in distinct fields, comment on the nature of the relationship with other major players in the international system, and outline specific missions of the armed forces. Finally, national security strategies often define the general force structure and procurement decisions necessary to fulfil the missions outlined. In the internal security field, the development of clear-cut strategies is rare. The setting of strategic priorities has often taken the shape of action plans, policy frameworks or other conceptual documents.

The scope of national security strategies has traditionally been state-centric. In the realist perspective widespread during the Cold War, grand strategies focused primarily on upholding the military conditions necessary for the survival of the nation-state in a potentially hostile international environment. This understanding, however, has changed considerably since the end of the Cold War. In today's complex security environment (e.g. Missiroli 2006; Kirchner and Sperling 2002), military means have become only one type of means amongst several to achieve desired outcomes. Security strategies have started to include a variety of objectives outside the classical military sphere. Public debates about widening the referent object of security policies – from state security to societal or human security – and a rise in non-military security concerns – for example, environmental, health or energy concerns – have resulted in a broader understanding of security in many security strategies.

At the same time, the blurring of internal and external security challenges has left a mark on current security strategies. While traditional security strategies were developed primarily for the realm of defence policy, today previously internal security concerns, such as terrorism and organised crime, take pride of place in many external security strategies. Several examples showcase the extent of this transformation. The French White Paper on Defence, for instance, places the threat of terrorism front and centre, concluding that 'the separation between internal and external security is fading' (Présidence de la République Française 2008). The first British National Security Strategy of March 2008 also acknowledges the wide-sweeping changes in the UK's strategic outlook:

> In the past, national security was understood as dealing with the protection of the state and its vital interests from attacks by other states. [...] Over recent decades, our view of national security has broadened to include threats to individual citizens and to our way of life.
>
> (UK Cabinet Office 2008: 3)

Finally, the US National Security Strategy 2010 confirms that the US is 'moving beyond traditional distinctions between homeland and national security' (The White House 2010: 10). Therefore, US engagement in pursuing its security interests increasingly depends 'upon the effective use and integration of different elements of American power' (p. 11).

On the whole, national security strategies have changed both functions and scope: state-centric concepts of security have given way to broader ones at the same time as traditional conceptions of military defence have opened up to include a wider set of civilian and military activities. Has this general trend been replicated during the process of strategy formulation in the EU? The following pages trace the upside-down evolution of the EU's institutional capacities and strategic frameworks for its internal and external security policies.

The evolution of EU security capabilities

As the policy field perhaps most closely linked to national sovereignty and decision-making, the development of a European security architecture was initially met with mistrust and opposition by EU Member States. Its relatively rapid institutionalisation during the past decade has therefore been an astonishing development in itself. Yet, this development has been driven to a striking extent by technical and institutional questions instead of political debates. In the internal and external security field, strategic questions took a back seat to debates about the development of internal and external security institutions and capabilities.

Since the beginnings of the EU's external security role at the Cologne European Council in 1999, progress in establishing the political and operational institutions for the Common Security and Defence Policy (CSDP)[3] has been swift (e.g. Grevi 2009; Menon 2009). Despite various setbacks during the deployment of the EU's first European Security and Defence

Policy (ESDP) missions, many observers have agreed that the EU has been remarkably successful in expanding its competence base into the field of external security.

However, one peculiarity of the EU's institutional development in this field has been the nearly exclusive focus on ESDP capabilities. A brief glance at the major documents published on progress in the EU's external security role since its inception – the biannual EU Presidency Reports and the European Council Conclusions on ESDP/CSDP – showcases the EU's 'capabilities first' approach to ESDP/CSDP. Also the biannual EU progress reports on ESDP have focused almost entirely on improvements in the EU's institutional architecture and capabilities. Stopping short at completely neglecting the strategic angle of the ESDP/CSDP, these documents routinely point to the EU's general commitment 'to preserve peace and strengthen international security in accordance with the principles of the UN Charter' (e.g. European Council 1999b, 2000).

Ever since the ESDP was declared operational at the European Council in Laeken 2001, the institutionalisation of the ESDP/CSDP has followed a capability-driven trajectory. Many observers of this process have similarly limited their discussions of the status quo of the EU's external security role to questions of institutional and capability development. The following issues have been discussed as particularly salient during the evolution of the EU's external role: the institutional fragmentation of EU security competences into first-pillar European Commission and second-pillar European Council activities and the resulting challenges of coordination and coherence (e.g. Gourlay 2006; Khol 2006); the challenges of capability development and military force generation through the ECAP process (e.g. Schmitt 2005) as well as issues of operational planning and deployment in a variety of individual ESDP missions. From its very beginning, the institutionalisation of the EU's external security policy field has proceeded through the rapid expansion of the EU's security capabilities, while at the same time avoiding the more difficult discussion of the strategic goals these capabilities should serve.

Progress in the internal security field has followed a similar trajectory. In 1999, the EU 'kick-started' the establishment of its Justice and Home Affairs (JHA) policy at the European Council in Tampere (European Council 1999a). Developing at least as rapidly as the EU's external security arm, JHA policies and institutions have 'mushroomed' during the past decade. Covering the whole range of justice, liberty and security issues that arise in the context of the EU's Area of Freedom, Security and Justice (AFSJ), JHA policies have become one of the fasted growing domains of EU action (see Monar 2006a: 495). Initially meant to enhance internal security cooperation across the EU's common borders to compensate for the establishment of an area of free movement in Europe, the EU's internal security policy field has considerably extended its scope and geographical coverage. In institutional terms, the Amsterdam Treaty transferred the issues of judicial cooperation in civil matters, immigration and asylum policies to the EU's first pillar. At the same time, the Schengen Agreement was incorporated into the EU's legal system.

With the adoption of the Treaty of Lisbon, the EU's competences in the JHA field changed dramatically again. The Treaty of Lisbon effectively replaced the previous unwieldy set of third-pillar legislative instruments with the EU's Community method – the 'ordinary legislative procedure' (see Ladenburger 2008; Donnelly 2008; Peers 2009 for detailed discussions). As a result, the binding rules of the single market (regulations, directives and decisions) now apply to JHA policies including judicial and police cooperation in criminal matters. The integration of internal security legislation into the EU's standard decision-making procedure was a huge breakthrough for policy-making in this field.

However, the internal security field primarily also developed in an incremental fashion (see den Boer and Wallace 2000 for a similar assessment of early developments). Particularly in the early days, larger strategic frameworks for internal security cooperation remained remarkably absent. The earliest forms of police and intelligence cooperation started out as informal meetings of law enforcement and intelligence professionals that responded to the rise in terror attacks during the 1970s. In 1975, the Rome European Council initiated the loose and intergovernmental TREVI cooperation as a framework for internal security cooperation. Later on, when these informal cooperation and information exchange bodies were brought into the framework of the EU's legislative framework, existing informal forms of cooperation were transposed into newly created formal EU bodies and committees. Left behind in the shadow of more high profile policy initiatives, the evolution of the EU's internal security capabilities has remained closely linked to the operational needs of internal security professionals. Particularly in contrast to ESDP's relatively high media exposure, the EU's internal security institutions have not received much attention. Building mainly on pre-existing forms of professional cooperation, institutional advances in internal security cooperation have been perceived as a largely technical and legalistic affair. Overall, the development of the EU's internal security system has been a story of incremental approximations of national criminal justice systems rather than one of the implementation of top-down strategies.

The creation of EU security strategies: better late than never?

Unlike the rapid creation of EU security capabilities, the development of strategic frameworks for the new ESDP and JHA capabilities proceeded at a much slower pace. Furthermore, the process of strategy development did not result in a formal national security strategy as outlined above. Instead, EU political priority-setting in the security field has been characterised by ad hoc, quick fixes to pressing short-term security issues at the expense of longer term strategic thought. In contrast to the core role that security strategies commonly play in determining policy in national political arenas, EU strategies have lagged behind the institutionalisation of a European security architecture. Mostly procedural in scope and focused on dividing competences among European actors, EU security concepts and frameworks were late to arrive on the scene while not having the same status as traditional national security strategies. Adopted in often relatively technical processes without much exposure to public debates, the influence of EU security concepts has been constrained by their often ambiguous formal status and by the relatively low relevance assigned to them. The following section compares the process of strategy development in the EU's internal and external security architecture.

Latecomer to the external security field: the European Security Strategy

In contrast to the widespread attention paid to sometimes rather technical questions of EU capability development, the EU's strategic ends for its external security arm have remained vague. Particularly in the early years of the ESDP, EU Member States studiously avoided potentially contentious strategic choices by deciding on the mandates of future ESDP missions on a lowest common denominator basis. Most missions were deployed ad hoc and to relatively safe and uncontroversial locations, while the comparatively more contentious EU military mission to the Democratic Republic of Congo in 2003 (Artemis) remained under the aegis of France as the lead nation. The choice for specific EU mission formats frequently followed a logic of feasibility – that is, what the EU *was able to do* at a given moment in time – rather than a strategic logic of what would fit into the overall security concept of the EU (see Kurowska 2008 for a discussion).

At the same time, the question to what ends the EU had created its set of civilian and military capabilities was routinely answered with reference to the relatively broad and unspecific aims of the UN Charter and the Petersberg tasks.[4] Outside these two conceptual frameworks, the EU's external security priorities were described by the vague label of 'crisis management'. Although it has become a common frame of reference for the EU's civilian and military ESDP missions deployed around the globe, observers agree that its 'meaning has not been clearly defined at the EU level' (Nowak 2006: 16). Also the Treaty of Maastricht's formulation that one of the objectives of the EU is the implementation of a common foreign and security policy, including the 'eventual framing of a common defence policy, which might in time lead to a common defence' (Treaty of Maastricht, Title V, J4), has remained largely unfulfilled. Even after the coming into force of the Treaty of Lisbon in December 2009, EU Member States remain reluctant to discuss the potential defence dimension of the EU's Common Security and Defence Policy.

With EU Member States unable to agree on specific scenarios for the EU's security and defence policy, strategy development initially proceeded very slowly. In effect, the EU did not have a security strategy at all during the first years of the ESDP's existence. In late 2003, the comprehensive European Security Strategy (ESS) was finally adopted (European Council 2003b). Yet, has it become the strategic 'saving grace' of European security policies? This chapter argues that not even the adoption of the ESS in December 2003 fundamentally changed the strategic outlook of the EU. The development of a common European security policy has remained a capability-driven process.

The ESS unites a wide variety of civilian and military security issues in a comprehensive framework. Nevertheless, it has remained relatively vague in its policy recommendations. Written by a small team of Javier Solana's policy planning staff, the ESS analyses the EU's security environment and acknowledges the increasing relevance of transnational security threats such as the proliferation of WMD, transnational terrorism and organised crime, regional conflict and the challenges associated with weak and failing states. Calling for a 'mixture of intelligence, police, judicial, military and other means' (European Council 2003b: 7), the strategy argued that these complex threats cannot be tackled by purely military means. At the same time, it acknowledged that the EU had created a number of different instruments 'each of which has its own structure and rationale' (European Council 2003b: 13). Thus, the challenge of the ESS was to 'bring together the different instruments and capabilities: European assistance programmes and the European Development Fund, military and civilian capabilities from Member States and other instruments' (European Council 2003b). Clearly comprehensive in its approach to security, the ESS has become the cornerstone of all major EU policy documents in the security domain. Its impact, however, has remained limited.

Instead of being perceived as a 'real' strategy that guides EU security-political actions, the ESS is widely seen as being just a general statement of principles. A former Chief of Staff of the EU Military Staff acknowledged that, while the ESS has generally been accepted in the EU security community as 'a rough guide for action, it was perhaps not a strategy document in the true military sense' (UK House of Lords 2008e: 12). This becomes obvious when the ESS's provisions are compared to the classical way of defining a 'grand strategy' as a plan of action that calculates the relationship between specific means and political ends. Indeed, the ESS qualifies neither as a military nor civilian strategy in the classical sense (see Quille 2004: 425; Duke 2004: 460; Toje 2005: 119 for similar assessments). Particularly in comparison with the US National Security Strategy, it 'reads more like an inspirational sketch' (Bailes 2004: 26).

Failing to clearly prioritise the EU's policy objectives in the field of external security, the ESS defines three general strategic objectives of the EU ('addressing the threats', 'building security in our neighbourhood' and fostering 'an international order based on effective multilateralism'). Yet, unlike other strategies, it does not indicate the conditions for the use of military force or civilian capabilities in the pursuit of specific foreign policy ends. Due to the lack of clear choices, the ESS has remained a general statement of intent, but has not played a critical role in defining European security interests. The December 2008 report on the implementation of the ESS did little to change this situation (European Council 2008). The implementation report called for a more capable, more coherent and more active EU. This was mainly a reiteration of the concerns and proposed solutions of the original strategy. The report simply reconfirmed the EU's original comprehensive approach to security. In brief, the traditional order of first developing a security strategy and then following its guidelines with the aid of specific instruments was turned upside-down in the case of the EU: it first started to develop a set of civilian and military capabilities and then decided on how to use it.

EU internal security: the proliferation of programmes and road maps

The process of strategy development played out somewhat differently in the EU's internal security field. Slower than the strategy development in the external security field, internal security policies remained based on a confusing set of sectoral road maps and programmes for a whole decade. It was only in 2010 that the EU adopted the Internal Security Strategy (ISS) (Council of the European Union 2010e), which tried to join up the different EU initiatives in the field into a coherent conceptual framework.

The EU's first policy framework on questions of internal security was initially known somewhat unceremoniously as the Tampere Programme (1999–2003). The special European Council meeting in Tampere in 1999 created the Area of Freedom, Security and Justice (AFSJ) and formulated a basic understanding of policy priorities in Justice and Home Affairs (JHA) matters. As its core principle, the Tampere Programme held that the 'challenge of the Amsterdam Treaty is now to ensure that freedom, which includes the right to move freely throughout the Union, can be enjoyed in conditions of security and justice accessible to all' (European Council 1999a). The follow-up 'Hague Programme' (2004–2009) further deepened the chosen course of EU internal security cooperation. It specifically highlighted the relevance of 'multidisciplinary and concerted action both at EU and at national level' on immigration and asylum issues alongside the prevention of terrorism (European Council 2004b: 4).

Despite progress on individual policy issues, neither programme can be qualified as a unifying and visionary strategic statement of EU internal security interests. The Tampere and Hague programmes aggregated a set of diverse policy interests instead – inter alia mutual recognition of judicial decisions, a common asylum system and cooperation against crime and terrorism – under the common roof of 'Justice, Liberty, and Security' policies. The third 'Stockholm Programme' (2010–2014) continues this trend, basing its substantive propositions on the policies of the previous decade. Its policy priorities highlight the need for rights- and citizen-based programmes. Debating the dilemma of reconciling security and liberty, the Programme stresses that 'law enforcement measures [...] and measures to safeguard individual rights, the rule of law and international protection rules [...] go hand in hand' (European Council 2010a: 4). Similar to the Hague Programme, it promotes a comprehensive approach to internal security governance and calls for further efforts in order to improve coherence between policy areas (European Council 2010a).

The three programmes were primarily technical documents geared towards the needs of EU security practitioners and law-makers rather than towards the general public. Thus, they have retained a relatively low profile in public debates. At the same time, the agenda-setting power developed by those programmes can be characterised as being considerably higher than that of the ESS. The European Commission has routinely translated the Tampere, Hague and Stockholm Programmes into concrete action plans and road maps that contain timetables and benchmarks for the adoption and implementation of specific policies (see e.g. European Commission 2010a). An annual report on the implementation of the different programmes rounds off the cycle of policy development. These reports, known as the AFSJ 'implementation scoreboard', monitor the adoption of legislative measures both at the EU level and within EU Member States. In short, policy programmes in the EU's internal security field are followed up by specific implementation strategies and a review process based on a system of benchmarks. In the shadow of more public and contentious discussions about the scope of the EU's external security capabilities, JHA actors have in this manner managed to formulate and implement a large number of policy initiatives during the past decade.

The first cuts at developing strategy in the internal security field were the EU's 'Strategy for the External Dimension of JHA' and its 'Counter-terrorism Strategy' in 2005. Both documents, however, essentially remained limited, only collecting a fragmented set of existing service-level initiatives into a single document. A horizontal and cross-pillar strategy that aims to link the EU's internal security and external security policies, the EU's Strategy for the External Dimension of JHA emphasises the role of internal security for the relationship between the EU and its neighbouring states. Focusing on common programmes to manage migration flows into the EU and to counter organised crime, terrorism and corruption at their roots, the strategy aims to improve the EU's internal security while at the same time supporting the EU's political objectives in its external relations (see Balzacq 2008 for an overview). Its substance was developed nearly exclusively within the EU's third pillar, with only limited input by external security stakeholders. JHA actors 'hijacked' the External JHA Strategy and effectively limited the access of the other services involved both in the drafting process and during the inter-service consultations (see Pawlak 2009b). The EU's Counter-terrorism Strategy, on the other hand, proved to be a step away from the post-9/11 EU Counter-terrorism Action Plan. Presenting a list of legislative initiatives to enhance the EU's fight against terrorism, the action plan and its accompanying road map resembled a lengthy laundry list rather than a comprehensive strategy. The 2005 Counter-terrorism Strategy summarised the different elements of EU counter-terrorism policy under a set of four headings (prevent, protect, pursue and respond; see Council of the European Union 2005b). Yet again, strategy clearly followed existing policies and developed incrementally.

The latest step in the process of strategy development has been the adoption of the ISS in February 2010. Initiated by the Spanish Presidency, the strategy aims to 'bring together in a sole document all the measures that have been adopted over the years and provide them with "a framework to set down strategic guidelines"' (Spanish Presidency of the Council of the European Union 2010). In late 2010, the transformation of the relatively generic strategy into an operational document was still under way. The plan is to put an operational plan for the strategy into place by 2014 (Belgian Presidency of the Council of the European Union 2010).

Echoing the outlook of other EU documents in the security field, the ISS understands internal security in an encompassing way as the protection of 'people and the values of freedom and democracy, so that everyone can enjoy their daily lives without fear' (Council of the European Union 2010e: 4). Based on a 'wide and comprehensive concept which straddles multiple sectors' (Council of the European Union 2010e: 2), the ISS is designed to be an 'indispensable complement' (Council of the European Union 2010e: 17) to the external ESS. The ISS lists multiple challenges to the EU's internal AFSJ[5] and outlines the EU's common tools and policies in response to this complex tableau of threats. Similar to the Counter-terrorism Strategy, the EU's set of responses is grouped into five main categories that address both causes and consequences of internal security challenges: preparedness, prevention, protection, response and recovery (Council of the European Union 2010e: 14). By joining up the EU's separate sectoral activities in the fields of law enforcement, judicial cooperation, border management, civil protection and disaster management into a single streamlined strategy, the ISS promotes a common European approach to countering internal security threats.

Optimistically entitled 'Towards a European Security Model', the ISS nevertheless remains relatively vague on the specific substance of this model. At its core lie the general principles of commitment to the protection of human rights and freedoms, the understanding that internal and external security have become interdependent, and a commitment to cooperation and solidarity between EU Member States (see Council of the European Union 2010e: 2). Whether or not the strategy will be able to develop the integrative momentum necessary to join up policy fields as diverse as preventive civil protection policies and repressive law enforcement activities remains uncertain. As it stands now, the ISS remains a summary of existing initiatives in the field of internal security. It does not promote a new strategic approach to the complex internal security challenges the EU faces. Instead, and very similar to the ESS, the document remains a declaration of intent that does not intervene into established power structures and interests in the field. Early studies of the ISS's role and potential impact agree. Monar (2010a: 37) finds that the ISS 'offers nothing more than a fairly insubstantial repetition of the main points already made in the Stockholm Programme'. While the presentation of EU internal security instruments in a single document is seen as commendable, Arteaga (2010: 3) also makes the point that the ISS 'falls short' as a 'means to achieve the purpose of acting as a catalyst, rationalising and integrating the internal security sector in the EU'.

A second shortfall is the lack of the ISS's integration into the wider field of security policy. Although the strategy in principle acknowledges the need to link internal and external security policies more closely, it effectively remains tied to a traditional understanding of internal security. It does not mention the EU's major external security players and does not define the relationship between internal and external security objectives and instruments in the EU (see also Arteaga 2010: 4; Monar 2010a).

On the positive side, however, the EU has managed to put internal security concerns firmly on its agenda during the past decade. The EU has not only developed a wide range of sectoral policies that deal with the various aspects of JHA, we have also witnessed a slow development of the EU-wide understanding of the need to develop a comprehensive European internal security model. The existing strategic document nevertheless stops short of this ambitious goal. The ISS provides a good overview of existing internal security initiatives, but is explicitly 'not aimed at creating any new competences' (Council of the European Union 2010e: 2) and does not mark a major strategic departure in the way the EU handles its internal security challenges.

Effects of incremental strategy development

The creation of the EU's internal and external security policies has followed a somewhat unusual path. Unlike the classical understanding of policy development through a 'policy cycle' that moves from agenda-setting to policy formulation to implementation to evaluation, we have seen that the EU security field developed, at least partially, in reverse. The development of security capabilities and instruments preceded the formulation of security strategies at the EU level. At the same time, more general debates about the direction and aims of European internal and external security integration were often left to small groups of security practitioners while not receiving much public attention. The chosen focus on often technical questions of capability development served as the lowest common denominator for the creation of an EU security architecture. It also avoided politically contentious questions about scenarios for its future use. What effects does this incremental process of strategy-shaping by stealth, rather than by design, have on the evolution of overarching security strategies for the EU? The following section argues that this peculiar process of security policy development has had both enabling and constraining effects on the evolution of security strategies.

Enabling effect: the multiplication of strategic ends

Intriguingly, the vagueness of EU strategies has had an enabling effect on security policy development. Although the EU's 'strategic void' has become a frequent argument to explain the only slow progress of European-wide security cooperation, it has provided an incentive for a dynamic process of policy innovation at the same time. As a result, EU security actors have been able to develop a variety of different strategic ends and priorities. In practice, different actors in the EU's decision-making system have pushed for specific and sometimes conflicting policy goals in the security field. In the external security field, the relatively large leeway built into the EU's strategic documents has enabled the ESDP's rapid extension of competences from an initially limited set of military peacekeeping scenarios to a broad range of external stabilisation and security sector reform (SSR) tasks. The wide scope of the ESS made this extension possible by leaving 'all doors open for potential future missions' (Hansen 2006: 5). One of the advantages of the rather general nature of the ESS was that it stayed 'broad-brush enough for all the EU members to read their favourite agendas into it' (Bailes 2005: 14). Similarly to the ISS, the ESS is not an immediately operational document (see Biscop 2004: 37). Nevertheless, it has paved the way for a broader debate about the aims and the future of the European security and defence policy. The EU's strategic outlook in the internal security field has long remained severely underdeveloped and the EU took a full decade to publish an ISS after the establishment of the AFSJ in 1999. Promoting the broad notion of a European model of internal security that balances freedom, security and justice in equal measures, the ISS has remained a projection screen that can incorporate diverse policy styles and goals. The two encompassing but relatively vague internal and external security strategies still coexist with a multitude of more specific lower-level policy programmes and frameworks. Developed as ad hoc solutions to acute challenges or resulting from specific organisational interests at the service level, a variety of strategic goals for the EU's security policies have emerged during the past decade. We can distinguish three to four major strategic ends for the EU's security policies. Emerging within distinct and often disjointed organisational fields, the three goals of 'stabilisation and governance', 'human security' and 'crime-fighting' can be identified as major determinants of EU policy-making in the security field. Stabilisation is mostly a goal pursued within the ESDP, human security was promoted by actors within the EU's development assistance programmes, while crime-fighting is strongly linked to the internal security field. A fourth goal – the 'eventual framing of a common defence policy, which might in time lead to a common defence' (Treaty of Maastricht, Title V, J4) – has remained largely unredeemed. Even after the coming into force of the Treaty of Lisbon, EU Member States remained reluctant to discuss the potential 'defence' dimension of the CSDP.[6]

Stabilisation

The predominant strategic aim of the EU's external security policies is the promotion of stability in its neighbourhood. The aim of creating regional stability and well-governed, sustainable political orders that do not interfere with the EU's internal security pervades policies towards Africa, the Balkans and the Mediterranean states. It is a frequent feature of regional strategy papers. The 1995 Barcelona Declaration on the Euro-Mediterranean Partnership already declared peace, stability and prosperity to be its general objective for the Mediterranean basin (Council of the European Union 1995). The 2003 'Wider Europe Strategy' – predecessor to the EU's current neighbourhood policy – similarly aimed at creating 'an enlarged area of political stability and functioning rule of law' in the states surrounding the EU's territory (European Commission 2003d: 3). The European Neighbourhood Policy (ENP) itself also focuses on reinforcing the 'stability, security and well-being' (European Commission 2004a: 4) of both EU and neighbouring states by promoting a series of governance- and stability-oriented measures in the EU's Southern and Eastern neighbourhood. It envisages a 'ring of countries, sharing the EU's fundamental values and objectives, drawn into an increasingly close relationship, going beyond co-operation to involve a significant measure of economic and political integration' (European Commission 2004a: 5). The follow-up declaration on strengthening this project emphasised again the EU's 'vital interest' in 'seeing greater economic development and stability and better governance in its neighbourhood' (European Commission 2006a: 2). The European Commission's regional strategy for the Horn of Africa is another example of a predominantly stability-oriented foreign policy strategy. It argues that 'stability in the Horn of Africa is also strategically crucial for EU security. Cross-border dynamics, such as illegal migration and trafficking of arms, drugs and refugee flows, are factors contributing to instability and tensions that spread throughout the Horn of Africa and beyond, and could even reach the EU' (European Commission 2006b: 5). The frequently voiced strategic concern to create stable regional orders in the EU's neighbourhood resonates strongly in the ESS. It argues that the EU should 'promote a ring of well governed countries' in its neighbourhood, as 'the best protection for our security is a world of well-governed democratic states' (European Council 2003b: 8, 10). The EU Concept for ESDP Support to Security Sector Reform provides another piece of the stabilisation puzzle, being a path towards its practical implementation. Building on the understanding that well-governed and democratically controlled security sectors contribute to political stability in a region or country, the EU's SSR Strategy aims at contributing to an 'accountable, effective and efficient' security system that 'can be a force for peace and stability, fostering democracy and promoting local and regional stability' (Council of the European Union 2005a: 4).

Finally, also several mission concepts for the EU's ESDP/CFSP operations have placed the objective of stabilisation at the top of their agenda. Particularly numerous police and rule of law missions[7] aim to strengthen the security institutions of states and regions in crisis and point to the practical relevance of stability-oriented mandates in the EU's Common Security and Defence Policy.

Human security

As the largest provider of development aid in the world,[8] the EU generally aims to reduce poverty around the globe and to promote good governance, human and economic development in the framework of the UN Millennium Goals. The EU has also accepted the growing consensus in the international development community that security and development policies are interdependent. Moving away from a purely economic outlook on development cooperation, development donors have increasingly accepted the need to foster the good governance of political and security institutions as a precondition for sustainable development (see in general Klingebiel 2006; Vennesson and Büger 2009). Both the 2003 ESS and the 2005 European Consensus on Development reiterate the need to integrate security and development policies. In the end, the Council Conclusions on Security and Development argued in 2007 that the 'nexus between development and security should inform EU strategies and policies in order to contribute to the coherence of EU external action' (Council of the European Union 2007d). Tasked with further developing work on security and development by the Council Conclusions, the European Commission's Directorate General for External Relations commissioned a study on the state of the security-development nexus in EU external relations. Distributed internally in early 2009, this inward-looking document assessed the EU's practices of coordinating its security and development policies in a number of empirical cases.

Building on the assumption that there can be no sustainable development without guaranteed physical security, a vocal group of civil society experts has begun to promote the strategic aim of 'human security' for the EU's external relations. In contrast to traditional forms of state or national security, their concept of human security refers to 'freedom for individuals from basic insecurities caused by gross human rights violations' (Study Group on Europe's Security Capabilities 2004: 5). In a report commissioned by Javier Solana, the Study Group advanced the idea that the EU should develop a 'Human Security Doctrine' for its external relations. An epistemic community (Haas 1992: 3) par excellence, this group of policy practitioners and academics shares a set of normative beliefs and a common policy enterprise: the advance of human security as 'a proactive strategic narrative' as well as an 'enduring and dynamic organizing frame for security action' (Kaldor *et al.*: 2007: 273; see also Matlary 2006).

Several EU policy programmes have used human security language to describe their goals. For instance, the Gothenburg 'programme on the prevention of violent conflict' argued that 'the international community has a political and moral responsibility to act to avoid the human suffering and the destruction of resources caused by violent conflicts' (European Council 2001a: 1). Similarly, the European Commission's Communication on Governance and Development held in 2003 that 'the concept of security is increasingly understood not just in terms of security of the state, but also embraces the broad notion of human security, which involves the ability to live in freedom, peace and safety. Security must be seen both as a national interest and as part of the individual rights' (European Commission 2003c: 8). A first outcome of the recent attention to security issues in European Community assistance programmes has been an increased focus on comprehensive security sector reforms, as enshrined in the 'Community Concept for Security Sector Reform' (European Commission 2006c). The concept enables the European Commission to address governance deficits in security sectors worldwide and is aimed at fostering the underlying peaceful conditions necessary for sustainable development.

Crime-fighting

The EU's second goal of fostering human security has to some extent been counteracted by a third strategic objective promoted predominantly by actors in the field of JHA. Faced with increasingly transnational forms of serious crime and terrorism, the EU's internal security agenda has become a central aspect of its external relations with its direct neighbourhood and further afield. First set out in the strategy on the 'External Dimension of Justice and Home Affairs' (Council of the European Union 2005c), internal security interests have started to play a large role in the conclusion of stabilisation and association agreements as well as in partnerships with states in the EU's southern and eastern neighbourhood.

Clear expressions of the 'internal security' objective underlying EU external security policies have been reiterated in all major JHA-strategy papers during the past decade. After the terror attacks of 11 September 2001 in New York and the attacks of 3 March 2004 in Madrid, JHA strategies targeting the EU's southern neighbourhood moved into the focus of JHA policy-makers. One of the earliest expressions of the EU's focus on JHA in its external relations was the 2002 Valencia Action Plan. In the context of the Euro-Mediterranean Partnership, it highlighted the strategic importance of the Mediterranean region for Europe and called for more inter-regional cooperation in the fields of 'justice, in combating drugs, organised crime and terrorism as well as cooperation in the treatment of issues relating to the social integration of migrants, migration and movements of people' (Council of the European Union 2002b). The 2004 Hague Programme for Justice and Home Affairs and the 2005 External Dimension of Justice and Home Affairs strategy once and for all staked out the claims of internal security actors in the EU's external relations. The Hague Programme (European Council 2004b: 42) for the first time outlined the contours of a strategy for the EU's external JHA policies and considered the 'development of a coherent external dimension of the Union policy of freedom, security and justice [...] a growing priority'. To improve the internal security of the EU, the Hague Programme specifically called for increases in the funding for counter-terrorism-related capacity-building projects in third countries (European Council 2004b: 21).

Similarly, the Strategy on the External Dimension of JHA stressed the need to build judicial and police capacities in third countries in order to respond to the needs of EU citizens. It therefore highlighted that the EU's relationship with countries seeking closer partnership needed to cover 'the full range of freedom, security and justice issues (e.g. counter-terrorism, organised crime, corruption, drugs, managed migration, human rights, access to justice)' (Council of the European Union 2005c: 7). In a similar vein, also the 2004 European Neighbourhood Policy and the Vienna Declaration on Security Partnerships (Council of the European Union 2006b) emphasised the increased internal security dimension in the relations between the EU and its neighbours.

Further, several civilian and military CSDP missions have incorporated crime-fighting tasks into their mandates. Particularly the EU's police missions in the Balkans have continued to play a very visible role in pursuing the EU's external JHA strategy. In Bosnia, Macedonia and Kosovo, CSDP missions train and support local police forces and are involved in reforming the national criminal justice systems. Mandated both to establish 'European-style' democratic policing (see Collantes Celador 2005) and to assist host countries in their fight against organised crime, these missions contribute to the EU's objective of strengthening its internal security through externalizing counter-crime policies.

Constraining effect: fragmented and conflicting strategic goals

As shown, the EU's security agenda is not of a piece, but has emerged through the interventions of a series of actors both at the EU's political and service levels. Because of the outlined incremental and often capacity-driven development of the EU's strategic goals, the EU's multiple strategic documents end up promoting different strategic aims in parallel. The negative implications are obvious: strategic vagueness should lead to the development of inefficient policy solutions. In the discussed case, this holds partially true: the 'sad fact that the EU has no strategic vision in foreign affairs' (Bet-El 2006: 14) has led to slow and cumbersome ad hoc decisions on the individual circumstances under which the EU is willing to deploy its civilian and military capabilities. The development of the EU Battlegroup Concept[9] illustrates the prevalence of operational level over strategic choices. Since it has not been developed within a specific strategic framework, it has been characterised as a 'concept in search of a strategy' (Gowan 2005: 17). In the internal security field, conflicts between EU Member States about a comprehensive approach to counter-terrorism similarly impeded the formulation of innovative policies and led to a lowest common denominator approach to fighting the threat of terrorism.

A further drawback has been the potential for conflict between proliferating strategic aims that cannot always be easily integrated into a single 'comprehensive' strategy. The goals of fostering stable governance structures, fighting crime and promoting human security do not always go hand in hand. Especially the recent development of the 'crime-fighting' goal in the EU's foreign relations policies collides with its more encompassing human security strategies. Following the assessment of the ESS that transnational security challenges can have direct and adverse effects on the European internal security landscape, the EU has promoted the new 'External Dimension of Justice and Home Affairs' as one of its central priorities in its external relations. Whereas crime-fighting before clearly fell into the competence sphere of third-pillar internal security actors, the convergence of internal and external security policies has led the EU to place particular emphasis on counter-terrorism and counter-organised crime capacity-building in its external police and judicial reform programmes.

Particularly the western Balkans and southern Mediterranean regions have come under increasing pressure to enhance their cooperation with the Union's fight against organised crime and terrorism (see Council of the European Union 2006a, 2006b). In these cases, the EU has been torn between its external policy goal of fostering democratic reforms and its quest for domestic security through fighting crime and stabilizing its neighbouring 'ring of friends'. Particularly the crime-fighting approach with its sometimes rather one-sided interest in enhancing the *effectiveness* of internal security bodies in third countries has 'not [been] positive' (Ball 2004; see also Youngs 2008) for improving their transparency and democratic accountability. As a result, the human security goal of developing well-governed security institutions that are able to provide a high level of security to the citizens of a recipient country collides with the EU's interest in diminishing the threat of organised crime to its territory. Although both policy goals could be complementary in principle, so far they have created a fault line that is cutting across the EU's security policies.

Conclusion

This chapter has outlined the 'upside-down' process of strategy development in the EU. In contrast to the centralised and top-down post-9/11 reorganisation of the US security architecture, the EU's reaction to the terror attacks of the past few years and more generally to an increasingly complex security environment has been characterised by a bottom-up and 'more of the same' approach. As a result, EU actors at different levels of the decision-making process have authored a long series of strategic documents: the EU's ISS, ESS, the Strategy for the External Dimension of Justice and Home Affairs, the Counter-terrorism Strategy, the European Neighbourhood Strategy and the Tampere, Hague and Stockholm Programmes, to name only the most relevant. None of the discussed documents, however, has been able to unequivocally answer the essential question of any strategic document: what is to be protected from whom with what means? Not even the two internal and external security strategies have clearly linked the EU's new security capabilities to specific political ends. Instead, the chapter found that a mostly capability-driven process of policy development has led to the emergence of several, sometimes contradictory, strategic aims in different EU policy arenas. Depending on the institutional location of the strategic claims made, the EU is meant to primarily focus on fighting crime, on providing for the security of individual human beings in crisis regions, on creating a stable neighbourhood in the EU's backyard or on defending the EU against external threats.

The comprehensive nature of the ESS and ISS did not alleviate this lack of clear priorities: on the contrary, they left the scope of the EU's security policies wide open. The observed bottom-up process of strategy-building during the development of EU internal and external security policies has had both enabling and constraining effects. On the one hand, strategic indecisiveness allowed for the 'mushrooming' of multiple policy initiatives and programmes, making the EU a very active security actor during the past decade. A flipside of the coin, however, is the lack of clear strategic priorities that has exacerbated the already pronounced fragmentation of the EU's security architecture. Boin and Ekengren (2009: 287) agree: 'Security as a strategic objective exists only in specific policy sectors.

Legislation is oriented towards known risks in pre-established sectors; over-arching programmes that draw together diverse initiatives are eschewed, at worst, or are strictly voluntary, at best'.

Despite the observed institutional and strategic fragmentation of the EU's security policies, the study of recent EU policy programmes and strategic documents revealed an increasing convergence towards the external promotion of stability and order as one of the EU's major strategic aims. Both the stability-oriented European Neighbourhood Strategy and the strategy for the external dimension of JHA have exemplified this trend. In line with the ESS's aim of promoting a 'ring of friends' around the EU, the two strategic aims of fostering stability and fighting crime in the neighbourhood have all but eclipsed the EU's classical crisis management functions outlined in the Petersberg tasks. Compared to stability and crime-fighting, the dimension of 'human security' appears less relevant in current EU security policy documents.

Although the European Commission routinely refers to human security as a strategic end in its developmental and external relations policies, CSDP missions do not specifically emphasise human security in their mandates. On the contrary, some CSDP mission mandates have started to shift their focus away from broader police reform and accountability issues towards enhancing the efficiency of law enforcement actors in the fields of border policing and the fight against organised crime. The mandate of the EU Police Mission to Bosnia is a case in point.[10]

The most intriguing finding of this chapter, however, is the highly apolitical process of developing security strategies for the EU. Avoiding political conflicts about the EU's strategic choices, technical questions took precedence during the development of the EU's security architecture and capabilities. While the ESS remained broad-brush enough to fit a variety of security interests, the ISS remained relatively devoid of a larger vision and mostly technical in its approach to internal security cooperation within the EU. Despite the eminently political nature of strategic questions, and turning the classical process of security strategy development on its head, the politics of European security policies were pursued at the service level, not the political level.

Finally, the chapter highlighted that post-9/11 strategy development in the US and in the EU proceeded in fundamentally different ways. Even though clear similarities between the content of the EU ISS and the US Homeland Security Strategy[11] can be identified, both the status of the strategies and their development differs considerably: the US Homeland Security Strategy was adopted in traditional top-down process after the 9/11 attacks and went hand in hand with the wholesale reorganisation of the US's internal security architecture. The ISS took shape nearly a decade later and has so far not become operational. In addition, it was not aimed at influencing the institutional structure of the EU's internal security efforts. Instead, it simply summarises and groups existing internal security measures into a set of categories. However, if we understand homeland security to be about the close horizontal integration of both preventive and repressive internal and external security policies to protect a citizenship against man-made and natural hazards, the EU ISS falls short of this larger goal. The ISS remains a document written by and for the internal security services. A truly horizontal and comprehensive approach to security provision would have to tie up the ISS's freedom, security and justice policies much more closely with the EU's external foreign and security policy framework.

Notes

This chapter partly builds upon a previous article, which was published as part of a special issue in *Perspectives on European Politics and Society* (Schroeder 2009). The author wishes to thank Patryk Pawlak, Xymena Kurowska, David Law and Jolyon Howorth for valuable comments on earlier versions of this chapter and Johannes Kode for excellent research assistance.

1 In March 2001, the US Commission on National Security (Hart-Rudman Commission) had recommended comprehensive institutional and procedural changes in the US national security architecture, including the creation of a National Homeland Security Agency. However, despite holding hearings on the National Homeland Security Act, Congress took no further action on the bill (US Department of Homeland Security 2008: 3).

2 Among others, the following US agencies became part of the Homeland Security Department: the Customs Service, Immigration and Naturalization Service, the Transportation Security Administration, the Office for Domestic Preparedness, the Coast Guard, the Secret Service and the Federal Emergency Management Agency.

3 The European Security and Defence Policy (ESDP) was renamed Common Security and Defence Policy (CSDP) after the Lisbon Treaty entered into force in December 2009.

4 The 1992 Petersberg Declaration of the Western European Union was later incorporated into the Treaty on European Union (TEU). The so-called 'Petersberg tasks' include humanitarian and rescue tasks, peacekeeping tasks and the tasks of combat forces in crisis management, including peacemaking.

5 The ISS lists 'terrorism, serious and organised crime, drug trafficking, cybercrime, trafficking in human beings, sexual exploitation of minors and child pornography, economic crime and corruption, trafficking in arms and cross-border crime' as major internal security challenges (Council of the European Union 2010e: 2).

6 Adding to the defence dimension, the Lisbon Treaty does, however, include a mutual defence provision in Article 27, which commits Member States to an 'obligation of aid and assistance by all the means in their power' if a Member State is the victim of armed aggression on its territory.

7 See www.csdpmap.eu/new.html for regularly updated overviews (accessed 16 November 2010).

8 The EU and its Member States provide over half of all official development assistance worldwide (see www.ec.europa.eu/development/how/monterrey_ en.cfm (accessed 16 November 2010).

9 The Battlegroup (BG) is a specific form of the EU's rapid response elements. It is a rapidly deployable, coherent and multinational battalion sized force (±1,500 troops), capable of stand-alone operations or for the initial phase of larger operations.

10 See www.eupm.org/OurMandate.aspx (accessed 16 November 2010).

11 Although it does not explicitly focus on homeland security, the EU ISS is in parts remarkably close to the substance of the US homeland security strategy. Both strategies include a similarly broad concept of security, focus on the need for concerted and multi-level responses to internal security challenges, closely link internal and external security, highlight the need for international cooperation and emphasise the merits of a culture of preparedness and anticipation.

4 The fight against international terrorism

Driver and yardstick for European homeland security

Raphael Bossong

This contribution takes stock of the European Union's (EU) fight against international terrorism, which has been critical to the construction of European homeland security. The first part surveys the historical evolution of EU counter-terrorism policy. After the first phase of event-driven and largely incoherent policy-making between 2001 and 2005, which led to a substantial increase in EU competences, one could speak of a mature policy agenda and a prevalent concern with implementation. The second part of this chapter presents a critical functional assessment of policy outcomes according to the objectives set out in the EU's Counter-terrorism Strategy. Measures 'to pursue', and 'to protect' against, terrorists seem to have grown substantially. In practice, however, they are undercut by a lack of focus and use at the operational level. Similarly, formal capacities 'to respond' to terrorism have been boosted, but there are doubts as to relevance in real crisis situations. Yet most importantly, the EU remains very limited in its activities 'to prevent' terrorism. This assessment leads to a sceptical view on the potential for comprehensive European homeland security.

A short history of the EU's fight against terrorism

Although several Member States have engaged in international counter-terrorism cooperation since the 1970s, the EU's involvement was comparatively slow to develop. After an early impetus in the 1980s, which led the creation of the so-called Terrorism Working Group, the emergence of EU Justice and Home Affairs (JHA) over the 1990s was mostly driven by the fight against 'illegal' migration and organised crime. Against this background, 9/11 was a genuine turning point in EU security policy (den Boer 2003).

The European Council (2001b) declared the fight against terrorism a new 'priority objective' of the EU, while the European Commission and the Council Secretariat quickly drew up a comprehensive policy agenda on the basis of pre-existing proposals for police and judicial cooperation (Kaunert 2007; Bossong 2008). This was most clearly the case with the

European Arrest Warrant (EAW), which came to be seen as a 'keystone measure' in the EU's counter-terrorism policy. The European Commission had worked on the EAW since the beginning of 2001 in the context of the Tampere Programme for the construction of Area of Freedom, Security and Justice (AFSJ). As a fully-fledged proposal – joined by a proposal for an EU-wide definition and criminalisation of terrorism – could, thus, be tabled already two weeks after the attacks 9/11; Member States could reach an agreement in record time (Mégie 2004).

Many other pre-existing proposals on the EU's security agenda were similarly accelerated, such as the creation of Eurojust or of the Monitoring and Information Centre for civil protection emergencies. Even the extension of EU competences into the area of aviation security – the most obvious response to the attacks of 9/11 – built on previous policy discussions, as the European Commission had already planned to present a Green Contribution on aviation safety in late September 2001 (Poincignon 2004). So, by and large, internal opportunities and timing determined the EU first counter-terrorism agenda.

External pressures only determined a minority of issue areas. Most importantly, the EU took a proactive role in the fight against the financing of terrorism on the basis of UN Security Council Resolutions and recommendations of the Financial Action Task Force, both of which reflected US interests. On other fronts, the EU could do comparatively little to support the emerging War on Terror. For better or worse, its international efforts were mostly confined to soft measures, such as diplomatic resolutions, support for international law or increased financial aid to vulnerable countries, while the European Security and Defence Policy had yet to emerge from paper.

Already by early 2002 the initial momentum for action had run its course, and the EU's comprehensive counter-terrorism agenda proved far too ambitious. As the EU's political response to 9/11 had not been accompanied by institutional reforms to speed up decision-making and to maintain political commitment (Bossong 2008), other security concerns, such as illegal migration, soon pushed terrorism from the top of the agenda. In addition, national implementation proved more cumbersome than expected, while front-line security actors did not leap at the opportunity to work with new EU policy instruments. For example, the entrenched reluctance of national police and security services to share sensitive information led to the quick dissolution of Europol's newly instituted Counterterrorism Task Force (Bures 2006).

This return to a more hesitant approach to EU security cooperation was only challenged by increasingly forceful US demands in matters of border and transport security. Despite long-drawn negotiations, the EU had no choice but to accept the transmission of Passenger Name Records (PNR) or the screening of shipping containers if it wanted to maintain the transatlantic flow of goods and people. This transatlantic cooperation was all the more remarkable against the background of the diplomatic crisis in 2002 and 2003. Trouble had already been brewing in relation to the Israeli–Palestinian conflict and Guantanamo Bay, before open conflict erupted over Iraq and brought EU foreign policy close to collapse. Yet the crisis over the Iraq also provided a new opportunity (Hill 2004). Member states demonstratively put their differences aside and agreed on the European Security Strategy as well as on a Strategy on Non-proliferation of Weapons of Mass Destruction, both of which emphasised the need to cooperate against international terrorism.

In March 2004 Europe was shaken by the terrorist attacks in Madrid that underlined the immediacy of the threat. In response, Member States declared their mutual solidarity and promised a significant acceleration of the EU's existing agenda in a high-profile 'Declaration on Combating Terrorism' (Council of the European Union 2004a). Despite some internal wrangling over the need and form of institutional reforms, this pledge was backed by a newly created office of the EU Counter-terrorism Coordinator. The European Commission also produced a series of critical reports on the implementation of key legislative measures, such as the European Arrest Warrant.

However, the Madrid attacks also led to a significant expansion of the EU's counter-terrorism agenda. Again, pre-existing policy proposal and entrepreneurship by EU institutions played a significant role. The Council Secretariat had just completed a review of the European Security Strategy, which generated various proposals – including the creation of a Counter-terrorism Coordinator. And discussions on a new long-term programme for the construction of the ASFJ informed a series of ambitious proposals by the European Commission. In particular, it pushed for a step change in cross-border information sharing and criminal justice cooperation under the so-called principle of availability. Yet Member States increasingly sought to act as policy entrepreneurs too, which generated frictions. For example, in parallel to the Commission's efforts Sweden pulled a proposal for simplified information sharing 'out of the drawer'.[1] Moreover, a subset of Member States pioneered increased security cooperation under the so-called Treaty of Prüm, which caused considerable unease in Brussels.

Over the next few months, the European Commission maintained a high level of activity to position itself in additional technical issue areas, where it could expect to face lower political opposition. This mainly revolved around improved information-sharing and coordination mechanisms in civil protection and response capacities to attacks with weapons of mass destruction. Moreover, the Commission started to develop the concept critical infrastructure protection (European Commission 2004c), which had been conceptually derived from US homeland security. Yet in contrast to the US comprehensive approach, the European Commission proceeded incrementally on the basis of existing regulatory competences for transport and energy networks.

By the end of 2004 the tragic murder of the director Theo van Gogh helped to maintain an interest in the fight against terrorism. Member states increasingly realised that they needed to work on the prevention of radicalisation and terrorism within their own borders, which was also inscribed into a new multiannual agenda for the development of the ASFJ. Still, one could also discern increasingly fixed limits to EU security integration. Despite renewed efforts of the European Commission EU-wide cooperation on criminal intelligence sharing proceeded at snails pace, while the Counter-terrorism Coordinator struggled to find a meaningful role (Lugna 2006).

A few months later, the London bombings of July 2005 served as another – but so far final – formative moment for the EU's counter-terrorism policy. The UK, which also held the rotating EU presidency at the time, mainly focused on overcoming the considerable resistance to mandatory retention of telecommunications data, but did not promote EU security integration across the board. The Counter-terrorism Strategy that was directly drawn from the UK's national approach rather provided a post hoc rationalisation of the EU's existing agenda (see also Schroeder in Chapter 3). The emergence of another Strategy for 'Combating Radicalisation and Recruitment to Terrorism' (Council of the European Union 2005g) could be seen as an exception to the relatively muted EU response to the London bombings. As mentioned above, discussions on this issue had been gathering momentum since 2004, but gained additional salience after it emerged that the attacks had been perpetrated by UK nationals. Yet, as will be elaborated in the second part of this chapter, this strategy did little to address the EU's fundamental obstacles to playing a meaningful role in the prevention of terrorism.

In 2006 the EU's comprehensive fight against terrorism increasingly developed along the lines of more specialised policy fields, such as the fight against the financing of terrorism or civil protection. One could observe familiar fluctuations in political attention, which undermined a more 'comprehensive' or strategic perspective in the EU's fight against terrorism. For instance, in the summer, the uncovered plot to blow up several transatlantic flights by liquid explosives led to a quick adaptation of aviation security regulations. But one could not make out any other significant initiatives to improve transport security or to address the underlying causes of the attacks. The increasing mobilisation of legislative and judicial actors added to a sense of retrenchment or 'fatigue' in EU counter-terrorism policy. The European Court of Justice ordered a revision of the procedure for the freezing of terrorist assets, whereas the European Parliament conducted a critical investigation into extraordinary renditions to the US.

2007 saw another series of failed or foiled plots; this time in Germany and Denmark as well as in the UK. By late summer this prodded Member States to appoint a new Counter-terrorism Coordinator after the post had been vacant for several months. Gilles de Kerchove had been a leading figure in the Council Secretariat and acted personally as an important policy entrepreneur over previous years, so that the post of Counter-terrorism Coordinator could be expected to rise in standing. The European Commission (2007b) presented another package of proposals, which underlined its increasingly regular involvement in a wide variety of internal security issues. These proposals largely consisted of items which had been under discussion since 2004, namely more stringent controls on the trade in explosives, the inclusion of acts of 'incitement' to the framework decision on combating terrorism and the creation of an EU PNR system.

From 2008 onwards the new Counter-terrorism Coordinator, the European Commission and the European Council consistently emphasised that the continuing development, enactment and implementation of existing policy programmes was their main priority. Accordingly, discussions on a wide variety of issues, ranging from counter-radicalisation, control of explosives to critical infrastructure protection, proceeded in an incremental manner. Further failed plots, such as the 'underwear bomber' in December 2009 or the air freight bombs from Yemen in 2010, had only a marginal impact in this regard.[2] Instead, senior officials and policy-makers in EU security policy mostly concentrated on the ratification of the Lisbon Treaty and its institutional consequences; that is, the creation of the External Action Service and of the Internal Security Committee. Due to the complexity of these processes, discussions on how to implement the Treaty's solidarity clause, which committed Member States to mutual assistance in case of a serious terrorist attack, was temporarily postponed.

However, during this period of institutional 'navel-gazing' the EU's fight against terrorism was also significantly influenced by the new US administration under President Obama. The US increasingly engaged with EU discussions on radicalisation and recruitment into terrorism and sought to accommodate demands for data protection. At the same time, the US pressured European Member States to support the closure of Guantanamo Bay or to accede to a revised mechanism for tracing financial transactions. In this context, the post-Lisbon decision-making powers of the European Parliament in matters of internal security were brought to bear for the first time, which generated heated negotiation process – but also to a more equitable outcome from the perspective of civil rights.

Otherwise, the EU's fight against terrorism could be said to have reached maturity by late 2010. Policy-making was mainly pursued through issue-specific policy subsystems or governance networks that often pursued increasingly technical measures and generally treated terrorism as one of several interrelated challenges. Despite periodically recurring media coverage of terrorist plots, there was little event- or crisis-driven momentum for ambitious EU security integration. Against this background, the next part of this chapter provides a functional overview of policy outputs according to the EU's own yardstick; that is, the Counter-terrorism Strategy. This could serve as a baseline for judging the EU's achievements before the Lisbon Treaty could manifest its influence across European homeland security cooperation as a whole.

Critical assessment and trends of policy outcomes

The following critical assessment shadows and partially contrasts the reports of the EU Counter-terrorism Coordinator who has increasingly taken to surveying the EU's efforts from an outcome-oriented perspective (e.g. Council of the European Union 2010a). Although the Counter-terrorism Strategy had no immediate impact on the EU's concrete policy agenda, it has become widely popular in policy as well as academic discussions, as it offers a coherent analytical framework. The Strategy features four objectives, which follow a clear deductive logic and could provide the outlines of a comprehensive concept of homeland security.

The main message is that the EU 'adds value' to the fight against terrorism (and security more widely) by means of a comprehensive approach. It acts before as well as after an attack, and addresses threats at the level of structure as well as agency. Yet precisely this broad approach generates problems when focusing on the fight against terrorism in a more narrow sense. Many measures under the loosely defined strands of protection, pursuit and response may lack focus and relevance or are simply unlikely to be widely used or implemented. Most importantly, prevention – arguably the most important objective – remains severely limited by complexity and a lack of relevant EU competences. In short, the dynamic developments in EU security cooperation since 9/11 may still fail to add up to a coherent counter-terrorism policy.

Pursue

As outlined in the first part of this chapter, numerous measures for police and judicial cooperation that were originally intended as building blocks for the ASFJ have been cast as tools to pursue terrorists across borders. The European Arrest Warrant and the associated framework decision on combating terrorism have been touted as the EU's main success stories in this regard (Verbruggen 2004). Many more measures could be added the strand of 'pursue', such as the framework decision on the retention of

Table 4.1 Objectives of the EU Counter-terrorism Strategy

	Before attack	After attack
Countering intentional threats	*Prevent*	*Pursue*
Controlling structural hazards/effects	*Protect*	*Respond*

electronic communication traffic data (European Union 2006a) or on improved information-sharing in relation to terrorism offences (European Union 2005). Another less visible contribution has been the peer review process of national counter-terrorism arrangements (Council of the European Union 2005e) that took its origins in the fight against organised crime and led to a number of domestic reforms in coordination and information-sharing mechanisms.

At the level of EU institutions and agencies, one could also point to a number of advances. Eurojust was not only set up more quickly than foreseen in the aftermath of 9/11, but is also by now operating quite successfully, including in terrorist cases. Europol was authorised to work on terrorism and to conduct data exchanges and related cooperation agreements with third countries. After a bumpy start of the so-called counter-terrorism task force, Europol now routinely prepares a variety of threat assessments on terrorism and handles a so-called 'analytical workfile' on Islamic extremists.

The most significant EU actions under the strand of pursue relate to the fight against the financing of terrorism. Financial investigations have been used to track the personal networks of terrorist suspects, and then to punish them in absence of hard judicial proof (Naylor 2006). Despite a growing number of legal challenges area (Guild 2008), the EU has steadily expanded its activities, which manifested in a separate strategy (Council of the European Union 2007a). For instance, it has continuously adapted the list of targets as well as the mechanism for freezing assets, toughened up its money laundering legislation and sought to better control remittances or donations to non-governmental organizations (NGOs). Finally, the EU has recently reached a new agreement on the US terrorism-finance tracking programme that covers international wire transfers

Nevertheless, the EU can only claim moderate success with regard to the pursuit of terrorism. While incomplete, slow or lacking implementation is a general problem for EU security policy, it has been particularly acute in matters of judicial and police cooperation (Monar 2007). At least before the ratification of the Lisbon Treaty, oversight mechanisms have proven to be notoriously weak, while Member States often faced considerable difficulties to match EU framework decisions with their diverse legal traditions (Alegre and Leaf 2004).

On the operational level, the exchange of information between national authorities and Europol remains unsatisfactory (Bures 2008), as the conservatism of police renders even domestic cooperation difficult.[3] National authorities also simply lack incentives to take on the added workload that is required by formal European cooperation.[4] Instead, most cross-border cooperation occurs on a personal and informal basis, which matches the autonomy-seeking preferences of police (Deflem 2004). Most fundamentally, the necessary trust for smooth interactions cannot be presupposed or easily created by EU legislation. Particularly judicial actors remain suspicious of the appropriateness and adequacy of legal provisions of other Member States. Therefore, EU police and criminal justice cooperation in the fight against terrorism develops in an incremental manner, which is underlined by an overall sense of saturation in this issue area (Coolsaet 2010).

Protect

Protection has been a very dynamic aspect of the EU counter-terrorism agenda. Member states' interest in controlling migration overlapped with US pressure for tighter border and transport security, leading to the introduction of biometric identifiers in travel documents and the transmission of air passenger data. Eurodac and the Visa Information System have also been linked to the EU's counter-terrorism effort, and may eventually be opened up to Europol and even national police authorities (Geyer 2008). More recently, the increasing activities of Frontex and efforts to create surveillance mechanisms for the EU's Mediterranean Sea borders have become entangled with the fight against terrorism (Council of the European Union 2010b).

The most straightforward result of 9/11 in matters of transport security has been the extension of EU competences into the area of aviation security (Poincignon 2004). In light of repeated failed attacks in recent years, the European Commission's regulatory power has been steadily expanded and consolidated (European Union 2008). A parallel development has taken place in the management of maritime security, which mainly reflects US demands for the screening of freight containers but also has become linked to the growing threat of piracy (Council of the European Union 2010a).

Finally, critical infrastructure protection has become an increasingly important component of the EU's internal security agenda. Critical infrastructure protection seeks to protect all core transport, energy and communication networks against 'all hazards', including terrorism. This broad approach has been flanked by a significant expansion of funding for research on security technology. Both in security research and critical infrastructure protection the European Commission has been keen to seize the initiative, as it matches its established competences in the areas of research funding and the regulator of transnational transport and energy networks.

In sum, increased border and travel security, security research and critical infrastructure protection could be regarded as a substantial array of protective measures against terrorism. Operational practice may look rather different, however. Critical infrastructure protection and security research are weighed down by financial constraints and inherent technical complexity (Fritzon and Ljungkvist 2007). The extensive delays of the second-generation Schengen Information System and the hesitant start of the Visa Information System furthermore illustrate the technical and practical challenges with increasingly sophisticated databases.

More fundamentally, one can question the relevance or effectiveness of such measures, as a comprehensive, yet reasonably cost-effective, protection from terrorist attacks is bound to remain elusive. States as well as private companies cannot continuously invest in hardening targets and modes of transportation, when terrorists can potentially strike everywhere (Enders and Sandler 2006). This basic dilemma explains, for instance, the limited progress with regard to the protection 'open transport systems' (Council of the European Union 2010a), even though this was the target for both the Madrid and the London bombings. Technology is also of limited use to reliably identify and to catch terrorist suspects in advance. Human intelligence, which – as discussed below – the EU is mostly excluded from, cannot be replaced (Müller-Wille 2008).

Finally, border security is also of doubtful effectiveness in the fight against terrorism, since it is radicalised EU nationals and not migrants – let alone illegal ones – that often pose the most serious terrorist threat. It is, of course, conceivable that terrorist suspects may be caught in an attempt to cross a border, especially if they come from 'terrorist training camps' in third countries. Nevertheless, one can question the proportionality of blanket border controls vis-à-vis covert monitoring of the international travel patterns of known suspects. After all, the most fundamental challenge remains the discovery of new threats and plots, which often emerge from within Europe's borders. These limits to protecting against terrorist attacks are not a reason for despair, however. Liberal societies have been very resilient in the face of more serious security threats (Mueller 2005) and should not tolerate the creation of overbearing surveillance systems.

Respond

The EU's contribution to responding to terrorist attacks mainly consists of a variety of civil protection mechanisms (see also Wendling in Chapter 7). The EU's Monitoring and Information Centre facilitates cross-border cooperation and asset-sharing in disasters and emergencies. Related rapid information-sharing is supported by the so-called ARGUS system and a variety of sector-specific networks, such as in health security (Rhinard 2009). Focusing more specifically on human-induced threats such as terrorism, the EU developed more political Crisis Coordination Arrangements (CCA) that would streamline decision-making in Brussels, and pursued an Action Plan to deal with the consequences of a possible weapons of mass destruction (WMD) attacks (Council of the European Union 2009b). Last but not least, financial assistance is provided to a network of special intervention units from several European Member States forces, the so-called ATLAS network, which facilitates the exchange of best practices and may even provide the basis for cross-border operations (Block 2007).

Yet despite these wide-ranging initiatives, there are clear limits to the depth and reliability of international cooperation. Ideas for a genuinely pooled EU civilian response capacity did not gain traction, as Member State with the most advanced capabilities worry about free-riding and a loss of costly assets. Similar to the case of police and judicial cooperation, trust and dense transnational contacts between civil protection forces also need time to develop and may often occur in formats beyond or beneath the EU level. And although special interventions units have been used abroad ever since the 1970s, it is highly doubtful that such decisions would be based on general EU provisions rather than direct bi-lateral and situation-specific negotiations. Exercises of the CCA mechanism have also revealed that real-time decision-making on highly sensitive matters cannot be easily latched onto the EU's formal institutional structures.[5]

Thankfully, European Member States have not been tested yet by a truly serious attack that could overtax their national response capacities. But it should also be remembered that functionalist considerations are only one consideration in the fight against terrorism, as governments seek to counter the political message of terrorists and to emphasize their continued control over public security. This could be witnessed in the aftermath of the attacks in Madrid and London when the Spain and the UK would only accept limited international assistance for investigative purposes.

From an external perspective, terrorism has also been highlighted in the European Security Strategy (ESS) and concepts or threat scenarios of the Common Security and Defence Policy (CSDP). But apart from largely symbolic efforts in Iraq, the Palestinian authorities and Afghanistan, missions to date have not been driven by, or effectively contributed to, the fight against terrorism (Berenskoetter and Giegerich 2006; de Vries 2008). And the CSDP's possible contribution to a WMD detection and response should always be seen in relation to the role of NATO. While the CSDP provided a catalogue of available capabilities of the Member States, the North Atlantic Treaty Organization (NATO) could draw on a much greater technical expertise and operational track record in case of serious military threats.

In sum, the EU can claim some success by facilitating the coordination if civil protection assets and the exchange of best practices. Yet Member States could neither be expected to generally relinquish national control over the use of assets, nor to be comfortable with high-profile EU assistance in response to a terrorist attack. In case of a WMD attack, which would genuinely overtax national capacities, NATO or channels of bilateral cooperation should be expected to dominate. Only time can tell whether the Lisbon Treaty and the solidarity clause could significantly transform these political obstacles to operational coordination.

Prevent

Arguably, prevention is the most important, but also the most challenging, component of an effective counter-terrorism policy. Unfortunately, the Action Plan that should implement the EU's Strategy on Combating Radicalisation and Recruitment (Council of the European Union 2005g) is not publicly accessible. Yet it is clear that the EU could only play a relatively weak role, as it faces several structural obstacles: the EU could not dramatically redirect its external foreign and security policy, is almost completely excluded from operational intelligence-sharing, and has almost no competences in matters of integration, education and social policy that are vital to countering individual process of radicalisation.

In the aftermath of 9/11, the EU claimed to fight against international 'root causes' of international terrorism (European Council 2001b). So far, however, the EU's contribution in this regard has been limited (Keohane 2008), as political disagreement among the Member States and institutional fragmentation barred a dramatic reversal or reorientation of its foreign policy. Despite several attempts to obtain a greater say vis-à-vis the US, the EU continues to play a very limited role in the hotspots of the Middle East or Central Asia. Countless diplomatic declarations and formal clauses in EU partnership agreements aside, the Western Balkans, which operate under the shadow of accession negotiations, are the only case where one can identify a substantive EU programme for counter-terrorism cooperation. In other contexts, EU 'technical assistance' to improve counter-terrorism efforts of third countries is of little significance (Wennerholm *et al.* 2010). As the EU Counter-terrorism Coordinator noted himself, financial sums remain small, and partner countries in Northern Africa often prefer to work on a bilateral level of EU Member States (Council of the European Union 2010a). Given the tensions between the fight against international terrorism and Europe's claims to normative power (Manners 2006), one could, of course, welcome this comparatively restrained EU role.

So the most serious obstacle to an effective EU role in counter-radicalisation is its lack of relevant competences and tools within its borders. Timely intelligence is the most valuable tool in preventive counter-terrorism work. Yet the EU's possible role in intelligence-sharing remains very limited (Müller-Wille 2008). Member states have simply refused to integrate their national security services at the EU level, while there are various informal European groups for intelligence cooperation, most notably the Club of Berne. The Counter-terrorism Group, which was founded after 9/11 to bridge this gap, has maintained a distance. The defence of sovereignty in matters of 'national security' is buttressed by a culture of secrecy. Sources and methods of work could be compromised if intelligence was widely shared. Alternatively, intelligence is used as a 'currency', so that it is not appealing to share it on the basis of general rules.

At the same time, the EU does not have human intelligence collection capacities of its own. Despite a growing role in providing general threat assessments, the EU's Situation Centre remains dependent on voluntary contributions from Member States' services.

Instead, EU officials mainly seek to support a 'soft' prevention at the Member State level. This started out with an initiative of the 2007 German Presidency to 'check the web' for radical websites (Council of the European Union 2007b). Since then a variety of other pilot projects on counter-radicalisation in prisons, imam training, public communication and community policing have been undertaken (*e.g.* Council of the European Union 2010b). The European Commission sought to play a part by financing an expert working group on radicalisation as well as a series of research projects and public conferences in this issue area. Yet there is still no firm consensus on the most important drivers and mechanisms of radicalisation. Last but not least, the diversity of Member States' threat profiles, as well as legal and institutional structures pose very high obstacles to cross-national transfers (Coolsaet 2010).

Summary and trends

The Table 4.2 sums up the above assessment of the EU's functional contribution to the fight against terrorism.

Against the background of an increasing stability or maturity of the EU's counter-terrorism policy that was outlined in the first part of the chapter, one can expect a continuation of these trends before the effects of the Lisbon Treaty could unfold over the medium to long term. Further measures to 'pursue' terrorists depend on the slow pace of harmonisation of domestic criminal justice structures and the creation of genuinely

Table 4.2 The EU's functional contribution to the fight against terrorism

	Before attack	*After attack*
Countering intentional threats	*Prevent* No operational prevention, weak structural role due to lacking competences in foreign and social or education policy	*Pursue* Advances in criminal justice cooperation and control of terror financing, but persistent deficits in implementation, information-sharing and trust
Controlling structural hazards/ effects	*Protect* Dynamic growth in travel and border security, critical infrastructure protection and security research. Yet measures lack relevance or face fundamental efficiency constraints	*Respond* Increased funds and programmes for civil protection (CBRN), new systems of crisis coordination. But weak role for CSDP and doubtful use in case of serioius terrorist attacks

interoperable databases. By contrast, measures to 'protect' against terrorist attacks will develop in a more dynamic fashion, as the European Commission can build on its legal competences in border and transport security, as well as critical infrastructure protection and security research. Yet even more than in the past, most measures will buttress the paradigm of 'all hazards protection', which underlines the decreasing importance of the fight against terrorism to the construction of European homeland security.

The EU's ability to 'respond' to major attacks and crisis will also be consolidated on a wider basis. Nevertheless, as long as civil protection policies have not made a more substantial contribution to countering intentional or political threats, the profile of the EU remains low. Finally, counter-terrorism experts in Europe increasingly focus on how to effectively prevent terrorism and radicalisation. The EU forms part of this wider discussion process, but could not overcome its structural limits with the ratification of the Lisbon Treaty. Member States maintain a firm grip on intelligence services as well as social policies, whereas the future role and impact the European External Action Service remains highly speculative.

Normative assessment

Broadly speaking, one can locate the debate on the legitimacy of the EU's fight against terrorism between two positions. One the one side, critical commentators regard EU counter-terrorism policy as part of a wider historical trend, whereby 'security professionals' and core government executives acquire ever more powerful tools for surveillance and the control of populations (Bigo and Walker 2006). Security actors have used the more removed and unaccountable EU structures to 'agree on things in Brussels they would not have obtained at home',[6] so that the increasing stability of EU counter-terrorism policy outlined above constitutes a normalisation of previously illegitimate practices. Therefore, the European Parliament and the European Court of Justice must challenge and retrench the EU's existing measures, while actors from civil society need to challenge the prevalent securitising discourse that presents civil rights and security as competing values.

On the other side, more mainstream analysts (e.g. Monar 2007) highlight that EU's counter-terrorism policy remains fragmented or weak, because it mostly represents a unanimous compromise of 27 Member States. Given that only a minority of Member States has been directly touched by international terrorism, it is unlikely that the EU would ever feature as a primary actor in this issue area. Instead, precisely those security measures that serve other overlapping security interests, such as the fight against organised crime or illegal migration, make better progress in EU security cooperation. The continued defence of national sovereignty also explains that the EU's counter-terrorism agenda has become increasingly focused on technical aspects, such as critical infra-structure protection – which limits the EU's impact on citizens' civil rights and liberties. This is not to deny that national executives have not occa-sionally moved ahead with EU policies that did not reflect a consensus among domestic actors. Yet over time, parliamentary and judicial actors have caught up, as evidenced in the revision of a number of counter-terrorism measures. In short, EU counter-terrorism policy continues to represent a bargain between the complex interests of Member States, making it perhaps not a perfectly efficient, but fundamentally legitimate enterprise.

Obviously, the analysis presented over the course of this contribution mostly supports the second position. Radical critics should explicate more clearly why the EU's counter-terrorism and security agenda has been frag-mented and heavily dependent on the rhythm of events, if there is struc-tural dominance of security professionals and executive actors. The pervasive problem of implementation and lack of interest at the opera-tional level also needs to be accounted for. Nevertheless, with sufficient hindsight one can discern a steady accumulation of surveillance and control technologies, which has been accentuated by repeated policy entrepreneurship to nudge ill-formed preferences in the direction of further security cooperation. So although one could not speak of an organised conspiracy for the creation of a European surveillance society, one could make out a lack of strategic direction, accountability and fore-sight. The revised decision-making and control mechanisms of the Lisbon Treaty have yet to prove to be an effective counterweight; especially if Europe is hit by another serious terrorist attack.

Conclusion

The EU has been surprisingly successful in promoting security coopera-tion under the banner of the fight against international terrorism. In the first few years, this was particularly the case with criminal justice measures that drew inspiration from the creation of the ASFJ, and border and travel security that reflected intense US pressure. Subsequently, the EU counter-terrorism policy was complemented by more technical initiatives and the notion of 'all hazards protection'. Taken together, this could constitute the foundation for a comprehensive notion of European homeland security.

However, this contribution also underlined the fragmented or hesitant nature of policy-making. From a historical perspective, the dynamic expan-sion of the EU's counter-terrorism agenda in the immediate aftermath of the attacks generated serious implementation problems. It took several years before a more incremental, realistic and sector-specific approach could emerge. Since then decision-makers have been less shocked by new plots, and have gone to increasing lengths to turn EU declarations into national legislation and operational practice. Nevertheless, path-dependency, US pressure and sheer expediency were more important than strategic decision-making and learning for the overall trajectory of this policy field.

The second part of the chapter developed this critical assessment on the basis of the EU's Counter-terrorism Strategy. The summary of each strand will not be repeated here (see Table 4.2). What needs to be underlined, however, is that the EU has yet to develop a genuinely focused and coherent response. For instance, despite its doubtful impact, border security remains an integral part of the EU's Action Plan on Combating Terrorism. And even though the Madrid and London bombings led a common learning process with regard to 'home-grown' threats, EU actions to counter radicalisation remain highly constrained. Instead, the growth of national pilot projects points to a rising importance of flexible and voluntary initiatives. Threat perceptions, preferences and security architectures of Member States remain too diverse to frame the fight against international terrorism as a genuinely shared priority objective of the EU.

Finally, one needs to consider fundamental normative constraints. The EU's fight against terrorism has been driven by political elites and has remained hidden from the view of ordinary citizens – with the exception of reinforced air passenger controls. The almost ritual reference of senior EU officials to Eurobarometer surveys that demonstrate popular support for increased international counter-terrorism cooperation does not change this state of affairs. Even if bottom-up approaches to security should not be idealised, the EU is a long way from the cultural and political roots that underpin the notion of homeland security. No matter how benign or effective the EU's actions may be, diffuse outcome legitimacy cannot replace genuinely vibrant and public discussions on how to respond to, and to live with, ever-changing threats to our way of life.

Notes

1 Interview with a national counter-terrorism expert, November 2007.
2 Currently, it is still unclear whether transport security would be significantly tightened again, or when increased information-sharing and interoperability of databases for improved threat awareness would come to fruition.
3 Interview with a national counter-terrorism expert, May 2008. See also Coolsaet (2010).
4 Interview with a European Commission official, March 2008.
5 The case of EU external crisis management shows that individual heads of state and large Member States are more likely to resort to informal mechanisms and direct negotiations.
6 Interview with a member of European Parliament, May 2008.

5 A 'coordination nightmare'?

Institutional coherence in European Union counter-terrorism

Javier Argomaniz

It has been stressed in the introduction how counter-terrorism has been a driving factor in the rapid development of homeland security in the European Union (EU). First, the hyperactivity that resulted from the events of 9/11 did lead initially to the rapid introduction of Justice and Home Affairs (JHA) measures that had been agreed at the 1999 Tampere extraordinary Council. Then the Madrid attacks raised alarm bells and fuelled new developments in infrastructure protection, response management and police, intelligence and judicial cooperation. Following this, the London bombings brought home-grown jihadist terrorism to the European consciousness, encouraging initiatives in the area of radicalisation and the terrorist and criminal use of the internet.

These policy developments have attracted increased academic interest, mostly from EU scholars. Yet comparatively less emphasis has been placed on the way these policies have been produced and the role of EU institutional actors in the process. These considerations are at the core of this contribution, which is concerned with the extent to which decision-making actors at the European level coordinate their efforts and maintain an interoperable and effective working relationship. It argues that the emergence of counter-terrorism as a policy domain has produced a significant expansion at the European level of bureaucratic actors with competing competences. Moreover, these processes and other institutional, political and legal aspects of the EU response have resulted in severe coordination demands that have the potential to undermine the EU's effectiveness as a counter-terror actor. The implications of these findings are not only uniquely relevant to the field of counter-terrorism but also raise important questions about the overall coherence of an EU homeland security framework.

In developing this argument, this chapter adopts Christiansen's definition of institutional consistency: 'the degree to which institution(s) operate a coherent and well-coordinated process of deliberation and decision-making' (Christiansen 2001: 747). It also follows Christiansen's (2001: 748) approach to conceptually separate institutional coherence into three different strands, namely: (1) inter-level coherence (i.e. relationships between

EU-level institutions and national authorities); (2) inter-institutional coherence (i.e. relations among EU institutions; and (3) intra-institutional coherence (i.e. internal politics of EU institutions).

The analytical focus is firmly placed here on the intra- and inter-institutional coherence dimensions. In essence, the intra-institutional sub-category refers to the mechanisms formulated to address the problem produced by internal fragmentation within the EU's two major decision-making bodies in the counter-terror domain; that is, the Commission and the Council of Ministers. On the other hand, inter-institutional coherence relates to the institutional resources devoted to the coordination of the work of the different actors within an institutional system. They can both be operationalised to tackle questions such as: how is coordination conducted at the inter-institutional and intra-institutional levels? What are the main weaknesses affecting such coordination? And what have been the EU's institutional responses to such shortcomings?

In an attempt to effectively accommodate these questions, the chapter is structured in the following manner: it first looks at the processes of intra-institutional coordination within EU's policy-making institutions and the mechanisms for inter-institutional coordination between EU actors. Attention is subsequently focused on the important shortcomings existing with regard to the institutional consistency of this policy arena and then the chapter finally concludes with a look at the impact that the structural reforms from the Lisbon Treaty have had on this form of consistency.

Intra-institutional coherence

The EU's two main policy-making institutions in the field of security, the Commission and the Council, are not unitary actors. They are internally divided and, depending on the nature of the policy issue or the coordination resources invested, this structural situation may result in limited institutional coherence. Christiansen, for instance, has reflected on a number of generic issues that have generally contributed to challenging institutional coherence within these two institutions: their rapid and remarkable growth during the 1990s as a result of enlargement, the expansion of their competences and the increasing complexity of the policies, and EU policy-makers' growing specialisation and clustering in policy networks (Christiansen 2001: 750). These shared circumstances aside, both the Council and the Commission have faced some very specific coordination problems associated with the nature of counter-terrorism as a policy and its original institutionalisation dynamics. Both institutions have established structures and mechanisms to improve internal coordination in this area and these are examined in turn.

Coordination within the European Commission

The Commission has the reputation of being notoriously bad at coordination (Jordan and Schout 2006: 98). For a start, the administrative structuring of the organisation in self-contained Directorate-Generals (DGs) naturally leads to internal divisions. The degree of autonomy and organisational isolation of each DG is high, a factor which is reinforced by their physical separation in different buildings scattered across Brussels. Moreover, Jordan and Schout have reported how the structure of the Commission, with its similarities with French-style bureaucracy and differentiated cultural make-ups, complicate relationships among the separate DGs (Jordan and Schout 2006: 99). It is not surprising that these structural relations have tended to encourage 'possessive territorialism' over particular policy dossiers. Due to the multidimensional character of most of the Commission's counter-terror policy initiatives, they often require the involvement of several DGs, ranging from Health and Agriculture (i.e. bioterrorism) through Research (i.e security research) to Transport and/or Energy (i.e. airport, seaport and container security). Moreover, and since the large majority of Commission DGs had traditionally lacked any involvement with counter-terrorism, the structures and expertise inherited from the past have not been designed to deal with these sensitive security issues.

As a consequence, the generic structures, networks and bodies available in the Commission have had to be supplemented by specific structures set up to tackle the high coordination demands of these policies. First, overall internal coordination is enhanced by the weekly meeting of the College of Commissioners, and immediately below, the weekly chefs de cabinet meeting ('Hebdo') setting the agenda for the College. Whereas the latter looks at problem-solving, the former is more focused on strategic matters and resolving differences between DGs on individual issues. An additional central player in the coordination process is the Commission President's Secretariat General (SG), which concentrates on guaranteeing coherence, transparency and focus on the main political priorities.

In parallel to the above standard procedures, the Commission has established two layers of coordination particular to policy formulation in counter-terrorism: an inter-service group presided at director level meeting on average twice a year and a separate high-level coordination group at DG and cabinet level. The latter group would include all DGs in the Commission[1] to provide strategic guidance on the basis of the Action Plan, the European Strategy, the European Council Conclusions and other strategic documents. It also allocates the responsibility of managing inter-service efforts in areas related to terrorism. Previous to the 2009 decision to divide it into DG Home Affairs and DG Justice, it was the DG Justice, Liberty and Security (JLS) that took the lead in coordination as well as policy delivery. Nonetheless there are a few specific areas where other DGs assume these responsibilities (i.e. DG Transport regarding airport security). In other cases, management is done jointly as with bio-terrorism, where the DG Health and the former DG JLS jointly managed and chaired Commission proposals. Complementing this top-level political and administrative coordination, operational organisation is the objective of a lower-level inter-service group on the Internal Aspects of the Fight against Terrorism. This group functions permanently and brings together all the DGs in the Commission with relevant responsibilities in the field of terrorism at the level of heads of units or directors. Here policy is discussed, perspectives reconciled, planning monitored on a working level basis and specific initiatives prepared.

In addition, and within this inter-service group, there is an extra layer of ad hoc subgroups that deal with differentiated areas, such as firearms and explosives, radicalisation, security economics and the protection of critical infrastructure. These subgroups have a reduced duration, are established for a particular task, and their composition is restricted on a need-to-know and effectiveness basis. As an example, a subgroup on Critical infrastructure protection involves DG Internal Market, DG Competition, DG Transport and others. These structures normally serve the purpose of preparing documents: communications, pieces of legislation or the establishment of a new instrument. Since 2010 DG Home Affairs officials convene and chair the subgroups at the start and during policy formulation. These subgroups are set up to involve and inform other DGs as well as to pre-empt potential discrepancies in the inter-service consultation process before the proposal is moved up to the College of Commissioners.[2]

Generally, this structure leads to little coordination problems within particular DGs, where the policy process is quite open, usually involving meetings with national officials and European sectoral bodies. On terrorism issues this often involves consultation with European agencies such as Europol or Eurojust. In fact, internal consultation and coordination occur relatively widely due to the existence of official frameworks and requirements, combined with an organisational culture of consultation at the policy formulation stage with national and interest group representatives (Stevens and Stevens 2001). On the other hand, inter-departmental relationships are significantly less fluid particularly when a specific proposal is controversial or generates the opposition from another DG. An important effort is often required from leading DGs whenever coordination needs to be guaranteed and it is up to the DG director's criteria to determine whether a particular proposal will be referred to inter-departmental discussion. So, coordination within the Commission of a cross-sectoral policy issue often depends on the perspective of the leading DG management. As a case in point, for the preparation by DG JLS of the proposal to criminalise the glorification, recruitment and training of terrorism, those DGs dealing with internet service providers and communication companies had to be contacted.[3]

When a controversy arises or coordination needs to be ensured, bilateral discussions can be established at different levels between unit heads, directors, DGs or Commissioners or, when it encompasses several DGs, the inter-service group can be convened to allow for informal discussion (Stevens and Stevens 2001). In relation to the above draft proposal, a steering group was established involving at least 10 different DGs affected by the initiative. The composition of the group is, in principle, made at the director level but it is common that the directors are replaced by those desk officers who are more closely involved with the matter. This leads to a process of electronic consultation including the proposal and the impact evaluation report and involving all the DGs taking part in the steering group. It represents another opportunity for those DGs to amend parts of the proposal before it is moved to the Hebdo meeting involving representatives from every DG. DGs that have not been involved in the steering group can then force further changes, leading in such cases to further discussions at the Cabinet level and new amendments to reconcile differing perspectives.

As Jordan and Schout (2006: 220) have demonstrated, consultation during the drafting of a proposal is highly dependent on the file officer assigned and the instructions from the lead DG but also on the working culture of the DG and, significantly, the political sensitivity of the topic in question. In fact when the topic is particularly controversial, preparatory discussions tend to be restricted to cognate DGs. This also affects the number of the steering group meetings: the more sensitive the initiative, the greater the necessity to ensure sufficient deliberation. It does also influence the composition of the steering group: hence other Directorates within DG JLS dealing with data protection and the protection of civil rights had to be included as the amendment proposal could have a potential impact on these issues.[4]

Coordination within the European Council

Internal coordination in counter-terrorism decision-making is a considerably bigger challenge in the Council. For a start, issue areas are often divorced at the Council of Ministers into separate deliberation procedures based on the ministers' remits. For example, terrorism financing has been discussed by finance ministers in isolation from foreign ministers and the JHA Council. The former deal separately with anti-terrorism financing clauses in third countries' agreements and the latter agrees on the exchange of police information in this area. At the Committee level, where working structures have rigidly followed the division of pillars, internal administrative and procedural divisions come to play an important part in fostering fragmentation. Here the main responsibility is divided into two separate working parties (WPs): the external COTER and the internal Working Group on Terrorism (TWG). It is not uncommon for both groups to present divergent angles on the same problem due to their differentiated composition and political loyalties; the former comprising senior officials from the justice and interior ministries and the latter diplomats from foreign ministries.[5]

In addition, technical matters of high relevance to EU counter-terror efforts, such as the financing of terrorism or critical infrastructure protection, are dealt separately within other working groups. This means that an issue area such as radicalisation and terrorism recruitment is managed by a myriad of committees. The TWG looks at the problem inside Europe and the foreign element is covered by COTER, but other WPs are also involved, particularly the Asian regional group where aspects such as interfaith dialogue, trends in Islam, cultural divide and prevention of ideological polarisation are discussed.[6] Even within the same side of the internal/external divide, it is not unusual to find more than a single working group dealing with the same matter. As a good example, COTER may deal with the Comprehensive Convention on Terrorism under negotiation in the UN; but in parallel the EuroMed committee works with the Maghreb countries to build a consensus position regarding the Convention, while this task is also under the remit of an independent UN working group.[7] The result is that a remarkable effort must be produced to link up the work of all these different groups and provide a coherent EU position.

In order to address these coordination needs, some formal mechanisms are available to manage these matters at distinct points of the hierarchy. At the WG level, COTER and TWG organise joint meetings on matters of mutual interest. They also issue a consolidated assessment integrating the internal and external dimensions of the threat. Moreover, the president of each working group can present the current state of play of their work on an issue at their counterparts' meetings. More recently, 'Friends of the Presidency' groups have been established for particularly complex terrorism-related matters when there is a need to involve more than a pair of working groups. These non-permanent working groups last one Presidency and are established to discuss a specific issue before producing conclusions that are adopted at Council meetings. In addition, ad hoc WPs can be established temporarily to improve coordination for a limited period. Hence in 2008 a JHA–RELEX Ad hoc Support Group was mandated to bring closer together the work of those working groups active in the external dimension of JHA.[8]

At the above level, coordination is also produced in parallel and separately within two different pillars by the Article 36 Committee and the Political and Security Committee (PSC), supported in the process by national officials from Permanent Representations. In order to bridge the internal–external divide, overall cross-pillar coordination would in principle be conducted by the Committee of Permanent Representatives (COREPER) but in this case the task is formally delegated to the Counterterrorism Coordinator appointed under the Secretary General of the

Council. This is 'to make sure that each working group is aware of what's going on in other working groups'.[9] The Coordinator acts as an interface by attending COTER and TWG meetings to brief on the work that is being produced in other sectors, explain and receive feedback on his initiatives and become informed of the matters discussed in these groups. The Coordinator can draw upon the resources of the Council Secretariat, which assists on institutional management by providing institutional memory and servicing working groups, linking their work with other permanent EU bodies and becoming a source of proposals.

Inter-institutional coherence

Intra-institutional coordination is however just an element of the broader issue of institutional coherence. The other side of the equation is whether the different bodies within the EU with a stake on counter-terrorism are fulfilling their role in an interoperable and interconnected manner; in other words, achieve inter-institutional coherence. This would indicate an absence of what Nuttall (2001: 8) defines as 'malign consistency': the existence of struggles for institutional power or, in other words, turf wars. Whereas Nuttall's analysis of the consistency of EU foreign policy focuses on the two separate bureaucratic apparatus, intergovernmental and Community, this analysis will add another layer by also focusing on the working relationship between those EU agencies operating in the field of counter-terrorism. In this regard, inter-institutional coordination in counter-terror matters within the EU has been addressed through formal structures, networks and bodies but also informal processes.

Commission–Council coordination

It is clear by now that the post-Lisbon European Parliament (EP) is becoming much more involved in the passing of internal security legislation and, as a result, the Counter-terrorism Coordinator and Commission officials are forced to engage the Civil Liberties, Justice and Home Affairs (LIBE) Committee early in the legislative process. Yet we must not lose sight of the fact that the development of these proposals continues to be managed by Commission and Council officials. Therefore fluid communication and interaction between these two actors overshadows any other consideration in ensuring effective counter-terror decision-making. This goal has been attempted through two instruments present in Nuttall's 'consistency model': institutional arrangements and political exhortations.

Under the latter type of response, the EU Counter-terrorism Strategy invited EU institutions to establish, during each Presidency, a high-level political dialogue bringing together the Commission, Presidency, the Counter-terrorism Coordinator and EP representatives to 'consider progress together and promote transparency and balance in the EU's approach' (Council of the European Union 2006d). The first of such meetings, convened in May 2006 by the Austrian Presidency, informed the EP on the state of a number of proposals prepared by the Council and Commission. The convening of the dialogue depends nonetheless on each Presidency's whim and some have declined to revisit this mechanism. This leaves the impression that this dialogue is more a half-hearted rhetorical effort to improve transparency than a conscious attempt at enhancing inter-institutional communication. It is difficult not to question in any case whether such ad hoc and irregular political engagements can do enough to strengthen institutional consistency.

Alternatively, organisational arrangements have also been put in place to encourage consistency. Thus, in 2005 a network of contact points consisting of one representative in each Permanent Representation was put in place. The network's mission is to improve communication between Commission and Council staff and capitals and to update the Action Plan (Council of the European Union 2007c). Cooperation is also fostered by the participation of the DG Justice and the DG Home Affairs Commissioners in JHA Council deliberations. This is reinforced by Commission officials taking part in Council Working Group discussions including TWG, COTER, informal expert and regional group meetings. The main rationale is to inform Member State officials about the state of play of their initiatives and future projects. The Commission often uses these meetings to 'test the waters': to consult Member States and receive feedback on draft proposals. According to a Commission official, ´the Commission does normally 40 per cent of the talking' in those meetings and

> we are a bit more part of the group than other participants in the groups because we are part of the preparation of the groups, we elaborate, we contribute to the elaboration of the documents of the groups, we're working directly with the Presidency and our colleagues in the Council Secretariat.[10]

In actual fact, Commission involvement depends on the individual, the subject matter and whether the Commission is working on a communication on the subject.[11] Nonetheless, the Commission's inclusion in these groups represent an opportunity for regular contact and a two-way exchange of information at the director level, providing both sides with broad knowledge of each other's activities.

At desk level, however, there are no formal structures of policy coordination between the Commission DGs and the Council Secretariat. A number of officials from both the Commission and the Council confirmed to the author that they had little knowledge of the activities of their counterparts.[12] Evidence from interviews with EU officials reinforces the view that, at this particular stage, and in the absence of formal mechanisms, communication and cooperation, when they occur, are mainly informal.

As a Commission official put it, cooperation has been improving in recent years 'because there are good personal relations perhaps more than anything else'.[13] Interviewees in the Council also emphasised the importance of this tool: 'An informal basis is the first form of cooperation, everything depends on who you know on the other side, who you can pick up the phone and call, you have to have some informal contacts'.[14] Informality has also characterised the working relationship between the Counterterrorism Coordinator and pertinent Commission DGs' directors, since the Coordinator's formal mandate is circumscribed to coordination within the Council. In those instances where the European Council has invited both the Commission and the Coordinator to work on a particular issue, although formally working in parallel, discreet contacts are usually established throughout the process before the work merges at the COREPER level.

Informal working relationships between the Commission and officials from the Council Secretariat are by no means an exception in EU policy processes. Although institutional dynamics point towards cooperation between officials from these two bodies, the development of these relationships is often reliant on personal contacts between individual officers. As it occurs in other policy fields such as Common Foreign and Security Policy (CFSP), informal relationships are often used as a way to address the geographical and institutional gap between Commission and Council institutions. Informal channels of communication have been opened at the director level and to a lesser extent the desk level; the latter pretty much dependent on the initiative of the particular individual officer. Informal networking then serves a variety of purposes from addressing information gaps, to preparing the agenda of joint meetings or consensuate a common position. This collegial atmosphere is facilitated by the fact that the expertise on these aspects is concentrated, at least at the director level, in a small group of officials who get to meet each other relatively often while dealing with various dimensions of the problem.[15]

Another factor that has encouraged informal coordination is the growing familiarity between policy-makers that comes from the experience of working on the same issues for a long period. In this way, the continuous assistance to formal coordination meetings leads to the nurturing of informal working relationships. Increasing interpersonal experience means also that boundaries in competences become increasingly clear and an understanding of the other person's work develops; an important issue in the external relations side where there has been an initial sense of competition between COTER and DG Relex.[16] It is clear from the above that informal networking is a trust-building process that contributes to ameliorate malign consistency.

Agencies

Coordination between the main European agencies tasked with counterterrorism varies strongly depending on the remit of the agency. Since the synergies are evident, Europol and Eurojust have aimed to develop a working relationship on terrorism matters. In fact, strengthening cooperation with Europol has been a Eurojust objective from the outset. The Eurojust's 2006 annual report reflected the ambitious goals in this regard by declaring the following cooperation priorities with Europol:

> to improve Eurojust's possibilities of obtaining information and better operational co-operation from Europol's Analytical Work Files (AWFs); to establish a secure network between Eurojust and Europol for the exchange of information; to develop the project on Joint Investigation Teams (JITs), together with Europol; to be more involved in the preparation for and conclusions of the Organised Crime Threat Assessment (OCTA); and to finalise, together with Europol, a report to the Council on common experiences and specific results.
>
> (Eurojust 2007: 15)

A first step was taken on 9 June 2004 with the signing of a cooperation agreement to enhance the exchange of strategic and operational data and improve the coordination of their activities. Admittedly, the negotiations for the agreement were rather difficult, caused by Europol management board's reluctance to meet some of Eurojust's data-sharing requests. This was due to the strict legal conditions that the onward transmission of data from Europol to third parties must meet and the fact that Member States 'own' the information that they transfer to Europol. A 'very long procedure for a very petty result' was how a Eurojust representative described the final agreement (UK House of Lords 2004: 29). Unsurprisingly, this dissatisfaction led to the signing in 2009 of a new operational cooperation agreement and a Memorandum of Understanding on confidentiality standards in handling the formal exchange of classified information (Europol 2009: 51). As a result, a steering committee is in place to monitor the implementation of the agreements and to develop strategies and priorities. This committee has become the main formal tool of collaboration between Europol and Eurojust in strategic matters (Europol 2007: 28). Its efforts are supported by ad hoc bilateral meetings between the presidents of both organisations.

Regarding operational cooperation, a secure communication link between the two organisations enabling the electronic exchange of confidential data has been activated. In addition, Eurojust has contributed to Europol's Terrorism Situation and Trend (TE-SAT) Report and has appointed national members and case analysts to be associated as experts in 12 of the existing 18 analysis work files (AWFs) from Europol. Both organisations have cooperated together to provide guidance to Member

States regarding the setting-up of the Joint Investigative Teams, through the production of a manual and periodic expert meetings. The fact that the number of cases dealt with by Eurojust involving Europol has quadrupled from 7 cases in 2006 to 30 in 2008 (Europol 2009: 51) illustrates how Europol–Eurojust cooperation has rapidly grown.

On the other hand, problems remain – restrictions on the use of the secure communication link by national officials have diminished its value as a tool. Furthermore, Eurojust is not associated with any of the Terrorism AWFs. Finally, data protection restrictions also impede Eurojust to access Europol's 'Check the Web' portal (Eurojust 2009). These and other examples contribute to the general view that there is 'an insufficient flow of information between the two organisations' and 'that they should try to work together more often' (UK House of Lords 2008d: 49, 153). In fact, the potential for further progress is constrained by their differences in institutional structure and legal basis; a problem exemplified by the lengthy negotiations of their cooperation agreement. Hence, a key aim of the two separate 2008 Council Decisions that transform Europol into a community agency and upgrade the mandate of Eurojust is precisely to help align their functioning. This promise has only been partially fulfilled, since political discussion on both texts occurred independently and, as a result, the opportunity for the full streamlining of their legal basis and institutional structure in a common system was clearly missed.

Apart from the links with Eurojust, Europol has also established a working relationship with the Secretariat Situation Centre (Sitcen) to produce joint threat assessments. Even if Europol has a liaison officer seconded to Sitcen (O'Neill: 2008), some friction has emerged in the process as they have tried to demarcate their separate responsibilities in the strategic analysis. Europol officers have acknowledged that an important obstacle in this joint activity is the different nature of the information and national governments' insistence not to let both channels communicate.[17] Operational agreements – similar to that signed with Eurojust – allowing for the exchange of personal data with the European Police College (CEPOL) and Frontex have also been negotiated (Europol 2009: 52). Europol cooperates with the Police Chiefs Operational Task Force (PCOTF) concerning counter-terrorism matters, including Islamist terrorism and terrorism financing (Deflem 2006). In addition Europol has links with organisations outside the EU framework such as Interpol and it also participates as observer in the Club of Berne's Counter-terrorist Group (CTG).

Sitcen's input is not reduced to Europol's Threat Assessments but also found in Eurojust and Frontex threat analyses (van Buuren 2009). On the other hand, there has been so far little practical cooperation between Frontex and other agencies involved in anti-terrorist work, although some collaboration with Europol started to develop by 2007, with this agency providing operational information and staff and contributing to some of Frontex threat and risk analyses (UK House of Lords: 2008a). Conversely, the Frontex Risk Analysis Unit also adds to the Europol Organised Crime Threat Assessment Report (Frontex 2007a). Contacts for further cooperation have been established with Eurojust and CEPOL but so far they have been very limited. Eurojust counter-terror unit director has stated that they have yet to formally interconnect with Frontex.

Finally, the heads of CEPOL, Eurojust, Europol and Frontex instituted in 2006 an annual meeting formally to exchange best practices and build on the vague aim of sharing ideas for closer working relationships (UK House of Lords 2008d: 51).

Regarding the relation between agencies and EU institutions, both Europol and Eurojust take part in the decision-making of the Commission and the Council on terrorist matters. The Commission regularly requests both of these agencies to submit comments on consultations and participate in their experts' meetings. The Commission, through DG Home Affairs, has also taken part in some Europol's Management Board meetings. Europol officials have argued that their relationship with the Commission in counter-terrorism is rather fluid in adjoining fields such as counter-proliferation.[18] Representatives from Sitcen, Europol and Eurojust also take part in combined TWG and COTER meetings and other Council working groups when discussing security issues of relevance. Europol was part of the Council's team that produced the peer evaluation report of national counter-terrorist arrangements. Similarly, the Counter-terrorism Coordinator holds regular meetings separately with the heads of the anti-terrorist units at Eurojust and Europol. Finally, the amendment of Europol and Eurojust legal bases, which involve the financing of these bodies by the Community budget, opens the door to the EP monitoring of their activities.

Apart from these formal and ad hoc structures set up to enhance institutional consistency, political obligations have been resorted to connect the activities of this constellation of actors. Thus, the Hague Programme called for the organisation of a joint meeting during every Presidency involving the chairpersons of the Article 36 Committee, the Strategic Committee on immigration, Frontiers and Asylum and representatives of the Police Chiefs Task Force, Eurojust, Europol, Frontex, the Commission and the Sitcen. The objective was to gain practical experience with the coordination and cooperation at the operational level by law enforcement and other agencies (Council of the European Union: 2005d). It is possible that two meetings per year are not sufficient to address the significant challenges to cooperation in the internal security arena, where terrorism is just one of a myriad of issues.

Consistency weaknesses

In spite of the diverse strategies that have been delineated above, there has been a general acknowledgement by policy-makers that there is room for improvement in the communication between the EU's counter-terror actors. Officials from the Council Secretariat and the Co-ordinator Office have stressed the complexity and challenges involved in the coordination practices and the existence of a serious problem in this regard.[19] Commission officials themselves have officially recognised that the situation is far from ideal: 'We have to be absolutely sure that they [EU bodies] are operating to full potential and they are operating with each other in the best possible way. Have we achieved that? No' (UK House of Lords 2005: 48).

What emerges from the analysis of official documents and interviews is that EU institutional arrangements have struggled to address inter- and intra-institutional coherence pressures in a congested organisational space. This notion needs to be further refined next by articulating a number of factors that have contributed to foster deficiencies in the institutional dimension of consistency.

Pillar structure

In spite of the fact that terrorism requires a multidisciplinary and complex response, the rigid legal division into pillars acts as an important obstacle to institutional consistency. As later discussed, Lisbon has nominally transformed the three-pillar system (Community, CFSP/ESDP and JHA) into a two-pillar structure with the communitarisation of JHA and the persistent intergovernmentalism of CFSP/CSDP, so the problem, although alleviated, remains. As Spence perceptively argues, this system has contributed to a dispersion of efforts and, it could be added, political responsibility (Spence 2007).

Moreover, this is a major hindrance with regard to those complex initiatives originating from the Commission involving a variety of measures with unclear policy demarcations. Thus, a policy proposal on the control of explosives may encompass areas as varied as the detection of explosives at customs control points, the security of explosives used in industry or scientific research policy. This means in practice that one single document on explosives control sent by the Commission to the Council may include in the same paragraph elements from more than one pillar. Here the Commission has flexibility in producing comprehensive proposals crossing a number of areas, as inter-service groups can be established to gather expertise and allow most interests to be represented. In contrast, the rules of procedure within the Council regarding the functioning of the working bodies are much more stringent and there is no possibility of the establishment of similar inter-service groups. Commission initiatives must then find their way through rigidly divided ministerial formations and their corresponding sectoral committees. The aforementioned proposal on control of explosives should be jointly discussed by a dozen of different working groups at the Council in order to involve all the relevant actors but this cannot occur as this would involve the meeting of a large number of national experts from different ministries and all Member States. No group has the responsibility of doing it and no systematic procedure to get all these groups together. This means that the multiple aspects of these measures end up divorced and discussed in separated and often unconnected Working Groups and Committees of senior civil servants. As a Commission official rather bluntly put it: 'the Council is in a mess in order to try to deal with our policies'.[20] As argued by the EU Counter-terrorism Coordinator himself: 'some legislation had been discussed in different groups within the Council, and so you have sometimes lawyers or police people discussing part of the same subject and sometimes there is a lack of consistency' (UK House of Lords 2008d: 155).

This hampers the efficiency of the EU as a policy-maker as progress may be blocked when no WP takes automatic responsibility for some cross-cutting initiatives. Continuing with the above example, the Commission proposal on the security of explosives was paralysed for 18 months because no WP discussed the proposal until the Portuguese Presidency allocated it to the Police Cooperation WP.[21]

As already mentioned, the establishment of Friends of the Presidency groups has been used to address these problems on a number of occasions. Yet these are by no means a panacea since they only last for a Presidency while negotiations of complex issues (i.e. the European Programme for Critical Infrastructure Protection (EPCIP), the Chemical, Biological, Radiological and Nuclear (CBRN) Programme) generally take a minimum of two years. Moreover the use of this solution is problematic due to such pedestrian obstacles as the limitations on the size of the Council rooms. More importantly, these temporary working groups burden Member States with the responsibility of the coordination as they must decide on which ministry would send the representative and the method for informing other departments. Coordination gaps at the national level make common the fact that some competent actors end up outside of the deliberative practices and it does not ensure that all the actors will be involved.[22] It is difficult not to agree with Nuttall when he argues that 'as long as the Union organises its affairs in separate pillars consistency will need to be managed' (Nuttall 2005: 96).

Overlapping competences

'Brusselisation', or transfer of decision-making authority to Brussels in counter-terrorism matters, has produced a plethora of committees, expert groups, agencies and other bodies. Such proliferation of actors has led to what den Boer (2003) has defined as a 'crowded policy area' emerging at the European level. In the words of an EU official, 'everybody thinks that they have to say something about terrorism'.[23] This overpopulation of actors is highly problematic in the sense that it overburdens coordination bodies. As an illustration, the Counter-terrorism Coordinator Office is stretched out due to the considerable number of working groups and committees within the Council that become involved periodically in specific counter-terrorist measures.[24] Moreover, the rapid growth in the number of competing bureaucratic populations is compounded by the fact that some of the EU structures in this field have been characterised by poorly defined mandates, including the Counter-terrorism Coordinator (Monar 2006b). The final result is inefficiencies in the form of overlapping competences between structures within and outside the EU framework. This is highly relevant, as Nuttall points out, since duplication is symptomatic of institutional consistency weaknesses (Nuttall 2005).

There are plenty of instances where duplication of tasks and expertise occurs in this field. As a case in point, the terrorist threat to Europe is separately assessed by at least four independent bodies: the TWG submits assessments on the threat on internal security, COTER on terrorism in third countries and regions, Europol produces a Situation and Trends report, and the Situation Centre at the Secretariat develops assessment reports on the internal and external dimensions of the terrorist threat. The fact that Eurojust has also become involved in collecting and analysing counter-terror information through its Case Management Team has raised concerns at the Coordinator Office in terms of duplication of efforts with Europol (UK House of Lords 2008d). On the other hand, technical assistance in counter-terrorism is provided by both COTER and DG Relex; the former focusing on a shortlist of priority countries and the latter providing third states with capacity-building assistance through the Instrument for Stability.[25] In a similar vein, both the Commission and the Coordinator evaluate the implementation of counter-terror instruments; the latter systematically through periodic reports and the former on ad hoc exercises covering measures that are deemed specially important or sensitive, such as the European Arrest Warrant.

Duplication may occur even within the same institution and in relation to very concrete tasks. In this way, terrorism financing within the Council is scattered across a diversity of formal and informal working groups since: COTER, the Multidisciplinary Group on Organised Crime (MDG) and the Clearing House WP are all involved. More importantly, the decision to separate DG JLS into two independent configurations has opened further opportunities for a confusion of roles since most counter-terror policies would necessitate the input from both DG HOME and DG JUST. Indeed, this division not only dilutes expertise but leads to increased bureaucracy, administration and coordination demands or the Commission.

Moreover, an overlap of sorts also exists between the Article 36 Committee and the Counter-terrorism Coordinator in managing counter-terror matters in the Council. The Article 36 committee mandate is limited to police and criminal justice, which is at the core of the European response to terrorism, resulting in clear potential for duplication. This is more relevant for those measures that target terrorism only as part of the broader fight against serious crime, including the European Arrest and Evidence warrants or the legislation on retention of telecommunication data. Finally, the mandate of the new Standing Committee on Internal Security (COSI) – tasked with facilitating operational coordination of Member States' competent authorities – intersects with that of the pre-existing PCOTF. The possibility for overlapping expands when structures outside the EU are considered. An interesting case is that of the Club of Berne's CTG and the Council's Sitcen, since some Member States tend to send the same representatives to both structures,[26] raising interesting questions over intelligence ownership. This also leads to repetition, particularly since the CTG also sends reports to EU bodies on Radical Islam (Council of the European Union 2004b: 3).

Following this pattern, Member States use both the PWGT (Police Working Group on Terrorism) and Europol as channels for the sharing of terrorism-related intelligence. Although it must be noted that security agencies have favoured informal and practitioner-created structures such as the PWGT over EU organisations for the sharing of confidential intelligence (Müller-Wille 2008). Finally, overlap exists between the PWGT again and the EU's PCOTF as both have served as platforms for high-level meetings with the heads of EU counter-terrorist units to share best practices and information.

Bureaucratic politics

As a result of the aforementioned instances of duplication and overlapping responsibilities, a degree of inter-institutional friction has emerged. Although clearly a fundamental issue, we will not be concerned here with conflicts of the political sort such as the EP's contestation of particular instruments based on concerns about their impact on civil liberties[27] but will concentrate instead on the antagonism between the Commission and the Council Secretariat within the process of decision-making. Although the pattern of the relationship between these two actors tends to be cooperative within the first pillar, competition has been a reality in the second pillar where demarcation lines between Commission and Council are rather blurred (Christiansen 2001). This has certainly been the case regarding the external dimension of counter-terrorism where initially DG Relex and COTER have considered each other as competitors for power and responsibilities as much as partners.[28]

This has often come as a result of the Commission's instinct to protect its independence from the Council's institutional influence and its competences in those counter-terror areas that fall under the common market. A well-known episode in this regard was the Commission's mixed reception of the appointment of the counter-terror Coordinator. Keohane has highlighted how Commission officials perceived the decision as an attempt by national governments to curb their role in this area (Keohane 2006). Indeed, Commission representatives took great pains to emphasise that the work of the Coordinator should be restricted to the inner workings of the Council and the overseeing of implementation. In other words, the role of the Coordinator *should* be complementary to that of the Commission. The former DG JLS director Jonathan Faull was very explicit: 'I do not believe that the co-ordinator has the resources, the mandate or the institutional position to co-ordinate operational action of the various bodies in the European Union' (UK House of Lords 2005: 46). Spence has also argued that the origin of the Commission's opposition to this post resides in its perception that the Council Secretariat was proposing structures that would put the first and third pillars at the service of the second by locating policy initiative and coordination under Solana (Spence 2007). The Commission's distrust of the Coordinator would then be symbolic of a broader debate on where the locus of political responsibility for this policy domain should reside.

On the other hand, inter-institutional rivalry can also be detected in the critical stance of some Council officials on the quality of certain Commission proposals. A Council official described, for instance, a particular Commission initiative on intelligence exchange as 'totally outlandish'.[29] Others have pointed out that the DG JLS 'lacked a little bit of expertise coming from the services' and sometimes the proposals did not respond to a clear need or were not realistic. The latter is a statement corroborated by Europol representatives. The Commission's argument is that it is precisely their role to raise issues and foster discussion:

> We have the responsibility to say there is a problem to be put on the table, we put the problem on the table, we have a discussion. If the discussion must start by 25 people pointing guns at us and shooting for hours and hours, let it be so. When they finalize shooting at us, they would have to say what they think about what is on the table, actually.[30]

This problem is also present at the Agency level. The 2004 European Council encouraged Member States to second internal intelligence officials from domestic services to Europol's Counter-terrorism Task Force; yet only two countries complied. This encouraged Europol to submit a formal complaint to the Council in 2005 that went unanswered (van Buuren 2009). A 2008 report attributed this situation to the preference of internal security services to engage in intelligence-sharing through the more opaque Sitcen as, in fact, 'the intelligence community is not very eager to work with Europol' considering the low level of security clearance by many Europol officials (UK House of Lords 2008d: 38). As a response to this situation, the EU Counter-terrorism Coordinator Office is exploring the possibility of overcoming this disconnection through stronger collaboration between national fusion centres; that is, the UK's Joint Terrorism Analysis Centre (JTAC) or France's *Unité de coordination de la tutte anti-terroriste* (UCLAT) and, at a later stage, European agencies.

These sporadic struggles for institutional power are highly relevant, since they highlight not only divergent approaches but also the persistence of 'malign consistency'. Importantly, this has affected the efficiency of the European response since contrasting approaches have occasionally resulted in the production of parallel and competing legislative proposals on the same matter.[31]

Limited coordinator actors

Notwithstanding the relevance of the above elements, arguably the key factor explaining the weakness in the EU's institutional consistency is the inadequacy of existing coordinating actors. At the apex of the structure, the European Council can arbitrate on strategic matters and put its weight behind proposals that would increase the general consistency of policies, such as the establishment of the Coordinator in the aftermath of Madrid. Its summitry format is however more suited to grand bargains and strategic decisions than to the small details of internal coordination.

On the other hand, the cross-pillar COREPER would appear well positioned to fulfil the role of overall coordination since it covers all the main separate counter-terror areas in its two manifestations: COREPER II addresses the JHA, the Common Foreign and Security Policy (CFSP), and the European Security and Defence Policy (ESDP) and terrorism financing; COREPER I deals with more technical matters such as transports, telecommunications and the environment (Council of the European Union 2004b). Yet COREPER has a very busy agenda and the ambassadors cannot easily extend the time they devote to this particular issue. In fact COREPER is already pressurised by a parallel problem in this field: due to the rigidity of the rules of procedure within the Council, and the fact that COREPER is the only body that has the legitimacy to address cross-pillar documents, permanent representatives are swamped by documents of great technical complexity.[32] This detracts ambassadors from concentrating instead on the political implications or mainstream guidance elements.

Following a recommendation from the Counter-terrorism Coordinator, in a 3 June 2004 decision, COREPER was invited to engage more systematically and regularly in the coordination of counter-terrorism. This would be achieved by following up the implementation of the Action Plan and discussing terrorism once a month, by giving stronger direction to the work being undertaken by Council committees and WPs, and by reporting to the JHA Council as well as to the General Affairs Council (Lugna 2006). Evidence from interviews confirmed that in reality this was more rhetoric than practice and there has not been any major change in the extent of the ambassadors' involvement in these matters.[33] In any case COREPER's oversight much depends on the Presidency. Whereas it played, for instance, a key role during the British Presidency in 2005, this was not continued in the same energetic fashion during the consequent Austrian Presidency. Immediately below COREPER, individual Committees within the Council such as Article 36 and the PSC have their mandate limited to their own pillars and cannot assist in bridging the internal–external divide.

Finally, and most importantly, the role of the Counter-terrorism Coordinator, a crucial post in this area has been beset with problems from the start. At their roots is the vague definition of its mandate established in the 25 March 2004 European Council Declaration. As already discussed, this circumstance led originally to institutional friction with the Commission. Moreover, the coordinator was first criticised by Member States' representatives for its ambassadorial role that they believe should be played by national authorities. It is safe to say that established actors have contested any perceived move by the Coordinator to step in their turf boundaries. This was a constant reality during the de Vries period as Coordinator and eventually disagreements between Member States over the exact scope of the position caused the decision for his replacement to be delayed by six months (EurActiv 2007). Although the abolition of the position became a possibility, the final verdict was to transform the post from a political figure to a more technical, bureaucratic position, a high-level civil servant with a lower public profile.[34] The appointee would be a 'qualified eurocrat' rather than a politician. This was a natural reaction given the displeasure of some important interior ministries with the high media profile that de Vries adopted for himself.[35] Indeed the fact that part of his job was to highlight Member States' inefficiencies in implementation did not help to endear him to the Interior ministers.[36]

Inherent in this debate is the well-known fact that the position has limited competences and resources. Keohane has described how the Coordinator has 'few powers, a small budget and no right to propose EU legislation in this area; nor can he call meetings of national justice and foreign ministers to set the anti-terrorism agenda' (Keohane 2006: 65). Neither can he formally coordinate the work of the Commission or the EP. The Coordinator can only persuade Member States to accelerate the implementation of measures but, according to the same author, 'only ten of the 25 governments take his role seriously and listen to what he says'. In fact, as stated above, de Vries became rather unpopular with Member States' ministers. This situation had much more to do with his decision to step down than inaccurate media reports connecting it to the critical EP report on the rendition policies.[37] If his powers are limited, the formal resources are equally notorious; formally the Coordinator Office is constituted just by the Coordinator himself and two assistants. In contrast a similar Council unit tasked with counter-proliferation has at least a dozen staff working full time. A member from the Coordinator's Office calculated that at least 15 staff would be necessary to have a more hands-on approach on the coordination process.[38] Although these limitations were rejected by other EU officials who reiterated the fact that the Coordinator can draw upon the General Secretariat staff for exercising its role, the reality is that he has no executive authority over them and can only cajole or persuade them to get things done. This further diminishes the possibilities of the Office to produce proposals leaving all policy initiative independent from Member States entirely to the Commission. It also obviously affects its ambassadorial role as there was little he could promise in its interaction with third countries' representatives that was in his power to produce. In this way, the Office evolved into a one-stop shop that was heavily stretched to fulfil the coordination, ambassadorial and implementation oversight roles that de Vries adopted for himself. These flaws have been very obvious for some time and Solana himself publicly acknowledged them when referring to the fact that de Vries' successor should have a 'deeper' mandate and enjoy 'a much closer relationship' with EU governments and institutions (EurActiv 2007). In actual fact the formal mandate and certainly the powers of the post have not changed much in practice.

Following from this, de Kerchove, aware of the sensibilities of the Member States with the work of de Vries, has followed a different pattern of action than his predecessor, concentrating on the more low-key coordination within the Council. De Kerchove's extensive EU experience and previous position as director of DG JHA within the Council Secretariat means that he is an ideal choice to oversee working relationships the inner Council. This background in JHA has also shifted the attention of the post towards the internal side in contrast with de Vries' emphasis on the external dimension. De Kerchove has also followed a more hands-on approach than his predecessor on information transfer within the Council and prioritised and raised the visibility of some particular dossiers.[39]

The Lisbon Treaty and institutional consistency: a positive development

The Lisbon Treaty constitutes the best opportunity to address the aforementioned institutional consistency weaknesses. This is achieved mainly through the communitarisation (i.e. introduction of the ordinary legislative procedure of qualified majority voting and co-decision) of the area of police and judicial cooperation in criminal matters, the core of EU counter-terror efforts. Although operational cooperation between police forces is still excluded from communitarisation, this alteration partly ameliorates the rigid structural division within the Council, enhancing coordination between the different WPs with counter-terror competences in what used to be the first and the third pillar. This change does nothing, however, to bridge the separation between the policy actors separately involved in the external and internal dimensions. Under the 'shadow of the pillars', the EU's foreign, security and defence policy remains inter-governmental and preserves its separate voting and decision-making methods.

In parallel, the involvement of new actors paves the way to new challenges. With the introduction of co-decision and the addition of the EP to the legislative process, the importance of fluent inter-institutional coordination has become even more important. The creation of a High Representative (HR) for Foreign Affairs and Security Policy merging the responsibilities of the SG-CFSP HR and the Commissioner of External Relations introduces a new powerful actor in the external dimension of the counter-terror response. The Representative also acts as one of the vice-presidents of the Commission and this entails new pressures on the Commission's working arrangements to ensure intra-institutional coordination between an increasing number of Commissioners with regard to its external policies. Such pressures and opportunities for conflict increase in a system with two new posts with competences in the EU's foreign policy (the new President of the European Council and the HR) to add to the Commission President's role in this area (UK House of Lords 2008b).

Under the HR, a new European Action Service has been set up to support Ashton's work and represent the EU overseas. This new bureaucratic machinery is being developed, but it can have the potential in practice to assuage the aforementioned degree of competition and rivalry between the Council and the Commission that has been present in the EU's external security policies. It does so by instituting a single independent structure that absorbs previously divided structures within the Council's General Secretariat and the Commission and includes officials from both of these institutions and staff seconded from national diplomatic services. As argued by Howorth, the question is whether 'the advantages of having this central pillar of cohesion will out-weigh the disadvantages of inter-agency complexity' (Howorth 2005: 196).

The establishment of the new HR figure has however represented a missed opportunity. As a result of these changes, the Coordinator has been placed under the SG of the Council, the European President Van Rompuy. Instead the alternative – being part of the HR Office – would have allowed the Coordinator's influence to extend to the Commission. Hence, the potential for a truly *EU* Coordinator became unfulfilled. This matter is not confronted either by Lisbon's COSI Committee on internal security operational cooperation, only formally tasked in 'helping' with the coherence of action by Europol, Eurojust and Frontex.

Conclusion

Although the Lisbon Treaty represents a step forward towards a more coherent EU response to the threat of terrorism, by no means does it constitute a panacea. An issue of concern remains, which is connected to a major question that this book addresses: whether a European approach that considers the constituent elements of its internal security as separate entities, instead of the dimensions of a broader 'homeland security' policy, is strategically sound. It does so by affirming that the fragmentation that is observed in such a broad policy complex is both aggravated and mirrored by the institutional incoherence observed in individual policy sectors, in this case, EU counter-terrorism.

This field serves as proxy to reflect on some of the intrinsic problems associated with the challenge of coordinating the work by a large number of institutional actors involved in a policy umbrella that runs across a number of very different areas, from social integration and community policing to the financing of crime to the exchange of intelligence. It is only logical to assume that these coordination weaknesses would be replicated and exaggerated in a potential EU homeland security arena. An open question to conclude this chapter would be therefore to wonder about how reasonable it is to expect a coherent EU homeland security on the basis of the intrinsic obstacles towards this goal that are found within its individual policy fields.

Notes

This contribution is based on the 'Institutional Consistency' chapter of the author's *Post-9/11 European Union Counter-terrorism: Politics, Polity and Policies* monograph (Routledge, 2011).

1 DG Fisheries and Maritime Affairs being the sole exception.
2 Interviews with Commission Officials, DG JLS, January 2006 and April 2008.
3 Interview with a Commission Official, DG JLS, April 2008.
4 Interview with a Commission Official, DG JLS, April 2008.
5 As a result, contrasting perspectives from both sides have emerged on issues such as the counter-terrorism clauses in third countries' agreements, where CFSP officials have expressed concern over the impact of potential penalties in the broader diplomatic relationship.
6 Interview with a Council Official, General Secretariat, January 2006.
7 Interview with a Council Official, General Secretariat, January 2006.
8 An alternative example is the group established by the 2007 Portuguese Presidency to discuss the Commission proposal on the control of Chemical, Biological, Radiological and Nuclear (CBRN) weapons. Interview with a Commission Official, DG JLS, April 2008.
9 Interview with a Council Official, General Secretariat, January 2006.
10 Interview with a Commission Official, DG JLS, January 2006.
11 Interview with an official from a Member State Permanent Representation, April 2008.
12 As an official from the Council (DG H-Justice and Home Affairs, January 2006) rather graphically put it: 'I don't have a clue what the Commission is doing'.
13 Interview with a Commission Official, DG Relex, April 2008.
14 Interview with a Council Official, General Secretariat, April 2008.
15 As argued by a high-ranked official, 'there are 50 people in Brussels working

on terrorism, they know each other, we all know where to find us'. Interview with a Council Official, DG H-Justice and Home Affairs, January 2006.

16 Interview with a Commission Official, DG Relex, April 2008.

17 Interview with Europol Officials, Serious Crime Unit and SC-5 Unit, January 2006.

18 Interview with Europol Officials, Serious Crime Unit and SC-5 Unit, January 2006.

19 Comments emphasising this point included: 'there is a real big coordination problem even within the Council', '[coordination] process indeed is challenging and very complex', 'do you want an honest answer? They don't [coordinate]', 'coordination could be done better' or 'sometimes they just don't know what people are doing'. These examples are by no means exhaustive. Interviews with Council and Commission Officials, January 2006 and April 2008.

20 Interview with a Commission Official, DG JLS, January 2006.

21 Interview with a Commission Official, DG JLS, April 2008.

22 Interview Council Officials, DG H-Justice and Home Affairs, April 2008.

23 Interview with a Council Official, General Secretariat, DG H-Justice and Home Affairs, January 2006.

24 Interview with a Council Official, General Secretariat, January 2006.

25 Interview with a Commission Official, DG Relex, April 2008.

26 Interview with a Council Official, DG H-Justice and Home Affairs, January 2006.

27 The most high-profile clashes include the EU–US Passenger Name Records Agreement, the EU–US agreement on the transfer of bank data and the EU terrorist lists.

28 Interview with a Commission Official, DG Relex, April 2008.

29 Interview with a Council Official, DG H-Justice and Home Affairs, January 2006.

30 Interview with a Commission Official, DG JLS, January 2006.

31 Some of the most relevant examples are the data retention directives, the US signing individual bilateral visa agreements with Member States or the EU–US Custom Security Initiative where the Commission even threatened to bring individual Member States before the European Court of Justice.

32 Interview with a Commission Official, DG JLS, January 2006.

33 Interview with an official from a Member State Permanent Representation, April 2008.

34 Interview with an official from a Member State Permanent Representation, April 2008.

35 Interview with an official from a Member State Permanent Representation, April 2008.

36 Interview with a Commission Official, DG JLS, April 2008.

37 Interview with a Council Official, General Secretariat, Counter-terrorism Coordinator Office, April 2008.

38 Interview with a Council Official, General Secretariat, Counter-terrorism Coordinator Office, January 2006.

39 More specifically: information-sharing on special investigation methods, radicalisation and recruitment, financing of technical assistance to third countries, and organisation of work within the Council and implementation of EU instruments. Interview with a Council Official, General Secretariat, Counter-terrorism Coordinator Office, April 2008.

6 The external dimension of European homeland security

Alex MacKenzie

This chapter demonstrates how agreements between the European Union (EU) and third states have added an external layer to European homeland security. Literature on the external dimension of EU security policies has often been thematically limited, emphasised certain agreements or focused on a certain area or country (Argomaniz 2009; Lavenex and Wichmann 2009; Pawlak 2009b, 2009c; Wolff *et al.* 2009b; Wolff 2009; Kaunert 2010a). However, these are only single parts of the puzzle that is the external dimension of European homeland security. In order to better explain the EU's role in homeland security, these agreements, and the threats that they combat, need to be brought together under the concept of homeland security. Although the external policies of the EU have rarely been coordinated into a coherent external strategy, the concept of 'homeland security' is an appropriate device for explaining European policy developments because of the horizontal implications of the agreements in question. In particular, the EU's role has grown substantially in the areas of border and trade security, which have clear importance regarding terrorism, crime, drugs, dealing with weapons of mass destruction and other threats. In addition, interestingly, the EU has now become an intelligence gatherer for the United States (US).

This demonstrates that third states – and particularly the US – are increasingly recognising the EU's value as a partner for securing their own homeland security. On the other side, the EU has generally benefited from this interaction because it has enabled it to take on an increasing role in homeland security. Crucially, as other contributors to this book have observed, counter-terrorism and US influence have been the key elements in creating this external layer of homeland security. Adding to this, the chapter shows that the direction that the EU has taken since 2001 has not necessarily been that of design, but security developments in Europe since then have in fact been the product of the environment created by 9/11 and the ensuing US influence.

In sum, this chapter adds to our understanding of the concept of European homeland security because it shows the EU's evolving external role in matters pertinent to security – something that would have been unlikely to develop in other circumstances. The historical development of the external dimension of European homeland security is now discussed.

The EU's role in European homeland security was virtually non-existent before 2001 because security itself was an area in which the EU had a minimal role. European countries had cooperated previously on counter-terrorism – in the intergovernmental TREVI Group in the 1970s (Bures 2006; Kaunert 2010a). However, TREVI remained intergovernmental until the Treaty of Maastricht in 1992, which brought this network into the EU framework. The EU's role in Justice and Home Affairs (JHA) was then amended and increased in the Treaty of Amsterdam in 1997 and the Treaty of Nice in 2001.

Importantly, the Treaty of Amsterdam established the Area of Freedom, Security, and Justice (AFSJ), which was subsequently expanded on at the European Council meeting at Tampere in 1999. External relations were expected to play an important role in the establishment of the AFSJ. It is worth noting that Section D in the Tampere conclusions emphasised the need to implement the changes made in the 1997 Treaty of Amsterdam. For instance, the conclusions stated that the 'Union's external relations should be used in an integrated and consistent way to build the area of freedom, security and justice' (European Council 1999a). In addition, it was suggested signing agreements with third countries on the basis of Article 38 of the Treaty on European Union (TEU) – or that which allows the EU to make agreements with third states for police and judicial cooperation in criminal matters (European Council 1999a). However, it is worth noting that no agreement of this kind was signed with third states until the post-9/11 period. This demonstrates the importance of 9/11 and transnational terrorism in establishing the EU's external relations in security matters.

9/11 catapulted the EU into an increased role in counter-terrorism specifically, but many measures brought in following 9/11 had horizontal implications. Internally, 9/11 acted as a wake-up call as it was realised that Europe had acted as a base for the planning for the plot – the notorious 'Hamburg Cell' is but one example (BBC News 2005). In this way, European economic integration was seen as having led to increased vulnerability, and the concern over transnational terrorism clearly acted as a catalyst to speed up the implementation of measures discussed at Tampere that may well have never seen the light of day without 9/11 (Zimmermann 2006; Kaunert 2007). The introduction of measures, such as the European Arrest Warrant (EAW), highlights how initiatives were introduced because of the need to combat terrorism, but they could also play a role in dealing with other threats as well. Terrorism itself is a threat that requires the cooperation of a range of areas of governance, including education, health, finance and intelligence (Keohane 2005; Lugna 2006). This internal progress with the AFSJ then enabled other actors to interact with the EU's security architecture (Kaunert 2010a).

The US in particular took advantage of the EU's efforts to improve internal security. Prior to 9/11, the US had frequently been rebuffed in its efforts to get the EU more involved in security matters (Rees 2006). Furthermore, the US had always wanted to shape the EU's internal security architecture to US preferences (p. 37). 9/11 provided the US with the perfect opportunity to boost cooperation. For the first time, the US administration considered that the benefits of interacting with the EU outweighed the risks (Archik 2010). This demonstrates the US desire to become more involved with the EU, and 9/11 provided the opportunity for this.

This chapter will be structured in six sections. The first section embeds this chapter within the appropriate literature, examining the external dimension of EU security and focusing on the roles of transnational terrorism and the US in helping to shape the EU's internal security policies. Second, the chapter examines air security, assessing the Passenger Name Record (PNR) Agreements that the EU has signed with the US, Canada and Australia, as well as the possibility of an EU PNR system. The third section looks at cooperation on trade security, particularly the agreement concerning EU–US cooperation on the Container Security Initiative (CSI). Fourth, the chapter turns to cooperation between the EU and the US in the area of Mutual Legal Assistance (MLA) and Extradition. The fifth section assesses the countering of terrorism financing, emphasising the Society for Worldwide Interbank Financial Telecommunications (SWIFT) Agreement along with the EU's commitment to an EU Terrorist Financing and Tracking Programme (TFTP) system. Finally, the chapter concludes with an examination of the external dimension of European homeland security. The agreements outlined here were chosen specifically because they each focus on a different area of cooperation, demonstrating the comprehensiveness of the EU's external relations. In addition, this chapter shows how these areas of cooperation have many horizontal implications, making external cooperation an additional layer of European homeland security. This chapter therefore argues that the EU's external role is an interesting and significant development for the creation of European homeland security.

The development of the external dimension of European homeland security

Students of European security are used to talking about the EU as a 'norm-maker'. This has been consistently demonstrated by the externalisation of EU security norms to its neighbours (Argomaniz 2009; Lavenex and Wichmann 2009; Pawlak 2009b; Wolff 2009). The external dimension of a policy field consists of '[t]he external projection of internal policies' (Lavenex and Wichmann 2009: 84).

On the other hand, internal security policies in the EU have seen significant US influence. Therefore, European homeland security has been an area that has seen the EU become a 'norm-taker' and recipient of US security norms, taking into account the externalisation of US security policies, with the US wishing to push its boundaries back to the furthest possible extent (Argomaniz 2009). The EU's position as a norm-recipient has been a feature of the transatlantic relationship since 2001. Furthermore, the EU has compromised on some fundamental values – such as data protection – in agreements relevant to counter-terrorism (Argomaniz 2009; Pawlak 2009c). Taking into account Europe's generally strong commitment to data protection (compared to the US more laissez-faire approach (Hailbronner *et al.* 2008)), it is clear that the EU has had to make compromises in its relationship with the US. In addition, transnational threats, such as terrorism, have led to the EU increasing its role in homeland security – sometimes at the expense of the Member States. Thus, the roles of the US and transnational terrorism have been instrumental in Member States pooling sovereignty on the basis of security interdependence.

Specifically, this US pressure and EU norm absorption manifested itself most vividly during the negotiations of the PNR, CSI and SWIFT Agreements. In short, the EU has, at times, had to adopt security policies that did not always reflect the European perception of the threat of terrorism or strategy of response (Argomaniz 2009: 120). According to Argomaniz (p. 120), this can be explained by '[s]tructural imbalances based on the nature of these two actors'. However, it must also be remembered that some EU Member States are more willing supporters of security over civil liberties and have been happy to outsource their security to the US (Aldrich 2009; Argomaniz 2009). In this sense, the UK and Spain have frequently prioritised security cooperation at the EU level due to histories of sectarian violence (Rees 2008). By contrast, Germany and Austria (as well as Greece and Hungary in the SWIFT Agreement) have sometimes pressed for greater controls on data protection (Monar 2010b). Furthermore, the US has often set the worldwide norms for border management because both the PNR and CSI Agreements extend far beyond Europe (Hobbing 2008; US Bureau of Customs and Border Protection 2008). In addition, more countries will in the future make use of PNR data (European Parliament 2010a). Although not all agreements with the US have led to norm absorption by the EU, it is quite clear that the EU has been heavily influenced by the US – as its future internal security policies develop to mirror those of the US, as shown by the discussions about the EU PNR and the EU Terrorist Financing and Trading Programme (TFTP) systems. However, the direction that these measures will take is yet to be seen.

This US influence would, however, have been in vain had the Member States not decided to move towards the construction of internal competences in the form of the Area of Freedom, Security and Justice (AFSJ). 9/11 provided the catalyst for the EU to gain more power in the creation of homeland security because of the realisation that Europe was a place of increasing interdependence. To highlight the impact that transnational terrorism had on the EU, Zimmermann (2006: 123) argued that 'on 21 September 2001, the EU prioritised the fight against terrorism, and accelerated the development and implementation of measures deliberated on prior to the events of 9/11'. These internal competences were created when measures discussed at Tampere were quickly implemented, and most had a use beyond the realm of counter-terrorism. These were the first concrete steps towards the construction of the AFSJ. Prior to interactions with third countries, it was necessary for internal competences to be constructed. Kaunert (2010a: 48) has pointed out that the construction of internal competences enabled the EU to become an international actor in the area of counter-terrorism. The construction of an AFSJ in the EU created an institutionalised structure with which external actors, such as the US, could interact (p. 41). Consequently, because of transnational terrorism, US influence and the AFSJ, the EU became a homeland security actor.

The post-2001 period has seen increased recognition of the EU by the US. In fact, the post-2001 period has seen the US sign international agreements with the EU for the first time (Kaunert 2010a). The fact that these agreements were made with some US officials having doubts over the effect that this may have on US bilateral relations with Member States demonstrates that the benefits of cooperating with the EU were considered to outweigh the potential risks (Archik 2010). This recognition, however, has not come without costs; namely, the EU absorbing US norms that would not necessarily have otherwise been adopted. Overall, however, the US has demonstrated, among other things, that it would rather negotiate with one partner rather than 27 and was willing to interact with the EU in security matters (Kaunert 2010a).

In sum, the EU has frequently been a recipient of US security norms in the post-2001 period. This came about as the result of the creation of the AFSJ in Europe, enabling the US to interact with a supranational structure in Europe. The external dimension of the AFSJ, however, would probably not have been possible without 9/11. These terrorist attacks led Member States to realise their vulnerability and to acknowledge that greater cooperation was necessary. As a result, the US was able to interact with the EU and influence the direction of European security norms – as well as global border management norms. In the following years, it was clear that US interaction also led to other countries requesting cooperation with the EU. If nothing else, the US had consolidated the EU's position, being primarily responsible for certain areas of security. This shows the true importance of recognition by the sole superpower. To some extent, the EU therefore became a homeland security actor because of its external relations. Furthermore, although there was some calculation with the introduction of measures discussed at Tampere, a comprehensive strategy for external cooperation on security issues has not been forthcoming. As a result, the EU generally found itself reacting to US activity.

Air security and PNR with third states

In short, PNR data are those that denote 'the travel record for a person, as used by an airline and travel agency databases' (UK House of Lords 2008c: 188). PNR data are thus basic types of information on passengers of airliners (UK House of Lords 2008c). Most of these data have been collected for many years by airlines and have also been used by law enforcement officials (most frequently under the heading 'Advanced Passenger Information' (API)). The difference between API and PNR is that API data contains information about the 'machine-readable zone of the passport, including name, date of birth, passport number and nationality' (Brouwer 2009: 2). By contrast, 'PNR data includes the data that are registered by the airline companies or travel agencies when a traveller makes a reservation, including the individual's name, seat number, travelling route, booking agent, etc.' (ibid.). In sum, the main difference is that PNR data are personal data sent by each individual before a flight and API data are more objective information (ibid.). When crossed with other data, PNR data are supposed to enable the tracking of passengers about whom a government has pre-existing suspicions (UK House of Lords 2008c). Therefore, these data are used for fighting transnational crime and preventing terrorism, but questions have been posed concerning potential abuse of the data, resulting in calls for purpose limiting the data to counter-terrorism and transnational crime (European Parliament 2010a).

Currently, the EU has a permanent PNR Agreement (from 2007) in force with the US, which was preceded by another permanent agreement (2004) and an interim agreement (2006). The reasons for this are explored in the subsequent section. In addition, the EU has concluded PNR Agreements with Canada and Australia. It must be pointed out that these agreements provide data to the third country in question, not to the EU. Thus, the EU can only derive benefits from PNR data if it sets up an equivalent PNR system (Argomaniz 2009). This seems a possibility in the future given the recent discussions concerning an EU PNR. Furthermore, the reason for the EU requiring PNR data appears to be all the more acute when taking into account that the European Parliment considers that other countries are likely to expect PNR data in the future (European Parliament 2010a). First, this is clear evidence of the US influence on worldwide border management – and the EU in particular. Second, the EU's external relations are important because under the new rules laid down in the Treaty of Lisbon, the European Parliament will be required to consent to all PNR agreements with third countries, making the European Parliament a more important external actor itself.

The EU–US PNR Agreement

In the aftermath of 9/11, the US looked for ways to improve its border security. The Customs and Border Protection Bureau (CBP), under the Transportation Security Administration (TSA), was required to find ways to improve US border security – before the CBP was made part of the newly created Department of Homeland Security (DHS) in 2002. On 19 November 2001, the Aviation and Transportation Security Act was passed. This was a unilateral decision taken by the US without consulting its international partners. Basically, this act required airlines flying into the US from other countries to hand the requested PNR data over to US authorities. If air carriers failed to do so, they could potentially face loss of flying rights and/or hefty fines of $5,000–$6,000 per passenger (Guild and Brouwer 2006; Argomaniz 2009; Brouwer 2009; Occhipinti 2010).

However, in Europe, this requirement for PNR data contravened Article 25 of the EU's Data Protection Directive (DPD) (95/46/EC), which prevented data transfer to countries without an 'adequate' level of data protection, such as the US (Fuster *et al.* 2008; Argomaniz 2009). In short, this put airlines in an invidious situation because they had the choice of either not handing over the data to US authorities and incurring fines, or handing over the data and violating EU laws, resulting in fines from the EU. If no solution was found, the access of European airlines to the lucrative US market would be denied. This forced the European Commission to come to an agreement with the US, and in February 2003 a temporary settlement was agreed (Argomaniz 2009). Then, in May 2004, despite serious opposition from European Data Protection authorities, the European Parliament Civil Liberties, Justice and Home Affairs (LIBE) Committee and privacy rights activists, the Commission concluded a permanent agreement with the DHS (p. 123). Problems were caused by the fact that US authorities requested 34 different types of data from the EU, among a number of other complaints (Spence 2007: 21).

The first PNR Agreement was eventually annulled by the European Court of Justice in 2006 (Joined Cases C-317/04 and C-318/04). The European Parliament initially challenged the agreement on the grounds of privacy of the individual; however, the European Court of Justice ruled that the agreement was in fact based on an incorrect legal basis in the first pillar (EU transport policy) because the purpose of the agreement was the 'enhancement of security and the fight against terrorism' (Brouwer 2009: 13). In consequence, an interim settlement was agreed with the US in 2006. In 2007, a third PNR Agreement (i.e. the second permanent agreement) was made on the basis of the second and third pillars, with the Presidency taking the lead. Agreeing on the basis of the second and third pillars sidelined the role that the EU institutions could play (Pawlak 2009b). This highlights the clash of interests at the EU level where some Member States in the European Council have frequently behaved with a preference for security and a willingness to 'outsource' their security to the US as they lack the necessary resources and are restricted by their legal systems (Argomaniz 2009: 129). In contrast, the European Parliament has pressed for stronger data protection constraints in all dealings regarding PNR and, later on, SWIFT (European Parliament 2007a, 2007b, 2009, 2010a, 2010b). To great criticism, the 2007 agreement apparently reduced the categories of data passed over to the US to 19, but it quickly became apparent that this had simply been achieved by merging data categories (Brouwer 2009: 13). However, the issues surrounding EU–US PNR are far from over, given that the European Parliament is due to vote on a new agreement in 2011.

In sum, the EU–US PNR saga demonstrates the EU's now important role in agreements relevant to security and demonstrates quite clearly the US influence over the EU, leading to the assumption that the EU was simply left to respond to US activity. An interesting point for the future is also how EU institutions will adapt to the changes made in the Treaty of Lisbon, having had their external roles enhanced significantly.

The EU–Canada API and PNR Agreement

The EU–Canada API and PNR Agreement was concluded in 2005. Compared to the EU–US Agreement, very little has been written about it. After 9/11, Canada quickly adopted a Customs Act requiring API data to be collected from 2002 and PNR from 2003 (Hobbing 2008: 8). This then obliged external air carriers to hand over the required data to the Canadian Border Services Authority (CBSA). Like the US, Canadian authorities would fine airlines that did not hand over the requested data (European Commission 2005c). As a result of the unpleasant experiences with the US, the EU quickly entered into negotiations with the Canadian authorities. The EU received a temporary derogation from the requirements requested by the Canadian authorities in order to draw up a long-term agreement (ibid.). An EU–Canada agreement on API and PNR matters was then concluded in October 2005. The EU–Canada Agreement expired in September 2009, but Canada wanted to continue accessing the data, so Member States were 'invited' by the Commission to continue submitting it to Canadian authorities until a permanent agreement could be prepared in 2010–2011 (European Union 2010a).

The EU–Canada PNR Agreement is interesting because it was agreed on the basis of the first pillar, in contrast to the PNR Agreement with the US (European Community 2006). This agreement was also hailed by Hobbing (2008: 2) as a model instrument due to its 'measured and legally balanced approach'. Furthermore, the European Parliament suggested that the Canadian and Australian PNR Agreements 'ensure higher standards of protection of personal data' than the US agreement, making it more tolerable to the European Parliament (European Parliament 2007a).

A memorandum by the Department for Transport Aviation Directorate (2007) in the UK suggests that '[t]he existing EU–Canada PNR agreement could be used as a model text with a change of legal base'. Thus, the Canadian PNR Agreement shows another element of EU external relations in that agreements were made that respect data protection. Overall, however, PNR Agreements in any form demonstrate a clear US influence on both the EU and Canada. In addition, Hobbing (2008: 2) raises concerns over the increasing tendency to abdicate civil liberties for security and stresses that the EU increasingly appears to follow security measures taken from the US toolbox. This demonstrates the US role as a global trend-setter in border management by impacting upon both Canadian and EU legislation.

The EU–Australia PNR Agreement

Little has been written about the EU–Australia PNR agreement. The PNR Agreement with Australia was concluded in June 2008. The Australian Customs Service (ACS) is the recipient of the data. As with the other PNR agreements, the rationale for the EU–Australia PNR Agreement appears to be counter-terrorism and fighting organised crime (Australian Minister for Foreign Affairs 2010). According to Australian sources, this was the first sign of broader cooperation between Australia and the EU, and this agreement was made necessary because Qantas, the Australian national airline, 'moved to a PNR information management system operating in Germany' (ibid.). In this case, nineteen categories of data were requested by the Australian authorities, but interestingly, they have stated that they 'do not want or need sensitive data', such as race and religion (Australian Minister for Foreign Affairs 2010; European Parliament 2008). Like the other two agreements, the Australian PNR Agreement will be voted on by the European Parliament in 2011. This is demonstrative of the EU's expanding external relations with third states. The EU–Australia PNR Agreement is further evidence that US influence has opened the door for other states to make PNR agreements with the EU. In addition, the European Parliament has consistently requested a general external strategy for PNR agreements to bring some conformity and coherence to external agreements on PNR (European Parliament 2010a, 2010b).

An EU PNR system?

As of 2010, the EU does not have a PNR system running, but there are plans to establish one. Currently, under Directive 2004/82/EC, EU Member States are obliged to hand API data over to each other (European Union 2004). Interestingly, this document gives regard to the initiative of Spain (ibid.), demonstrating initiatives by Member States in the aftermath of the Madrid bombings of 11 March 2004.

At present, the UK is the only EU Member State that has a fully-functioning PNR system, but France and Denmark have legislation in place to create one (UK House of Lords 2008c). The proposed EU PNR system is intended to be a specifically European measure, which was suggested as a result of a Commission anti-terrorism package several months after the third PNR Agreement was made with the US – despite some strong European concerns about the US system (Pawlak 2009c: 5). More specifically, the Commission put forward a proposal for EU PNR on 17 November 2007 (European Parliament 2010b). It was then first discussed in 2009 in a Multidisciplinary Group on organised crime (Pawlak 2009c: 5). Since then, EU PNR has reappeared in documents several times; among them the Stockholm Programme (European Council 2010a) and the new Internal Security Strategy (Council of the European Union 2010e). Nevertheless, EU PNR is not yet close to being implemented and its future remains uncertain.

An EU PNR system would demonstrate two points: the increasing role of the EU in homeland security, and the influence of the US over the EU. The former point is demonstrated by the fact that EU PNR would be a standard PNR system for all European countries[1] – an area of security in which the EU would simply not have become so involved without the influence of transnational terrorism and 9/11. Furthermore, an EU PNR would be intended to combat terrorism and crime in particular. The US influence is evident from the fact that EU PNR retains many aspects of what made the EU–US PNR Agreement so controversial (see Pawlak 2009c: 5–6). Also, Pawlak (pp. 5–6) has gone as far as suggesting that the Commission does not mention the US PNR system or those being established in other countries in an attempt to avoid 'any association with the US PNR initiative in order to reduce internal opposition in the EU. The linkage between the EU and the US PNR systems would be more difficult to make if there were not a surprising similarity between the Commission's proposal and the provisions of the EU–US PNR Agreements'. In short, this section has highlighted the EU's growing role in European homeland security by examining both the proposals for an EU PNR and the EU's external relations with regard to PNR. It has also emphasised the key role played by the US in this policy area.

Trade security and the CSI

The CSI was another initiative that originated in the US. Once more, the decision was taken unilaterally by Washington. In the aftermath of 9/11, the CBP looked for ways to improve US trade security. The greatest concern emanated from the fact that 12 million containers were shipped into the US every year and, of these, only 2 per cent were thoroughly inspected (Occhipinti 2010: 125). The potential for shipping a bomb or any other threatening device into the US was obvious. Consequently, CSI came into existence in 2002. The target of CSI was not simply European ports, but all of the US main trading partners. Only countries that made the requested security arrangements would be able to ship cargo to the US. In short, this had the potential to cut off European countries from the lucrative US market (Rees 2008).

CSI requested that shipping to the US receive its own terminal. US officials would scan US-bound containers side by side with the other country's officials, and high-risk cargo would be subjected to x-ray and radiation scanners (US Bureau of Customs and Border Protection 2008). In 2003, a further stipulation was added to CSI: the so-called '24-hour rule', which requested shippers to report the contents of a US-bound container to US authorities at least 24 hours before being loaded onto a US ship (Spence 2007; Occhipinti 2010). In response to this, European countries quickly made bilateral agreements with the US. However, the Commission looked upon US action as a violation of the customs cooperation accord of 1997 and viewed Member State actions of negotiating bilateral agreements as potentially jeopardising the Community customs union (Occhipinti 2010: 125). Thus, the Commission initiated proceedings against the Member States before the European Court of Justice and, at the same time, requested a mandate for an EU–US agreement (Cameron 2007; Spence 2007). The US was open to an EU–US agreement, but the US pointed out that this should not delay the implementation of security measures. At first, negotiations moved slowly, notably because of the Commission's particular concern over the 24-hour rule and attempts at pushing for reciprocal arrangements (Spence 2007; Occhipinti 2010). However, given that most European countries had already implemented the 24-hour rule, the Commission relaxed its stance (Occhipinti 2010). Occhipinti (2010: 126) shows that 'once Commission competence over European ports was established, the EU-US negotiations proceeded smoothly'. This action helped to consolidate the Commission's lead in this area, adding trade security to its portfolio.

An agreement was then signed in 2004. The text of the agreement states that it aimed to 'deter, prevent, and interdict any terrorist attempts to disrupt global trade by concealing terrorist weapons in global sea container trade or other shipments, or by using such shipments as weapons' (European Community 2004). Once more, this shows the priority attached to the combating of terrorism. The CBP website claims that, as of 2008, 58 foreign ports were working under CSI and 35 customs administrations had committed to joining it (US Bureau of Customs and Border Protection 2008). CSI now covers 86 per cent of all maritime containerised cargo destined to the US (US Bureau of Customs and Border Protection 2008). Within Europe, there are now twenty-three CSI ports in ten EU Member States (Occhipinti 2010: 126). This shows the global extent of the CSI.

The CSI provides further evidence of US influence on the EU and demonstrates the EU's role in trade security. Thus, again, the CSI shows the prominence of the EU's role in another aspect of European homeland security, which potentially goes beyond combating terrorism given that the CSI is also relevant in dealing with crime, weapons of mass destruction (WMD) and any other dangerous items that could potentially be brought into Europe or the US by cargo container.

Judicial cooperation and the Mutual Legal Assistance (MLA) and Extradition Treaties

The MLA and Extradition Treaties were initiated by the EU in the wake of the terrorist attacks on 9/11 in the US. On 20 September 2001, the EU Justice and Home Affairs (JHA) Council decided that a series of measures needed to be taken in order to enhance cooperation with the US in criminal matters (UK House of Lords 2003). In an exchange of letters between the then Head of the European Council, Guy Verhofstadt, and President Bush, it was suggested that an agreement be made on penal cooperation with regard to terrorism. The US expressed an interest in such an agreement (ibid.). Such an idea was supported again by the Member States and the President of the Commission at the European Council meeting in Ghent on 19 October 2001 when it was decided that mutual legal assistance and extradition should be an area of cooperation between the EU and US (ibid.). This demonstrates just how much influence terrorism had on the post-2001 evolution of the EU in the area of JHA.

The conclusions from the informal meeting at Santiago de Compostela on 28 February 2002 then led to the adoption of a negotiation mandate on 26 April 2002 (ibid.). On the basis of Articles 24 and 38 TEU – which stipulate that the conclusion of international agreements in third pillar matters is to be allowed by the Council on a recommendation by the Presidency – an agreement was finalised in the spring of 2003. The mandate was then expanded beyond terrorism, which included temporary surrender for trials, exchanging data, setting up joint investigation teams, giving evidence (via video conference) and establishing single contact points (ibid.). During the phase of parliamentary scrutiny, more changes were made where provisions were withdrawn, which related to the extradition of own nationals and the narrowing of the political offence (ibid.).

Even so, some Member States were slow to implement the agreements, and Rees (2008: 101) has noted the 'inordinate' amount of time it took some Member States to pass the MLA agreement in their own parliaments. As a result, the agreement only came into force on 1 February 2010. Undoubtedly, agreements of this level of sensitivity – which include discussions about the death penalty – take a long time to negotiate (Council of the European Union 2009c). In short, the US had to commit to not enforcing the death penalty on anyone extradited from Europe to the US.

It should be noted that all pre-existing bilateral agreements between the US and EU Member States remain in place, and the EU–US agreements simply work as a common base where agreements did not exist in the past. In addition to this, the EU–US Extradition Agreement made possible extradition between the US and Bulgaria, Latvia, Malta and Romania for the first time (Occhipinti 2010: 115). The EU-US MLA Agreement also represents the first MLA agreement between the US and Bulgaria, Finland, Malta, Portugal, Slovakia and Slovenia (ibid.). Furthermore, it establishes a legal basis for international joint investigation teams, eases restrictions on banking secrecy, and the sharing of evidence for prosecution (ibid., p. 124). Interestingly, the US also sought an assurance that it would be given equal consideration under the European Arrest Warrant (ibid.). Thus, the EU-US MLA and Extradition Agreements modernised outdated bilateral agreements and made possible mutual legal assistance and extradition between the US and some Member States for the first time. In addition, the MLA Agreement established a legal basis for other forms of cooperation, which may develop further in the future. The MLA and Extradition Agreements are also cases where the EU initiated agreements with the US. They are also examples of agreements that may be used to deal with threats beyond those posed by terrorism.

Tracking terrorist financing and the SWIFT Agreement

SWIFT is a Belgian, European-based company responsible for worldwide financial messaging and facilitating worldwide bank transfers (Fuster *et al.* 2008). In short, SWIFT sends standardised financial messages of 9,000 banking organisations, securities institutions and corporate customers in 209 countries (SWIFT 2010). Most importantly, SWIFT is responsible for roughly 80 per cent of the electronic transfer market. Crucially, these messages frequently include personal data of the payer and payee (Fuster *et al.* 2008: 192). As a result, the US saw a benefit in the use of SWIFT data. The US TFTP was instigated by the US Treasury (UST) after 11 September 2001 and SWIFT was obliged to cooperate with the TFTP because a mirror of its data was kept in Virginia – the main server being based in the Netherlands.

The TFTP had been kept fairly secret until it was leaked in the *New York Times* on 23 June 2006 that SWIFT had provided the US with access to bank data. It appears that this came as a surprise 'almost for everybody' (ibid., p. 194). Fuster *et al.* (ibid.) point out that '[f]rom a European perspective, the main problem with data processing as foreseen by counterterrorist US law is in general terms not the absence of checks and balances to ensure data protection, but the exclusion of non-US citizens from access to such protection in the cases where it is granted'. In 2009, SWIFT relocated its mirror from the US to Switzerland, which made it necessary for the US to request data from Europe. This required the signing of an EU–US agreement.

Member States recognised the benefits of TFTP. For example, the US passed on over 1,500 leads to European governments, some of which have led to arrests and the prevention of terrorist attacks (Archik 2010: 5). More tangibly, TFTP data prevented terrorist attacks on transatlantic flights in 2008 and led to three arrests, among other examples (Occhipinti 2010: 137). This demonstrates how TFTP has been of benefit to both sides of the Atlantic.

A SWIFT Interim Agreement (for nine months) was concluded by the Council on 30 November 2009 – one day before the Lisbon Treaty granted the European Parliament consent over most international agreements, including that concerning SWIFT. However, this interim agreement was rejected by the European Parliament in February 2010. In particular, the European Parliament – as in the case of PNR – raised substantial concerns about the transfer of bulk data to the US, criticised the actions of the Council and resisted US pressure (Monar 2010b: 145). The Commission then renegotiated the agreement. A second SWIFT Agreement was accepted by the European Parliament in July 2010. The new agreement was somewhat different from the original agreement in several ways. First of all, the new agreement includes a role for Europol as a clearing house, which gives the 'green light' to the transfers of data. For the purposes of this chapter and the development of European homeland security, one of the most interesting articles was the inclusion of Article 11, a vague mention of an EU TFTP, as well as a commitment by the US to help set up this equivalent system (European Union 2010b). Furthermore – and perhaps most interestingly of all – the SWIFT Agreement gets the EU involved in intelligence-gathering for the first time. In this way, it could be a key moment in the evolution of the EU.

An EU TFTP?

EU TFTP appears to have arisen on the EU policy agenda on 17 September 2009 with the European Parliament's Resolution on SWIFT suggesting that the Commission might look into the possibility of proposing a European system (European Parliament 2009). As mentioned above, this again appeared in the second EU–US SWIFT Agreement. There are still great uncertainties surrounding the creation of this system, but the primary purpose of the EU TFTP appears to be to prevent bulk data being sent to third countries and allow for the processing and analysis of European data on European soil. This would mean that only processed information and leads would be sent to third countries. The idea of an EU TFTP raises many questions about how the Member States would manage it, where the data would be stored and a plethora of other problems (EurActiv 2010). A major problem that arises in that respect would be whether to stop sending European data to the US, which is not likely because, for the US, it would mean handing over part of its own role in homeland security – and a vital part actually – to another actor. However, the European Commission is due to present its findings on the possibilities of an EU TFTP sometime in 2011.

Here, several scenarios are possible. The EU could establish its own TFTP (clearly influenced by the US) and stop the transfer of data to the US. Or the EU and the US could come to some kind of agreement over such a system once it is in place. Another possibility is that the EU does not establish such a system, which is probably the most likely outcome at this stage. If the EU does establish such a system (with US help, as set out in the SWIFT Agreement), it raises an interesting point on US influence over the EU. US behaviour towards the EU would have actually helped create a more important actor, which would be able to oppose greater US influence in the long run. In short, US influence in the short-term would actually have been detrimental to long-term US goals. For now, however, this remains mere speculation. On the other hand, this raises the possibility of a more independent and ambitious EU.

Also, an intriguing development is that the more pro-integration EU institutions (European Parliament and Commission) may push initiatives into agreements with third countries. This could prove to be very interesting in the future. EU TFTP may bring the EU Member States to a crossroads: either they continue to be satisfied about the outsourcing of their security to the US (Argomaniz 2009) or they enable the EU to establish itself as a more important component of European homeland security. The consequences of this, however, are yet to be seen.

Conclusion

In conclusion, 'European homeland security' is a useful concept for explaining the role that the EU now fulfils. Furthermore, the EU has clearly become more involved in certain aspects of European homeland security. Together, the EU's agreements with third countries bring the EU into air security, trade security, mutual legal assistance and extradition, and countering terrorism financing. These agreements, as demonstrated, frequently have horizontal implications and this helps fill the gap where previous literature has analytically restricted the discussion along thematic lines. As a result, previous literature has not appreciated the full utility of these agreements.

The main reasons for the proliferation of external relations regarding issues concerned with homeland security are: the creation of the AFSJ, the effects of international terrorism, and the ensuing (and somewhat questionable) US influence. Crucially, terrorism acted as the catalyst for the creation of each of the above agreements. Also, PNR agreements will soon be expected and requested by other states, so this ensures an expanding role for the EU institutions in external relations in the future. For these reasons, the European Parliament requested from the European Commission an external strategy for PNR, which shows an attempt to increase coherence in the EU's external relations.

US influence has been obvious, but must also be understood in a context where some EU Member States have been content to outsource their security to the US. Furthermore, the discussions about EU PNR and EU TFTP systems raise serious questions about US influence on the EU. However, in another way, this influence was unavoidable given the US government's actions in the aftermath of 9/11 and their view that Europe posed a threat to the US. Frequently, the EU has simply reacted to US- originating homeland security policies, demonstrating a lack of design in the EU's homeland security role and a lack of genuinely coherent external strategy. Understandably, these measures have raised questions about the EU's commitment to civil liberties and have demonstrated a preference for security. Thus, in some ways US influence proved beneficial to the EU, but a price has been paid for this recognition and interaction.

Even so, it will be interesting to follow the development of the EU PNR and EU TFTP systems in order to establish the extent of US influence – if they develop at all. EU TFTP is without doubt the most ambitious project on the basis of it requiring cooperation on sensitive issues – including intelligence cooperation. Thus, there are understandable doubts about whether EU TFTP and EU PNR will come into existence. However, what this does demonstrate is how the EU is becoming more involved in European security. Also, the EU–US SWIFT Agreement sees the EU involved in intelligence for the first time. Thus, the agreements since 9/11 have consequences beyond the realm of counter-terrorism and one may therefore highlight the EU's expanded role in homeland security. This chapter has demonstrated how the EU's external relations and security-related agreements since 2001 have added an external layer to European homeland security due to transnational terrorism, the following internal EU developments, as well as the ensuing US influence.

Note

1 EU PNR may or may not include intra-European flights, but it will include flights from outside the EU into Europe.

7 The development of European Union emergency and crisis management structures

Cécile Wendling

From the terrorist attacks on 11 September 2001 to the London bombings in 2005, from the 2005 Pakistan earthquake to the Lebanon crisis of 2006, from the Haiti earthquake to the Hungarian toxic red mud crisis the last decade has witnessed a large number of major emergencies and crises leading to reviews of performance of the actors in charge. At the same time, demands on the European Union (EU) emergency and crisis management response increased, as disasters grew both in size and frequency, a trend which is supposed to continue notably because of climate change (European Commission 2010d). The necessity to adapt the administrative and political system to the new international security challenges became an issue at EU level at the end of the 1990s, as both natural risks and man-made threats often trespass boundaries. Therefore, to enhance emergency and crisis management capacity and to deal with the imminent threat of major transnational catastrophes (natural or man-made), the EU has developed a community mechanism in the field of civil protection, which is managed by the European Commission under the label of 'Community Civil Protection Mechanism' (CCPM). This mechanism was established by a European Council decision in 2001 and aims to deal with natural, industrial and man-made catastrophes both inside and outside the EU borders (European Union 2001). Moreover, in 2005, the EU adopted the so-called 'Emergency and Crisis Coordination Arrangements' (CCA) dealt with by the Joint Situation Centre (SitCen) within the EU Council, which are there to be activated in case EU interests are at stake both inside and outside the EU borders (European Council 2005). Both EU tools were adopted to enhance cooperation among Member States in the event of crises and emergencies.[1] With consistency and effectiveness being two of the major issues in crisis management, what were the reasons behind the creation of these two structures? Looking at the CCPM and then at the CCA from their creation until 2009, this chapter will identify the elements of constraint, opportunity and repositioning, which led to the existence of the CCPM and the CCA by the EU. Drawing upon sociological neo-institutionalist literature, this chapter investigates the development of EU emergency management tools and attempts to explain divergences between original strategic planning and final policy design.

Emergency management is an important part of homeland security, which is often neglected by researchers in Europe although it is included by most US researchers in their work (Comfort 2002). This difference is linked mostly to the historical context as the US Department for Homeland Security has, since its creation, included the Federal Emergency Management Agency in its structure. At the EU level, homeland security is not a concept in use in most of the literature. European homeland security is not linked empirically to one particular organisational structure, but is split between numerous actors. The Monitoring and Information Centre (MIC) and the SitCen, which are studied in this chapter, are two of the European security actors which are the focus of this book. An important point to keep in mind when analysing European security policies is the step-by-step implementation of a comprehensive approach at the European level. It means that all actors in charge are in a process of better integrating their action to enhance effectiveness and efficiency and secure the EU (Wendling 2010). With the emergence of this new concept at the EU level, it makes sense to look both empirically and theoretically at the protection of the European homeland as a whole instead of focusing only on one particular instrument or one particular sector. In particular in the field of EU crisis management, the concept of 'comprehensive approach' is gaining momentum with several official texts pushing towards greater harmonisation of EU security actors in charge (see Council of the European Union 2010c). This process is cumbersome, however, as this chapter shows by highlighting the differences between the MIC and the SitCen and the way they have developed historically.

First, this chapter presents the sociological neo-institutionalist theories that can explain the gap between the originally planned EU emergency and crisis management model and its implementation. Second, the chapter investigates this gap by analysing the case of the CCPM. Third, the chapter explores this gap by examining the case of the CCA. Finally, the chapter concludes on the two cases and identifies the drivers of EU emergency management in practice.

A sociological neo-institutionalist approach

Sociological neo-institutionalist theories focus on how bureaucracies navigate between formal organisational models as planned and the constraints and opportunities that they face in practice. As a matter of fact, the neo-institutionalist literature focusing on organisations and recent studies on the politics of security policies offer different reasons for the emergence of such a gap (Kurowska and Pawlak 2009b).

First, the literature explains that when conforming to the institutional rules adopted conflicts with the requirements of day-to-day practices, decoupling can occur, leading to a repositioning of the organisation. Therefore, new EU tools of emergency management could emerge diverging from the initial strategic planning. 'Decoupling' occurs if the prescriptions of institutional contexts contradict the requirements of the technical field contexts, as argued by Greenwood *et al.* (2008), who draw upon the early work of Brunsson (1985). This argument of technicality could apply in this study, as civil protection is a field where the technical aspects of intervention in a crisis are paramount. Civil protection involves fire protection technical knowledge, but also chemical, biological, radiological and nuclear (CBRN) expertise and so on. Due to the technicality of the operation, decoupling could occur, leading to a situation where the emergency management in practice could develop differently from what was originally planned. A second hypothesis on the decoupling effect due to the technicality at the EU level is the following: at EU level, the decision-making process itself can be very technical. The administrative procedures are cumbersome. Indeed, different actors from the European Commission and Council can intervene at different moments, which can change a decision taken during a crisis and, hence, the crisis management itself. To a great extent, organisations are exposed to inconsistent demands from their environment (Brunsson 2002). Facing inconsistent demands is difficult for an organisation because organisations are supposed to follow consistent rules. Therefore, 'organisational hypocrisy' occurs. This argument is of interest in the EU context where 27 Member States must agree on the use of the new emergency management tools. According to Brunsson, to win legitimacy and to survive, organisations adapt their 'talk' and 'decisions'. Organisations will 'talk in a way that satisfies one demand, decide in a way that satisfies another' (Brunsson 2002: 27). Therefore, a gap will occur between the organisational model and the way the organisation operates in practice, decides in practice and talks in practice. Hence, double-talk and inconsistencies in the practice of an organisation can be explained by the external pressures of the inconsistent environment. This could explain why new EU tools for emergency management did not emerge as formally planned, but rather in an accidental way. The external pressure coming from Member States could explain the emergence of the CCPM and the CCA at the EU level.

Second, the literature says that a gap can occur between formal planning and practice due to the development of 'margins of initiative' by the actors in charge (Crozier and Friedberg 1977). Indeed, when European Council decisions are put into practice, some grey areas can emerge during the implementation phase, in which the margins of initiative of EU actors can either be broadened or restricted with regard to the initial official legal model. Grey areas are defined in this chapter as places where the organisational model can be interpreted in one way or another by institutional actors. These grey areas can be the source of friction, dilemma or doubt (Selznic 1948). Due to the possibility of existence of these grey areas, a gap between the formal administrative model adopted and the concrete implementation in the organisation to which it refers can emerge, particularly in the case of the administration (Bezes 2005). As no organisational model can exhaustively plan and totally describe the whole range of empirical situations, organisation in practice will differ. Crozier and Friedberg show how individual actors can 'play' with these gaps to develop 'margins of initiative' (Crozier and Friedberg 1977). In this case, the gap between the formal organisational model and the implementation in practice also depends on the capacity of individuals to play with the rules, to develop their own margins of action. Thus, not only external pressures, but also the capacity of the actors in charge to play with the rules must be taken into account to explain the gap between the model as adopted and the model as implemented. In other words, EU officials can become institutional entrepreneurs (DiMaggio 1988: 14). It means that, in the phase of emergence of a new organisational structure, they can seize the opportunity to play with their margins of initiative to influence the way the new structure will be used.

Finally, the literature identifies the role played by legitimacy in understanding the gap between the strategically planned model and the implemented one. Beyond the questions of external pressures and the individual capacity to play with the rules, it is all about legitimacy (Meyer and Rowan 1977). Actors create and adopt new tools to gain 'external legitimacy'. On the contrary, internally, the organisations maintain different habits when it comes to implementation. As a result, the organisational model is decoupled from the organisational architecture and structure in practice.

This chapter is not stressing, like Meyer and Rowan, that the original organisational planned model is purely artificial. This chapter shows indeed that this early model has an impact on the implementation. However, the chapter demonstrates that there still is a gap between the organisational model as adopted and that which is implemented. This is why it is necessary to study how individual actors deal with external pressures when it comes to implementation on an administrative day-to-day basis, and how they develop their margins of initiative. In other words, neo-institutionalist theories are suited to explain what has happened at the EU level in the field of emergency and crisis management. But to do so, they need to incorporate some agency aspect. Therefore, this study will investigate the 'tug-of-war' between Member States and EU officials when it comes to the implementation of EU tools of emergency management.

This chapter tests four hypotheses. First, the chapter examines whether, due to the technical constraints of civil protection, a gap occurs between the EU emergency and crisis management model as planned and that as implemented. Second, the chapter investigates whether, due to the EU bureaucratic technical constraints of decision-making, a gap occurs between the EU emergency and crisis management model as planned and that which is implemented. Third, the chapter evaluates whether, due to the capacity of actors to play with their margins of initiative, a gap occurs between the model as planned and that as implemented. Finally, the chapter studies whether, due to the necessity of maintaining external legitimacy as emphasised by sociological neo-institutionnalists, a gap occurs between the model as planned and that as implemented.

The emergence of the community mechanism: a successful repositioning?

A European Council decision of 2001 created the CCPM, an advanced emergency management mechanism relying on the MIC in Brussels at the European Commission.[2] The MIC is the centre where emergencies are managed at the EU level: it gathers the requests of affected countries and coordinates the offers of the states participating in the CCPM in order to have them match the request. Since 2002, the mechanism has been activated for more than 37 emergencies,[3] among which several forest fires in Italy, Cyprus or Greece, the 2005 Pakistan earthquake, but also the 2007 floods in Bolivia.[4] The MIC was also involved more recently in Haiti and Hungary. The mechanism can be activated in two different institutional and legal contexts depending on the situation (war or peacetime). The decision of the modality of activation is in the hands of the state presiding over the EU when the crisis strikes. So far, the mechanism has only been activated under the modality of a 'peace situation', even when it was a case of war situation, such as in Lebanon in 2006. This led to a situation where completely unarmed teams were in the middle of an armed conflict. This rather unanticipated development, which led to the activation of the mechanism both in Lebanon in 2006 and in Georgia in 2008, is examined in this section.

The pillar structure introduced in the Maastricht Treaty was a result of Member States' concerns about their sovereignty in more sensitive areas; the field of security and crisis management is not an exception. Concerns about sovereignty did not facilitate the emergence of solidarity when a crisis struck. As a compromise, Member States developed the community mechanism. According to the 2001 European Council decision creating the mechanism, two institutional settings were possible: a pillar I activation for peace situations, where the European Commission could monitor the crisis directly, and a pillar II activation for war contexts, where the European Council would take the leadership. However, this strategic decision was never successfully implemented.

In contrast with all the security issues that were legally linked to pillars II and III, the CCPM was also included in pillar I even though it could be activated for crises inside and outside the EU borders, and for both natural and man-made crises (Council of the European Union 2003e). The legal reason for that development is that EU treaties do not include any specific section on emergency management per se. All the activities and decisions linked to the CCPM were originally made under Article 308 of the Treaty on European Union, which requires decisions to be taken unanimously. This article was presented by some interviewees as the 'garbage can article' ('*article poubelle*' in French).[5] It means that it is often the article referred to in the absence of any clearly stated legal basis. This article is presented by them as broad enough to include all the issues that are possibly on the fringes of the European treaties. How does this work? Interviewees from officials in the European Commission and in the European Council explain the legal situation as follows. According to the legal basis, when a country outside the EU borders requires assistance, the European Commission must coordinate with the Member State presiding over the EU. If the Presidency decides that it is not a war situation, it is not declared to be part of 'civilian crisis management' (which legally characterised pillar II issues), and the organisational entities of the European Commission can therefore intervene and deal with the crisis itself. If, on the contrary, the Presidency declares the situation to be a war context, that is, part of 'civilian crisis management', then the CCPM is activated under pillar II, and then decisions must be taken at Council level. But because no implementing rules have been drafted – there was no agreement on how this could work out in committee meetings – no one knew in practice how a pillar II activation of the CCPM could work. It therefore seemed dangerous to test it during a crisis. In addition, interviewees mention that it would have taken too much time to reach the Committee of Permanent Representatives (COREPER) level of decision-making, whereas the crisis asked for a rapid response.

As a result, even where armed conflict was evident, such as in the case of the Lebanon crisis, the Finnish Presidency authorised the activation of the CCPM under pillar I, although they had first considered the option of using the CCA and then the option of using a pillar II activation of the CCPM.[6] Similarly, during the Georgian crisis of August 2008,[7] the French Presidency was initially reluctant to activate the CCPM under pillar I, but eventually did so because they feared that an activation of the CCPM under pillar II would be too slow in practice.[8] So, from a legal point of view, the CCPM was based on both pillars I and II. However, in practice, it has always been used in the sole context of the pillar I architecture, even in war contexts. It means that, technically, it was not feasible to strictly follow the planned legal model of decision, because Member States could not find an agreement on pillar II activation. As a consequence, decoupling occurred. The technical EU context of decision-making linked to a pillar II activation was not made clear enough for the actors to be able to rely on it when a crisis strikes. Moreover, EU actors facing the external constraint represented by the Member State presiding over the EU – which feared using an unclear pillar II framework, but also feared doing nothing – used their margins of initiative to activate the CCPM in a pillar I framework even in a war context, putting civil protection forces unnecessarily at risk in the field. They drew upon the legitimacy acquired during normal pillar I activations for natural disasters in order to stretch their framework of intervention. Taking advantage of the technical constraints of EU decision-making and their opportunity to become a recognised player of 'all-hazard' crisis management, they managed to reposition the mechanism as a pillar I 'all-hazard' mechanism.

Thanks to the use of the pillar I architecture, EU officials could deal with a large number of crisis management aspects themselves due to the lack of implementing rules to allow a Pillar II activation of the mechanism. Certainly, the European Commission has exploited this situation to address various crises, but in practice the staffing level was too low and imposed material constraints, which limited the margins of action of the European Commission officials in charge. The MIC running the CCPM did not have enough employees who were qualified to be on-duty officials. Moreover, on-duty officers were normal European Commission officials who were in charge of on-duty shifts, in addition to their other administrative tasks. Indeed, during the Lebanon war, only 23 people worked at the MIC in shifts of two or three days. It meant that, in a normal situation, two officers were on duty, whereas the others dealt with their day-to-day administrative work at the Civil Protection Unit. The two on-duty MIC officers did not actually sit in the MIC room. They were in their office (or at home during nights and weekends). They came to the MIC room in case of emergency. So, in a nutshell, when the MIC is operating 24/7, it is difficult for the MIC on-duty officers to be able to cover simultaneous emergencies on a long-term basis, as there are only two of them on duty. As a European Commission official stated in an interview, 'even if the MIC wanted to deal with a large number of emergencies, this would not be feasible, not given the current conditions'.[9]

This section made it clear that EU officials could develop their margins of initiative and be in a situation of CCPM activation restricted to a pillar I setting, even in a war situation, contrary to the planned legal framework. This was possible because of the lack of consensus among Member States on drafting the implementing rules of a pillar II activation and because of the strong experience and legitimacy acquired in the context of pillar I activations. This development shows that there is a discrepancy between legal frameworks and practice, which makes strategic planning for European homeland security a difficult task. This section therefore confirms hypotheses 2, 3 and 4.

The birth of the emergency and crisis coordination arrangements: an unsuccessful repositioning?

The SitCen is an organisational structure which was created at the EU level to gather intelligence in the different Member States and share it on the basis of the North Atlantic Treaty Organization (NATO) model. The objective was to provide the European Council with high-quality information. In 1998, when the European Security and Defence Policy (ESDP) was first developed, no structure existed to allow Member States to share intelligence. There was only some exchange of confidential information in the form of diplomatic telegrams. Intelligence was a matter of bilateral cooperation and not part of EU homeland security policies. Since its creation, the SitCen has recruited intelligence analysts from Member States and has facilitated information exchange through the creation of secure communication networks. For instance, it has installed secure communication channels with the five operational military headquarters. Its main objective was to produce reports on long-term strategic trends to help the Council in its decision-making, but the SitCen has faced difficulties on the road to becoming the EU Central Intelligence Agency. Intelligence services agree to share information on a bilateral basis, but not at the EU level. Therefore, the SitCen has strategically moved towards becoming an actor involved in emergency and crisis management at the EU level.

In 2005, the Council developed cross-pillar integrated crisis management procedures linked to SitCen and referred to as the CCA. 'The arrangements are designed to enable the Council and the European Commission to successfully respond to any major emergency or crisis that may affect several EU Member States, or the interests of the Union as a whole' (European Union 2006b). This gave an opportunity to the SitCen to enlarge its activities and become a Council-based actor that could be a potential EU-based coordinator in times of crises. The sources on which the SitCen relies are open-source materials, military intelligence, non-military intelligence and diplomatic reporting. According to the seventh report of the UK House of Lords Committee on the EU,[10] the new missions of the SitCen include contributing to early warning (in conjunction with other Council-based EU military staff) in case of emergency, situation monitoring and assessment when crises occur and providing facilities for crisis task force. This means that the crisis steering group and crisis support group, which are activated in case of emergencies, could be based at the SitCen in the event of a major crisis.[11] This could have been a case of successful repositioning but due to various constraints, the SitCen could not really become an EU crisis manager.

The CCA in practice only included the organisation of on-desk exercises by the SitCen to test the adequacy and efficiency of the CCA internal procedures. There was no full activation of the CCA for real crisis situations during the long period of their emergence, although this could have been the case, for instance, for Lebanon or Georgia, where interests of EU Member States were at stake.[12] Indeed, from its creation in 2005 until the implementation of the Lisbon Treaty, no full activation took place. Hence, the SitCen only coordinated and provided the main operational backbone for conducting such exercises: 'The Joint EU Situation

Centre has already carried out exercises that have explored the likely needs of a EU crisis co-ordination mechanism in the event of an incident both outside and inside the EU' (European Council 2005). Moreover these exercises were always 'table-top', based in Brussels, and made using fictitious scenarios. For instance, the first exercise of the CCA took place on 30 October 2006 with a simulation of a major terrorist attack targeting different European cities. On 13 and 14 September 2007, a second exercise of the CCA was conducted. It was a simulation of the perpetration of a biological attack. It focused on managing all the consequences of such a biological risk for European citizens. Since then, a lot of different exercises have taken place. For security reasons, it is not possible to quote the lesson-learnt reports of these exercises. What can be said though is that these exercises were mainly 'table-top' exercises based in Brussels. This means that the CCA were mainly tested without any involvement of the nationally based decision-making actors. This is a limit to the validity of the exercises, as in real time the national Brussels-based actors (the members of the Permanent Representative Committee) would need to coordinate with their capital (Prime Minister office, etc.), which would make the decision-making process in Brussels much more cumbersome. The second point that can be made on these exercises is that the scenarios were chosen by the country presiding over the EU. In the case of the biological attack exercise, the choice was, for instance, linked to the priority of the Portuguese Presidency to focus on European protection against contamination via biological agents (European Union 2007). This choice, which is politically grounded, might not reflect the most probable threat on EU soil. In a nutshell, the CCA have never been fully activated in practice. And even their activation during exercises could be characterised as restricted in scale and scope.

There are two reasons for which the CCA can be seen as extraordinary EU modes of governance. First, the CCA rely on ad hoc structures of crisis management; namely, the Crisis Steering Group and the Crisis Support Group. The role of the Crisis Steering Group is to contribute to the building of a common understanding of the crisis among the Member States. Its assessment draws upon information provided by the Crisis Support Group, which is composed of experts (e.g. CBRN experts, medical experts, etc.). The role of the Crisis Steering Group is to suggest possible EU responses and to elaborate potential scenarios. The Crisis Steering Group is also in charge of monitoring the implementation of the response. It is composed of high-level cross-pillar actors, such as the Presidency, the EU High Representative, the Representatives of the affected Member States and the European Commission. The SitCen and other agencies, such as Europol, might contribute. Permanent structures have a role to play as well, as they will be requested to provide all the necessary administrative support. For instance, the Council Secretariat will prepare papers for submission to the Crisis Steering Group. The SitCen will be requested to give an assessment of the threat. Even the MIC assistance can be required. But, in a sense, the characteristic of the CCA is to involve more people in the crisis management process than it is normally the case. Indeed, the CCA procedure goes beyond the normal involvement of usual respondents.

Second, the activation of the CCA is linked to the definition of different stages of emergency. Only a crisis that involves various Member States can lead to the activation of the CCA. In this sense, it creates new opportunities for existing structures (e.g. SitCen, Council Secretariat) to reposition themselves and gain in terms of legitimacy should an emergency occur, but only if the crisis is of a large magnitude.

Having such ad hoc structures linked to the assessment of the level of emergency had consequences. As these types of extraordinary modes of governance were new (compared to the MIC and the CCPM), this created a context of fuzziness described by actors in interviews. For instance, the organisational locus of the CCA was not clear. It could be placed in a secure room of the SitCen. The difficulty was to make a high level of confidentiality possible without hindering communication between the Representatives in Brussels and their capital. One interviewee stressed the fact that he was willing to sit in the Crisis Steering Group, but not 'naked'. He mentioned that, so far, he had not been allowed to enter the SitCen rooms made available with a mobile phone and that due to this situation he could not imagine how he could possibly communicate with his capital to take appropriate decisions.[13] The permanent national contact points for the CCA could be the same contact points as for the CCPM or different ones. For instance, for Italy, it was a different contact point. However, in the UK, both the CCPM and the CCA had their national contact point in the Cabinet Office (i.e. in the Civil Contingencies Secretariat).[14] This would also create a very complex situation, should the CCA be implemented in real emergency situations. The coexistence of ad hoc and permanent structures made the routine of emergency response more fragile as this suddenly had the consequence of creating new bodies for a short period of time. EU actors not being used to those new ad hoc structures found themselves confronted with doubts and fears. They did not activate the CCA, neither for the 2006 Lebanon crisis nor for the 2008 Georgian crisis. The CCA could not become legitimate between 2005 and 2009, even if SitCen officials tried to develop their margins of action thanks to the development of these emergency modes of governance.

To sum up, the CCA were a strategic move of the European Council to tackle the issue of emergency and crisis management, but were never fully activated in practice between 2005 and 2009.[15] The main reason for that was a lack of legitimacy. New ad hoc structures of crisis management linked to extraordinary modes of governance were not considered legitimate. As a consequence, no one pushed for the activation of the CCA in real crisis situations. In this case, it was not the technical aspects (both operational and political) that can provide an explanation, but rather hypothesis 4, concerning legitimacy. A lack of legitimacy hindered the SitCen in its attempts at developing its margins of initiative. Therefore, although the CCA had been planned to be activated, these arrangements were not in crisis situations.

The unanticipated mode of emergence of European homeland security?

Neither the CCPM nor the CCA were used as initially planned in their first years of existence. The CCPM were only activated in the modality of 'peace activation', even during war situations. The CCA were never fully used during real crisis or emergency situations between 2005 and 2009. Why did the emergence of European emergency management follow such a divergent track? What lessons can be drawn for European Homeland Security in the making?

In the case of the CCPM, the technicality of the EU process of activation in a war context and the lack of consensus among Member States led to a situation where Commission officials could stretch their margins of initiative beyond the legal framework and intervene in a war context using the modality of peace activation. This was made possible thanks to the legitimacy they had achieved at the EU level following the successful numerous activations in times of peace. On the contrary, in the case of the CCA, the fact that no full activation took place, even during the Lebanese and Georgian crises, is due to a lack of legitimacy of new structures of emergency management linked to extraordinary modes of governance.

The technicality of the decision-making process itself (and not the technicality of the civil protection operation) led to this situation of unwritten law. Indeed, agreement was reached on activation in pillar I, whereas no agreement was ever reached on the process of activation in pillar II. In fact, on 17 June 2003, the Political and Security Committee had reached an agreement on a draft joint declaration by the Council and the Commission on the use of the CCPM in crisis management referred to in Title V of the Treaty on European Union, and hence included in pillar II. Nevertheless, it remained a 'political agreement with no implementation details'.[16] This situation is the result of long discussions amongst the representatives of the Member States, which led to the expansion of the first draft to a seven-page document – which was too cumbersome to be adopted by all the members unanimously – followed by a reduction to a three-page document, which has thereby become too general to be used to define the design of a pillar II activation. A certain degree of path-dependency can be observed. Once actors have become used to pillar I activations of the CCPM, they have tended to rely on this, without going back to a complex bargaining to settle the rules of implementation under pillar II. This situation has been reinforced by the fact that, so far, pillar I activations have been satisfactory, even in a war context.[17] In addition, a process of skill formation, both at the MIC and national levels, can be highlighted with training, exercises and the accumulation of real activations from 2001 onwards. Moreover, every disaster has been followed by 'lessons-learnt' meetings and a 'lessons-learnt' document, which have increased the awareness of actors on what to do next.[18] This has enhanced the ability and willingness of actors to choose the pillar I CCPM activation to which they are now used. Hence, Commission officials have had the legitimacy to stretch the pillar I activation framework to war situations having incrementally developed the mechanism.

Moreover, what is striking in this study is the difficulties linked to the birth of EU emergency modes of decision-making due to the EU organisational structure and architecture. Indeed, emergency decision-making must be quick. This is in contradiction with the principle of consultation used at the EU level to take decisions. For instance, an activation of the CCPM in a pillar II situation would entail a complex organisational process of consultation with a large number of EU actors:

> If the presidency considers that the assistance requested might fall within EU crisis management, it will so inform Member States and the Commission. In those cases the presidency, following consultations with the Member States and the Commission in the appropriate Council bodies, may establish that the assistance requested falls within EU crisis management.
>
> (Council of the European Union 2003d)

This organisational process would be too long to lead to a swift answer of the EU. Another solution adopted for the CCA was to create extraordinary modes of governance. It meant that an ad hoc organisational structure, the Crisis Steering Group, would be created in case of an emergency with the inclusion of a restricted number of EU actors (i.e. only those directly affected by the emergency). In practice, this idea of a smaller COREPER, gathering only the countries affected, could not work because EU Member States were not willing to be excluded from the decision-making process. This led to a situation where a gap emerged between the formal modal and its implementation. This deviation from the formal model has become institutionalised, as an 'unwritten law' has emerged out of a constant CCPM pillar I activation every time a crisis has occurred, while there has not been any activation of the CCA and the CCPM pillar II. Hence, the cross-pillar CCA could not develop their legitimacy.

Conclusion

Among the hypotheses tested in this chapter, the one having the strongest explanatory power is that of legitimacy (hypothesis 4). This question of legitimacy seems foremost in the hands of EU bureaucrats, who can manage to impose their legitimacy or fail to do so when it comes to the making of European Homeland Security. This is why the chapter shows that the main actors having an impact on the development of European homeland security in the sense of designing its institutions are first EU bureaucrats. The process that they follow at the EU level when drafting the first official documents is of paramount importance, because if their draft implementing rules do not lead to the emergence of a consensus among Member States, the Council decision will not be implemented as foreseen. This was true for the pillar II activation of the CCPM, but also for the CCA.

What were the consequences in reality? First, this situation led to institutional frictions between different EU officials about the most appropriate EU setting to be used to respond to an emergency, as two competitive models existed, the CCPM and the CCA, which were competing for legitimacy. Second, it created unnecessary duplications at the EU level – two crisis centres with all the necessary IT equipment and personnel – although one was used and not the other. Third, it led to the adoption of organisational structures that were not designed to save as many victims as possible, but to satisfy as many political interests as possible. This fostered the emergence of suboptimal organisational designs at the EU level. It led to sending European civil protection forces unarmed in a war situation, potentially putting their lives at risk in the field.

Where are we now? How far are we in the process of integrating EU crisis management actors in a European homeland security strategy? The Lisbon Treaty is a turning point because it introduces a new legal basis. The new legal framework changes the way emergency and crisis management actors are organised at the EU level. The creation of the European External Action Service (EEAS) offers opportunities to improve consistency between disaster response and possible political and security-related elements of the EU's overall crisis response. During the Haiti earthquake crisis, the SitCen was activated and played a role in coordination with the civil protection actors of the MIC. Moreover, civil protection (MIC) and humanitarian aid actors (Humanitarian Aid & Civil Protection Directorate General of the European Commission (ECHO)) have been brought together so as to have one response centre integrating both aspects of emergency management. This new crisis room will be implemented soon and named the European Emergency Response Centre. The Lisbon Treaty has also introduced a new solidarity clause, which will bring EU Member States together in case of emergencies. The question of its use in practice is to be clarified in the coming months. Drawing from this chapter, it seems here too some gaps could emerge between the legally defined solidarity clause and the implementation modes, which will be used in the future, as questions regarding the interpretation of the clause are still open to debate in the field of emergency management. If the concept of homeland security was not well received in Europe so far, it seems that, incrementally, the interplay of new institutional frameworks (e.g. solidarity clause) and new security concepts (e.g. the comprehensive approach) could make it a reality with both the greater integration of EU Member States in the face of disasters and the greater harmonisation of the action of EU actors of emergency and crisis management (MIC, SitCen, etc.).

What are the consequences for theory development? This chapter opens the way to a qualitative use of the sociological neo-institutionalist theories based on process-tracing, which reconciles institutional processes with agency aspects. Incorporating the margins of initiative of actors into a neo-institutionalist framework allows for a better understanding of the institutional constraints and their instrumentalisation by officials, especially in the field of European homeland security, which consists of a broad range of actors at the EU level. Moreover, it shows that further research is required on the cognitive aspects of institutional design when exploring the role of bureaucrats drafting the first documents at the origin of a policy. Do new organisations come from the routines of bureaucrats, who prefer to rely on the implementing rules they know and stretch them to the maximum, rather than engage in further cumbersome bargaining with Member States? Or are EU officials under the pressure of Member States, which prefer to find solutions by default, rather than risking frontal confrontation on issues in the making, such as emergency management? Using cognitive studies could help differentiate between rather accidental and rather planned organisational designs. Finally, theoretically, the use of this comprehensive approach calls for an integrated approach to European security policies. The theoretical security field, which has developed essentially by sectors in Europe, might not be relevant anymore. It will be more and more about 'whole of government' approaches, unity of effort among security actors to protect Europe and EU citizens. Both practitioners and researchers will have to adapt to this challenge.

Notes

Interviews were conducted to gather data for this article. Because of the sensitivity of the topic of emergency management, confidentiality was ensured to all interviewees, whose names are therefore not mentioned. The author would like to thank all those who accepted to be interviewed for this study, as well as Patryk Pawlak and Christian Kaunert, who read and commented on earlier drafts of this manuscript.

 1 The literature often distinguishes between natural and technological risks leading to emergency and man-made risks leading to crises. The CCPM and the CCA are both designed to be all-hazard. They deal both with emergencies and crises.
 2 The MIC is now called the 'European Emergency Response Centre', following the implementation of the Lisbon Treaty and the recent merger of the civil protection unit with the humanitarian aid Directorate-General (DG) ECHO of

the European Commission. The ECHO and MIC crisis rooms are set to merge in order to strengthen coordination.

3 This number does not include five exercises for which the mechanism was activated as though a real emergency were taking place. It includes, however, the times that the Mechanism was activated on standby.

4 For a list of all the emergencies which led to the activation of the mechanism, see www.ec.europa.eu/environment/civil/index.htm.

5 Interviews with EU officials, Brussels, March 2007 and November 2008.

6 Statement made by the Finnish Representative during a PROCIV meeting in 2007.

7 This crisis opposed Russia to Georgia and led to several fires due to bombings in Georgia.

8 Interview with an EU official, Brussels, August 2008.

9 Interview with an EU official, Brussels, July 2007.

10 Parts of this report are available online, see www.parliament.the-stationery-office.co.uk/pa/ld200203/ldselect/ldeucom/53/5313.htm.

11 The Crisis Steering Group is an ad hoc organisational structure which acts as central coordinating body in the event of an emergency. It consists of the following high-level cross-pillar actors or their representatives: Presidency, Secretary General, Commission, Member States affected and Joint Situation Centre. The Crisis Steering Group is assisted by a Crisis Support Group composed of senior officials with relevant expertise.

12 In particular the Baltic States.

13 Interview with a French official, May 2007.

14 Interview with a British official, February 2007.

15 A case of 'stand-by' activation, but not full activation, was the Mumbai terrorist attack.

16 Interview with an EU official, Brussels, June 2007.

17 As stated in 'lessons-learnt' documents.

18 Interview with an EU official, Brussels, August 2008.

8   The fog of border

The fragmentation of the European Union's border policies

Patryk Pawlak and Xymena Kurowska

The European Union (EU) has developed a number of frameworks and instruments related to the management of its external borders, which have stimulated a substantial scholarly interest (Carrera 2007; Marenin 2010; Wolff 2010; Zapata-Barrero 2010). The number of border management tools has substantially expanded and includes simple fences and more sophisticated optical and electro-optical sensors, information technology (IT) intrusion detection systems, biometrical and patterns sensors and systems, manned and unmanned aircrafts, as well as intelligent surveillance means. Altogether, the border management security market amounts to €22 billion in the US and €10 billion in Europe. In addition, a multitude of 'stakeholders' has largely expanded to include not only traditional border management actors (e.g. the DG Justice and the DG Home Affairs in the European Commission, Interpol, Europol or the Customs Cooperation Working Party), but also the European Union Anti-Fraud Office (OLAF), the United Nations High Commissioner for Refugees (UNHCR), the Fundamental Rights Agency (FRA), the European Maritime Safety Agency (EMSA), the Global Monitoring for Environment and Security (GMES) programme, the Joint Research Centre (JRC), the European Union Satellite Centre (EUSC), the European Defence Agency (EDA) or the European Security Research and Innovation Forum (ESRIF). Operational cooperation on border management is mostly structured around the activities of the European Patrol Network and the External Borders Agency Frontex (joint operations, Focal Points, Rapid Border Intervention Teams, risk analysis, training, technical assistance to Member States), which is the focus of the next chapter. The implementation of these measures is supported through the use of burden-sharing tools like the Schengen Facility (e.g. €400 million for Romania and Bulgaria in 2007–2009) and the External Border Fund, which amounts to €1.82 billion for the period 2007–2013, the major part of which is distributed among Member States depending on their burden regarding external border controls and visa policy. Several new legislative proposals are in the making concerning, among others, the amendment of the Schengen Borders Code, setting up an Entry Exit System (EES) and a Registered

Traveller Programme (RTP), as well as the start of operations of the Agency for the operational management of large-scale IT systems in the Area of Freedom, Security and Justice (AFSJ).

These developments give rise to an intricate system for the defence of the EU's realm where the construction of the border depends on its dislocation, both political and spatial. The three clusters of border policy repertoires described in this chapter, surveillance, smart borders and integrated border management, epitomise the emerging practice the EU has engaged in. They reflect the 'pushing-out of borders' in two distinctive ways: through technological devices and a particular relationship with the neighbour. The latter relies on attempts to prevent the border-related threat from entering the EU's realm by shifting increasing responsibility to contain it onto the neighbour. This move is accompanied by conditionality (e.g. the pressure towards readmission tied with the promises of visa facilitation) and the projection of the EU political and social model geared at a systemic reform of the neighbour. A quote from the EU Internal Security Strategy (ISS) reflects the rationale underpinning this logic: 'The quality of our democracy and public confidence in the Union will depend to a large extent on our ability to guarantee security and stability in Europe and to work with our neighbours and partners to address the root causes of the internal security problems faced by the EU' (European Council 2010b: 9). Here the externally assisted reform, most explicitly in our case integrated border management and security sector reform, turn into modern state-building.[1]

Such processes are facilitated by the massive role of technology and the extensive co-option of academic research for the generation of border management solutions, a development that involves a growing number of actors active at and around the border. These actors no longer solely represent the Member States and EU-level policy-makers, but also stand for the interests of industrial players, civil liberty organisations and research consortia. The involvement of such actors points to broader developments in contemporary international security practices where the state is one party among many.[2]

The aim of this chapter is however more specifically to outline how the defence of the EU's realm is executed through a multifaceted and often hardly coordinated web of sectoral strategies. Such fragmentation is not simply to be blamed on policy-makers who supposedly notoriously fail to coordinate and communicate effectively. Instead, the actors are themselves thrown into interdependencies they cannot have full knowledge of and control upon, quite apart from their own participation in ongoing contestation of border policies. In this respect, an ineluctable predicament of the social world; that is, finding out in 'which game' one is, rather than assuming that this is common knowledge and everybody has complete information (Kurowska and Kratochwil 2012), is particularly evident in the EU's border policy problematique. To capture the ambiguity involved, we use the term 'fog of border'. Borrowed from military strategy concerned with the 'fog of war', a concept ascribed to Clausewitz, it denotes the uncertainty regarding one's own capacities, those of the adversary (and various partners across levels) and the intent of the other party. We extend this term to bring in the need of continuous figuring out by the participants of where their interests lie and how to go about securing them under the condition of a limited grasp of the evolving situation. Thus, we restate our argument presented elsewhere (Kurowska and Pawlak 2009b) that policy is a discursive battlefield with strategic interaction constituting the framework for action, and that policy-making, comprising a wide range of participants with diverse agendas and values, concerns to a large extent the formation and maintenance of certain interpretations of the policy at different levels.

New border paradigm: from territorial to smart borders

The discussion about European integrated border management can be traced back to the Laeken European Council in 2001 when the control of the EU's external borders emerged as a means of fighting terrorism, illegal immigration networks and trafficking in human beings (European Council 2001c). The issue gained in importance on the wave of the EU enlargement and in particular through programs like PHARE, TACIS and CARDS, which emphasised the need to cooperate with neighbouring countries in managing shared borders (Hobbing 2005). The Hague Programme adopted in 2004 stated that 'an optimal level of protection of the area of freedom, security and justice requires multidisciplinary and concerted action both at EU level and at national level between the competent law enforcement authorities, especially police, customs and border guards' (European Council 2004b). It specifies that 'the further gradual establishment of the integrated management system for external borders and the strengthening of controls at and surveillance of the external borders of the Union' are all important components of the European approach to borders.

The process of policy definition resulted in the development of a European model of border management, which encompasses five major elements: (1) border control, including relevant risk analysis and crime intelligence; (2) detection and investigation of cross-border crime in coordination with all competent law enforcement authorities; (3) the four-tier access control model (measures in third countries, cooperation with neighbouring countries, border control, control measures within the area of free movement, including the return); (4) inter-agency cooperation in border management (border agents, customs, police) and international cooperation; and (5) coordination and coherence of the activities of Member States and institutions and other bodies of the community and the EU (Council of the European Union 2006c). This approach is reflected, among others, in the so-called 'Border Package' adopted in February 2008 with the objective to set out a comprehensive border management strategy that would respond to the challenges of globalisation (European Commission 2008a). It is composed of three Communications, which focus on the next steps in border management in the EU, the creation of a European Border Surveillance System (EUROSUR) and the evaluation and future development of Frontex, respectively. The provisions of the Lisbon Treaty have facilitated the implementation of this model. According to Article 77 of the Treaty on the Functioning of the European Union (TFEU), the EU should propose a policy approach that would allow adopting 'any measure necessary for the gradual establishment of an integrated management system for external borders'. The Stockholm Programme of December 2009 complemented the changes prescribed in the Treaty and suggested that Frontex as the agency responsible for the management of the external borders should play a major role in the implementation of these provisions. In order to improve coordination between the different actors involved, the Lisbon Treaty has also created the Standing Committee on Operational Cooperation on Internal Security (COSI), which relies mostly on national and EU threat assessments and priorities.

The transversal nature of border protection has further strengthened the idea that interoperability and inseparability between various policy tools should be one of the objectives in policy design. The ISS, which was adopted in 2010, emphasised the need to exploit potential existing synergies between law enforcement, border protection and criminal justice systems. One of the identified prerequisites was the exchange of information between all actors involved and the promotion of 'a coherent approach to the development of information technology and exchange of information' (The Future Group 2008). The idea of an EU Information Management Strategy based on the principle of availability[3] was supposed to offer a solution. The report submitted by the Friends of the Presidency group on the technical modalities to implement the principle of availability set as the objective the establishment of

> business processes which can facilitate the quick, efficient and cost-effective means for exchanging data [...]. The technical solution must be designed to meet current and future business needs, taking into account functional and technical requirements. Its functionality and interoperability should be maximised and it must be easy to expand and modify.
>
> (Council of the European Union 2005h)

In practice, such an approach means not only enhanced cooperation between Member States and the EU bodies, but also an exchange of information between large-scale IT systems created for law enforcement and border protection purposes, including the Second Generation Schengen Information System (SIS II), the Visa Information System (VIS), Eurodac, as well as the exchange of information extracted from criminal records.

Crucially, the realisation that many threats can actually be prevented from reaching the borders of the EU results in an increasing 'pushing-out' of borders away from the EU's realm. Border management is no longer only about maintaining security by protecting physical borders, but is also about protecting borders by shifting their meaning and moving them in space and time. This is achieved partly by increasing reliance on technology (e.g. the development of the European Border Surveillance System, profiling). As Laitinen (2008: 8) put it,

> in the 21st century border management must be intelligence-driven. This is a prerequisite of all actions taken regarding borders. Effective border management does not exist without sophisticated systems of data collection and analysis followed by its timely dissemination to officers making decisions on the ground, such as the eligibility for crossing of a person or cargo. [...] That is why the concept of a 'virtual border' is so important; because the management of a border starts even while gathering intelligence or issuing a visa in third country. The physical border is, so to say, the 'last border line'.

The following sections provide an overview of the most recent developments in three areas of border management: the creation of smart borders, border surveillance and the externalisation of border management, including the extended role of Frontex which, according to the EU ISS Action Plan, constitutes the focus of strengthening security through border management (European Commission 2010a).

Smart border checks: facilitating mobility while improving security

The implementation of the concept of 'smart borders' has accelerated in the United States (US) after the 9/11 terrorist attacks (Koslowski 2004a, 2004b; Pawlak 2007, 2010b, 2010c). According to the White House and the Department of Homeland Security (The White House 2002b; The White House 2002c; The White House 2002d), the future border 'must integrate actions abroad to screen goods and people prior to their arrival in sovereign United States territory, and inspections at the border and measures within the United States to ensure compliance with entry and import permits' (US Department of Homeland Security 2002). This preventive approach was also adopted by the EU, which highlighted in the ISS that it aims to 'emphasise prevention and anticipation, which is based on a proactive and intelligence-led approach as well as procuring the evidence required for prosecution' (European Council 2010b). Transforming this policy objectives into concrete actions is mostly possible thanks to technological advances, which 'may make it easier for citizens to cross quickly at external-border posts through automated systems, advance registration, frequent-traveller schemes, etc. They improve security by allowing for the necessary controls to be put in place so that borders are not crossed by people or goods which pose a risk to the Union' (European Council 2010b: 27). The main assumptions and objectives of the EU model of smart borders are set out in the Commission (2008a) Communication 'Preparing the next steps in border management in the European Union'. The solutions proposed in that Communication resemble greatly the US implementation tools, which raises legitimate questions about the way in which the EU border management policy is being made (Pawlak 2009c, 2010a).

Whereas increasing security is undoubtedly one of the objectives of border management, the other side of the coin is the impact that more stringent measures may have on human mobility. Consequently, facilitating border crossing for *bona fide* travellers while at the same time fighting illegal migration becomes one of the aspects in new approaches to border management. The answer from the European Commission was RTPs. Those offer a voluntary pre-screening process and eventually a 'Registered Traveller' status for low-risk travellers, which in the future will allow for using automated gates when crossing the external border and consequently result in better use of resources and saving time at border checks. For the moment, automated border checks are proposed for the citizens of the European Economic Area (EEA) in possession of an e-passport. Automated Border Control (ABC) (automation through e-passport) operating with either iris-based or fingerprint-based systems are currently implemented in a number of EU Member States, including the Netherlands (PRIVIUM), France (PARAFES), the UK (miSense and miSense Plus), Germany (ABG), Portugal (RAPID) (Frontex 2007b). For instance, the French PARAFES (*Passage Automatisé Rapide des Frontières Extérieures Schengen*) is open for the nationals of the EEA and operates with biometric elements included in passports and collected upon enrolment. Registration offices are located within the airport premises and are equipped with computers connected to a specific national police database, which allows for the verification of the eligibility of passengers.

Another proposal is the introduction of an Entry Exit System (EES) which is supposed to help identify potential 'overstayers' by the means of automatic registration of the time and place of entry and exit of third-country nationals. Like RTPs, the EES will rely on biometric data collected from third-country nationals upon their visa application at the consulate of a Member State. The information will then be verified at border crossing points and alerts will be issued in cases where individuals have previously abused conditions of their stay. Both the RTP and the EES were conceived as a response to growing passenger flows at the EU's external borders (European Commission 2008b). Third-country nationals who do not require any visa to enter the EU territory will be requested to make an electronic application through an Electronic System of Travel Authorisation and provide information about their travel details and travel documents. In addition to the measures proposed in the Border Package, the EU has presented proposals for the establishment of a European Passenger Name Record (PNR) system similar to the one operated by the US (Brouwer 2009; Hobbing and Koslowski 2009; Pawlak 2009c). The system relies on the PNR data collected by air carriers and then submitted to competent authorities in EU Member States – a Passenger Information Unit (PIU) which will be responsible not only for collecting the data, but also for carrying out risk assessment (Council of the European Union 2009c). The proposal mentions the benefits that the PNR system will offer to law enforcement agencies to prevent a crime, watch or arrest people before a crime has been committed or for investigations, prosecutions, and the unravelling of networks after a crime has been committed (European Commission 2011a).

These policy developments were accompanied by a simultaneous advancement of large-scale IT systems. The application of the Dublin Regulation and the determination of responsibility for asylum applications have largely been possible thanks to Eurodac (European Union 2000), which became operational in January 2003. The evaluation report published by the European Commission in 2007 pointed to certain inefficiencies in the implementation of the Eurodac Regulation, including the late transmission of fingerprints by some Member States. The Schengen Information System (SIS) and a proposed second-generation SIS II are other good examples. The SIS allows the consulates and border guards to check third-country nationals, wanted persons and those to be refused entry to the Schengen area or put under protection. According to the data from 2007, the SIS contained at that time approximately 15 million reports on issues such as stolen vehicles, lost or stolen identity papers, or people wanted for arrest for extradition. To complement the architecture of large-scale IT systems, the European Commission has proposed the Visa Information System (VIS), which should become operational in 2012 allowing the authorities to verify the authenticity of a visa and the identity of its holder by introducing biometric data (photograph and fingerprint) during the application procedure. The VIS aims to improve the administration of the common visa policy by setting up a central database and facilitating the exchange of data between Member States.

Part of the problem with those measures – as identified by their critics – is that they favour 'a routine collection of data of individuals who are in principle not suspected of any crime' with very limited evidence that such measures are necessary at all (European Data Protection Supervisor 2008). The criticism about potential costs, the transparency of the process and a need for a more structured approach should have been taken into account in light of problems that other countries have encountered while taking similar steps (General Accountability Office 2009a, 2009b, 2010). A major objection towards new measures addresses their introduction in a fairly uncoordinated manner, which raises the question of whether there is any strategic thinking behind them. As the European Data Protection Supervisor (EDPS) (2008) observed, 'no assessment was made of the functioning of either the existing instruments, the instruments that are about to be implemented, or measures still under discussion, including SIS II, VIS, Advanced Passenger Information (API) Directive, EU PNR, Schengen Border Code (with amendments), proposals for allowing law enforcement authorities to access the VIS-Eurodac and other databases and information systems by changing the purpose for which they were established'. With regard to the EU PNR, the EDPS has observed that there should be an 'in-depth and comprehensive analysis' of all those systems before new forms of control are introduced (European Data Protection Supervisor 2007). The EDPS on many occasions has warned against a 'risk of overdrive' and expressed his concerns that 'far-reaching proposals intended to contribute to the monitoring of travellers (e.g. SIS II, VIS, review of Eurodac Regulation, Passenger Name Records, etc.) are succeeding each other rapidly, making it difficult for stakeholders to have a comprehensive overview. Even though the European Commission claims that the orientations were already defined in Hague Programme, this programme does not qualify as a comprehensive master plan which would help stakeholders to have the full picture (European Data Protection Supervisor 2009). In terms of costs, the assessment is not different. Most recently, Germany and Austria have criticised the European Commission for delays in making the SIS II operational – it was supposed to be running by 2007, now 2013 is mentioned as a possible date – despite a 1,000 per cent budget increase from €15 million to €143 million (Council of the European Union 2010d). Furthermore, inter-operability between those systems, although desired from the perspective of law enforcement and border protection, carries numerous risks for citizens, especially in terms of the protection of their personal information and hypothetically the right to free movement. The practice of ethnic profiling and data mining – on which several new measures rely – constitute a significant intrusion into personal life. This is even more worrying in light of the tendency in the last few years to use data collected by private institutions for law enforcement purposes (Guild 2003; Carrera and Geyer 2007; Guild *et al.* 2008; Guild and Geyer 2008).

Border surveillance

Another challenge for the EU's border management policy is improving the surveillance of borders by boosting detection capabilities, sharing relevant information within and between Member States, and sharing relevant information, including pre-border intelligence information. This relates for instance to the detection and interception of small boats that are used for illegal migration or cross-border crimes like drug trafficking. Spain, for instance, has implemented the Integrated System for External Surveillance (*Sistema Integrado de Vigilancia Exterior*, SIVE). This operational system, which is supported by technical equipment, allows for border surveillance and provides real-time information to command and control centre and transmits orders (Serrano 2010b). Since 2006, the EU Member States have also engaged in the multilateral cooperation project 'Seahorse', which has resulted in the establishment of the Seahorse Network and Seahorse Cooperation Centres in Spain, Portugal, Morocco, Mauritania, Senegal and Cape Verde. The evolution of the network towards 'Seahorse Mediterranean' bringing together countries from the Mediterranean basin is under way (Serrano 2010a).

A 'system of systems' approach: EUROSUR

In terms of managing migration, EUROSUR is a tool to increase the situational awareness and improve the reaction capabilities of border protection authorities in order to 'detect, identify, track and intercept persons attempting to enter the EU illegally outside border crossing points' (European Commission 2008c). It aims to prevent cross-border crime and reduce the number of illegal migrants entering the EU. It is supposed to help achieve those objectives by enhancing information-sharing and cooperation between Member States at the tactical, operational and strategic levels. EUROSUR enables the exchange of information and intelligence within a 'system of systems' meaning that it merges the data from the existing systems (i.e. national systems, SafeSeaNet) and available surveillance tools (e.g. satellites, unmanned air vessels) in order to provide a more complete picture. The backbone of EUROSUR is the national coordination centres operated by Member States, which, with limited support at the EU level (Frontex and GMES), are also responsible for the implementation of the system (Seiffarth 2010). The EUROSUR Pilot Project, developed in close cooperation between Member States and the DG Justice, Liberty and Security, connected six national coordination centres and Frontex, although the latter had access only to a limited amount of information (see European Commission 2008b). Using the results of security research projects funded by the Seventh Framework Programme (i.e. integrated projects and the MarBorSur demo), the EUROSUR Pilot Network was primarily designed as a tool for the exchange of agreed 'common interest' information, initially in form of alerts and incidents, between the members of the EUROSUR Network. The events are grouped in three categories: (1) illegal migration (illegal border crossings, incidents related to facilitators); (2) related cross-border crime (human trafficking, smuggling); and (3) crisis (natural disasters, violence, armed conflict) (Ameyugo 2010). Analysis and operational information are foreseen at a later stage. Despite criticisms about the questionable added value of systems like EUROSUR[4] (European Data Protection Supervisor 2008), European policy-makers have already announced that 'future security solutions will need to be embedded in a network of legacy security systems, interact with them and provide benefits of their synergies. More and more security solutions will therefore become part of complex "system of systems"' (Laitinen 2008: 8).

Research and science to serve security

Security research is one of the major drivers behind such a rapid development of border management instruments. Its importance is reflected in a number of security research initiatives that have emerged in the last few years, including the report of the Group of Personalities in the field of Security Research (European Commission 2004b), the European Security Research and Innovation Forum (European Security Research and Innovation Forum 2009) and the work of the Joint Research Centre (Joint Research Centre 2005). In addition, under the Seventh Framework Programme for Research (FP7), the European Commission has earmarked €1.4 billion for security research. The three calls issued under the FP7 have provided funding for 67 cooperative projects and support actions.[5] The following sections discuss some of the funded projects.

The Transportable Autonomous Patrol for Land Border Surveillance system (TALOS) is a project implemented within the Seventh Framework Programme by a consortium of 14 institutions and organisations, including research and development (universities and research institutes), industry (telecommunication companies, aerospace industry) and small- and medium-size enterprises.[6] The objective of the project is to develop and test an 'adaptable land border large area surveillance system capable of detecting, locating, tracking and tracing individuals and vehicles crossing the border', adapting to topographic conditions and capable of engaging intruders by unmanned ground or air vehicles (European Commission 2009a). The implementation of the project is structured around a close cooperation with end-users and border guards in several EU Member States who provide general supervision of the project goals and activities, an evaluation and assessment of the project results and assistance in the deployment of project results.

The Wide Maritime Area Airborne Surveillance (WIMAAS) is a capability project implemented by a consortium of 14 partners from ten EU Member States. The aim is to create a 'common operating picture' through 'detection, localisation, identification and tracking of targets' that may pose a threat. More specifically, the project intends to explore potential benefits resulting from the employment of air vehicles with zero or reduced crew. However, scenarios instantiated by WIMAAS are not limited to illegal migration or drug trafficking, as they also include terrorist hijackings of large cruise liners, illegal fishing, the smuggling of weapons of mass destruction or Saharan pirates (European Commission 2009a).

The Global Monitoring for Environment and Security (GMES) is similar in terms of scope. It is designed to 'establish a European capacity for the provision and use of earth observation based application supporting environment and security issues'.[7] Conceived as a joint initiative of the European Commission and the European Space Agency, the main contributions of the project are improving prevention and increasing preparedness and response capacities in case of trans-regional security threats. Under FP6 and FP7, the GMES implemented two major projects: LIMESS (developing prototypes and testing earth observation applications and services, which can provide useful for maritime surveillance or humanitarian relief and reconstruction) and G-MOSAIC (developing methodologies and services in support of EU external security-related activities by providing geo-spatial information). For instance, the geo-spatial mapping and monitoring cross-border situation awareness were tested on the border between Poland and Ukraine where a 'Border Permeability Index'[8] was used. The tools for maritime surveillance were implemented in order to monitor migration routes over the Mediterranean Sea. Border area surveillance in the Sahara desert and coastal surveillance in Somalia exemplify further possibilities of LIMESS. Several other demonstrations have been carried out for the DG External Relations in Darfur, for the EUFOR Operational Headquarters in Chad or for the United Nations (UN) during crisis management operations after the earthquake in Haiti (di Federico 2010). Based on its experiences, the GMES has defined its 'target security community of users' to be composed of EU institutions (Council, Commission and agencies), national administrations in Member States (Ministries of Foreign Affairs, Defence and Interior), as well as civilian organisations (UN agencies, NGOs) (di Federico 2010).

It is remarkable that the scope of these projects extends beyond the traditional definition of border security and incorporates implications of potential regional conflicts or catastrophes. In that sense they respond not only to their primary border protection mission, but also to broader security objectives (e.g. preventive engagement and a more comprehensive approach to security) outlined in the European Security Strategy (ESS) of 2003. Their capacities may provide assistance in peacekeeping and peace enforcing, crisis management, damage assessment and reconstruction. In areas of maritime surveillance and border monitoring, they provide information that is useful for protecting transport and fighting piracy or the observation of civilian and military activities close to borders.

The externalisation of integrated border management

As prescribed in the four tier model discussed earlier, the cooperation with third parties has grown to constitute a crucial aspect of the EU's border management policies seeking in-country and international coordination among the various services involved in border management issues. In the context of external assistance, the concept was first defined within the Community Assistance for Reconstruction, Development and Stabilisation in the Western Balkans (CARDS)[9] and operationalised through the Guidelines for Integrated Border Management in the Western Balkans drafted in October 2004 in a Commission Staff Working document.

This section provides a survey of the tools that relate directly to the externalisation of integrated border management. The regularity that emerges reflects two broader tendencies: the 'pushing-out' of borders wherein the burden of traditional border protection is shifted to a third party, and the tendency to state-build through the promotion of integrated border management; that is, by a systemic transformation of third countries via the endorsement of technical solutions and the values embedded in them.[10]

As described before, the reliance on and the idealisation of technology constitutes a foundational element of the dislocation of the EU's border. In focusing on different modes of the externalisation of border policies, this section looks in particular at readmission agreements and mobility partnerships; some aspects of security sector reform, and the enlargement of the mandate of Frontex towards third countries. The first cluster indicates the shifting of responsibility for the handling of irregular border activity onto the neighbouring countries to contain the spill-over into the EU realm. Visa facilitation agreements are often accompanied by readmission agreements . Visa liberalisation forges a clear conditionality situation. The earmarking of EU funds for the establishment and maintenance of centres for irregular migrants on the territory of the other party seeks containment, while attempting to comply with the basic human rights that the EU embraces. The second cluster situates the concept of integrated border management within a larger enterprise of promoting systemic reform in fragile countries. A number of operations launched within the Common Security and Defence Policy (CDSP) feature this component, mostly under the banner of 'security sector reform'. Similarly, while based on different *modus operandi*, the EU Border Assistance Mission to Ukraine and Moldova (EUBAM), an EU flagship project, has over the time of its deployment grown to incorporate and vehemently promote integrated border management reform in the two countries (see Kurowska and Tallis 2009). The third cluster follows the robust, if mostly uncodified, enlargement of Frontex activities. It shows how these practices amount to a light form of state-building with an 'on-the-job' transfer of practices seen as the core of building an effective border regime.

Readmission and mobility agreements

Readmission agreements reiterate and define the obligation for a country to readmit its citizens. Some readmission agreements set out the conditions under which the state parties are obliged to readmit citizens of third countries who have passed through their territory, although such an obligation cannot be deduced from international law (Council of the European Union 1999). As they should facilitate the swift return of irregular migrants, they are supposed to be a major element in tackling irregular immigration. Sceptics claim that there is a risk that readmission agreements pose a threat to the human rights of irregular migrants and to the right of those in need of international protection not to be subjected to *refoulement* (Council of Europe 2010a). EU readmission agreements (see European Commission 2011b), together with visa facilitation negotiations that often accompany their drafting, are part and parcel of an EU security regime towards the neighbourhood (Trauner and Krause 2008). They are concluded to facilitate the removal of 'persons who do not or no longer fulfil the conditions of entry to, presence in or residence in the requesting state' (European Commission 2002c: 26) and the EU is in the process of active cooptation of neighbours into this process (see Cassarino 2010).[11]

The endorsement of readmission needs to be reconciled with the fundamental rights that the EU seeks to advance in its external action; yet, this is far from automatic. The recent Return Directive[12] set out certain procedural guarantees for third-country nationals subject to return (including the respect of the principle of *non-refoulement*) in compliance with fundamental rights, particularly the EU Charter of Fundamental Rights. Important non-state actors,[13] however, have voiced their concerns over premature returns to Afghanistan, Iraq, Somalia and Sri Lanka. In 2009, the Council of Europe Commissioner for Human Rights, Thomas Hammarberg, called on governments in Europe 'to avoid forced returns of minorities to Kosovo and to regulate the status of those in their host country until conditions in Kosovo permit their safe return'. The development of the Italian–Libyan cooperation on readmission arguably constituted another clash between the fear of irregular migration and the commitment to promote human rights; in this instance, regarding the fate of the migrants and the support of oppressive regime.[14] In April 2005, the European Parliament voted on a resolution stating that the 'Italian authorities have failed to meet their international obligations by not ensuring that the lives of the people expelled by them [to Libya] are not threatened in their countries of origin'.[15] The reinforcement of the bilateral cooperation in May 2009, when Italy set out to intercept migrants in international waters before they could reach the Italian coasts to force them back to Libya, triggered a vehement UNHCR reaction against Italy's reinterpretation of its responsibilities under the principle of *non-refoulement* enshrined in the 1951 Geneva Convention (Council of Europe 2010b).

The multiplicity of humanitarian organisations is one aspect of the increase of non-state stakeholders in EU border policy. In fact, the recent evaluation of EU readmission agreements specifically recommends case-by-case participation of NGOs and international organisations, in particular those on the ground as they have better access to information (European Commission 2011b: 10). Private business and security corporations have been further busy lobbying the notion about the lower cost and higher effectiveness of their service, which arguably also secures less visibility and better operability of the removal procedures. As Thomas Gammeltoft-Hansen shows, privatised migration control encompasses the use of private contractors to run immigration detention facilities and to enforce returns, the use of private search officers both at the border and at offshore control zones, and an increasing market for short-term visa exemption agents (Gammeltoft-Hansen 2009: 233). The outsourcing of migration controls to private contractors (e.g. the GEO Group, European Homecare, Group 4 Securicor, International Trading Agency Overseas Escorts Ltd, RSI Immigration Services Ltd, Global Solutions Ltd) has become a widespread practice and a lucrative business in the EU over the last 10 years (Hayes 2009: 12). The UK, the Czech Republic and the Netherlands have meanwhile outsourced parts of the management of their detention facilities and their escorting for removal operations (Cassarino 2010).

Mobility partnerships involve a large array of issues ranging from development aid to temporary entry visa facilitation, circular migration schemes and the fight against illegal migration including readmission.[16] They were initiated in 2007 as part of the EU's global approach to migration, framed as 'novel approaches to improve the management of legal movements of people between the EU and third countries ready to make significant efforts to fight illegal migration' (European Commission 2007a) and presented as a paradigmatic 'shift from a primarily security-centred approach focused on reducing migratory pressures to a more transparent and balanced approach' (European Commission 2008d). They envisage commitments from the partner countries geared towards discouraging irregular migration through targeted information campaigns, efforts to improve border control, including through operational cooperation with EU Member States and Frontex, and efforts to improve the security of travel documents against fraud or forgery. In exchange, they offer improved opportunities for legal migration for partner country nationals; assistance to develop capacity to manage legal migration flows; measures to address the risk of brain drain and to promote circular migration or return migration; and the improvement and/or easing of the procedures for issuing short-stay visas (European Commission 2007a: 4). With these prescriptions, the rationale behind mobility partnerships form an integral part of the externalisation of integrated border management.

Integrated border management within security sector reform

The broadest definition of integrated border management can be found in the security sector reform area, which views the practices of providing security and order as a political arena populated by numerous state and non-state actors. From this perspective, integration means the creation of a systematic network of actors, powers, resources and authorities all working together towards the common good of security through effective and fair border controls (Marenin 2010: 68). The EU has been busy promoting this model through some of its CSDP operations, association agreements in the western Balkans, as well as various justice and security projects of the European Commission, including EUBAM, its flagship project in the eastern neighbourhood. The model operates on the assumption that external capacity-building assistance for border and security systems can prevent the influx of irregular migrants and threats at borders next to one's own borders. Based on the premise of intensive cooperation among border agencies internally and internationally, it involves passing on risk analysis techniques, human resources policies, standards of training, communication and information exchange procedures, the development of border-related infrastructure and the procurement of relevant equipment. As such, externally assisted integrated border management reform aspires to fundamentally transform the security sector of the third party to meet the basic Schengen and EU standards. Critically, the number of state actors engaged in the process is high and comprises at least the Ministry of Interior, the military, the intelligence community, the police, the customs and border guards services, as well as the Ministry of Justice and the courts. Non-state actors further involve human rights NGOs, think-tanks, private security providers and academics. The range of participants accordingly widens to encompass external experts and EU bodies. The number of stakeholders with political and institutional agendas makes integrated border management reform a highly contentious, rather than merely a technical, process, which, once properly planned and stated, would be implemented without dispute or difficulties.

Apart from the case of the association agreements in the western Balkans mentioned before, the EU has sought to promote the practices of integrated border management through some aspects of CSDP operations, in particular EULEX Kosovo.[17] EUBAM has also proven a success story in this regard. So has the cooperation with third countries pursued by Frontex. Since its deployment in 2005, EUBAM has significantly enlarged its mandate and managed to build trustful enough relations with the borders and customs services of Moldova and Ukraine, as well as higher political echelons, in order to facilitate the introduction of integrated border management, which did not feature in its initial mission statement (Kurowska and Tallis 2009). It did so by, first, helping bring together the border-related state actors within the relevant countries; second, facilitating the Moldovan–Ukrainian cooperation in border-related matters; and, third, aligning these actors with Frontex activity, including through the participation in joint operations. The inevitably bumpy path towards this aim has, however, resulted in both Moldova and Ukraine adopting integrated border management reform strategies, initially in a bottom-up manner and now through formal provisions. On 27 October 2010, the Cabinet Ministers of the Ukraine approved the concept of integrated border management in line with a plan of priority actions for 2010 on Ukraine's integration into the EU. On 27 December 2010, the government of Moldova approved the National Strategy on Integrated State Border Management for 2011–2013, which explicitly acknowledges the input of EUBAM, in particular in the development of a risk analysis system, and the role of the working arrangement with Frontex. The structure and contents of the strategy clearly reflect the integrated border management model as promoted by the EU. The strategy also envisages the training of border guards according to the curriculum developed by Frontex.[18]

The enlargement of the mandate of Frontex[19]

Article 14 of the Frontex Regulation tasks the agency with facilitating operational cooperation between the Member States and third countries in the areas under its remit, within the context of the EU external relations policy and in the framework of working arrangements. Frontex cooperates with third countries in the framework of working arrangements. This cooperation takes the form of 'letters of intent', aimed at establishing a structured dialogue with non-EU countries and setting the scene for operational cooperation to counter irregular migration through border controls. The further development of structured operational cooperation with neighbouring countries has been singled out as the agency's 'overriding priority for 2010', including by pursuing alternative routes of ad hoc cooperation when the competent authorities indicate that they are not ready or willing to conclude formal agreements (Frontex 2010a: 10).

Frontex is engaged in the externalisation of integrated border management in multiple ways. Through capacity-building projects for third countries, concrete technical solutions are endorsed. As defined in the current Regulation, Frontex should assist Member States in training national border guards, as well as in establishing common training standards across the EU. Yet the provision of training also acts as a means for enhancing operational cooperation with third countries[20] and Frontex-designed training curriculum is increasingly adopted in third countries, such as Moldova as mentioned before. Third-country representatives routinely participate in joint operations. The Frontex General Report 2009 reveals, for instance, that Albanian, Croatian, Moldavian, Russian, Serbian and Ukrainian border guard officers actively participated in six joint operations during that year (Frontex 2010a). The participation of third countries in joint operations serves the build-up of a particular *esprit de corps*, the streamlining of procedures, and the promotion of particular values, as explained before, as joint operations are often perceived as an occasion to 'train on-the-job'. Many Member States further see international cooperation with third countries as being of major importance for the impact of joint operations on the combat against illegal immigrants crossing the external borders. The success of the joint operation Hera in 2008, targeted at illegal migration flows coming from West Africa to the Canary Islands, is a case in point.[21]

Frontex has grown to be an important border actor and, as the external evaluation report assesses, the fact that Frontex has not taken over the responsibility of guarding the external borders does not always seem to be clear to a number of stakeholders – including some Member States (COWI 2009: 6). This is reflected in the de facto change of its role in joint return operations. There currently appears to be a mismatch between the legal basis and reality: while the legal basis only talks about Frontex 'assisting' Member States, Frontex has already taken on a 'coordinating' role in cooperation with leading Member States (European Commission 2010b: 16).

Conclusion

The objective of this chapter was to explore the complexity of the EU approach to border management. As we have tried to show, the EU border management – as a major component of homeland protection – is much more than the sum of its parts. It responds to a variety of policy objectives, including state-building, security sector reform, crisis management, counter-terrorism and law enforcement. This chapter has also highlighted a number of trends that underpin the EU's border management repertoire: the importance of technology and research and the impact it has on the policy-making process, the increasing role of new policy and issue networks including private companies and civil liberty organisations, and consequently the redefinition of the whole border management profession. A more extensive investigation of these trends is definitely due.

By describing this policy area as 'the fog of border', we have brought to bear the need of the continuous figuring-out by the participants of where their interests lie and how to go about securing them under the condition of a limited grasp of the evolving situation. A glimpse through this fog reveals a technology-driven and highly business-like policy area with a dominant managerial mindset, preoccupied with risk analysis, cost-efficiency and the needs of end-users. The vast number of issues involved, of which we have discussed only some, coupled with the multiplicity of public, private and institutional actors with diverse agendas has exposed a discursive struggle, a process we refer to as 'the politics of security policies', pervaded by contested ideas about the meaning of border, its security, and the appropriate tools for providing it. While strategic inter-action with actors in the pursuit of their interests constitutes the frame-work of action, we conclude that the outcomes are far from being strategically laid out and pursued. This is because of the many necessarily poorly coordinated players in the field, but also the external inspiration of the policies and the 'fog' of the social game where no one has complete knowledge of and full control over the design and implementation of any project.

Notes

1 State-building can be defined as the externally assisted construction and recon-struction of the institutional infrastructure. While there are highly invasive forms of external regulation, such activities are regarded as a legitimate way of assisting disadvantaged communities if they are sought or requested. For the discussion of the EU's policies of state-building as a crisis management; in other words, crisis prevention – strategy; see also Kurowska and Seitz 2011.

2 In this context, the most extensively researched illustration of this phenome-non is private security and the role of non-state activists (e.g. Abrahamsen and Williams 2010; Keck and Sikkink 1998. The practices of modern research con-sortia and consultancy and their influence on state practices await scholarly attention.

3 The proposal for a Council Framework Decision on the exchange of informa-tion under the principle of availability submitted in 2005 has not been imple-mented, but has provided a basis for two other initiatives: in June 2004 Sweden proposed a Framework Decision on simplifying the exchange of information and intelligence between the law enforcement authorities of the Member States of the EU and in May 2005 seven EU Member States signed the Prüm Conven-tion aiming to enhance cross-border cooperation, particularly in combating terrorism, cross-border crime and illegal migration.

4 For instance, the EDPS argues in one of his opinions that one of the main objectives of EUROSUR (assistance in identifying illegal immigrants coming to the EU by sea) cannot be realised if these persons have not been to the EU before and such information can be provided through Eurodac, SIS or VIS. See European Data Protection Supervisor 2008.

5 The projects that got funding for border security-related research include: TALOS (land border), WIMAAS (sea border), AMASS (sea border), OPERA-MAR (sea border), GLOBE (land border), EFFISEC (land border), SeaBILLA (sea border), I2C (sea border), OPARUS (land border), ARGUS 3D (air border) and PERSEUS. The fourth call for €230 million was published in July 2010 with a focus on research and development related to border control at check points.

6 See www.talos-border.eu.

7 See www.gmes.info.

8 It combines walk criterion (classification of terrain according to the easiness of walking) and hide criterion (classification of terrain according to the easiness of hiding).

9 For more information about the programme, see www.ec.europa.eu/enlarge-ment/how-does-it-work/financial-assistance/cards/index_en.htm. For the updated concept of integrated border management, see Guidelines for Integrated Border

Management in the Western Balkans 2007, see www.ec.europa.eu/enlargement/pdf/financial_assistance/cards/publications/ibm_guidelines_en.pdf (accessed 22 February 2011).

10 For an illustration of the approach based on instilling EU values during daily operational cooperation, see, for example, an interview with Ilkka Laitinen, Executive Director of Frontex, conducted by Eurasylum, www.eurasylum.org/Portal/DesktopDefault.aspx?tabindex=2&tabid=19 (accessed 22 February 2011).

11 So far, the EU has signed readmission agreements with 12 countries: Albania, Bosnia and Herzegovina, the former Yugoslav Republic of Macedonia (FYROM), the Republic of Moldova, Montenegro, Russia, Serbia, Ukraine, Pakistan, Hong-Kong, Macao and Sri Lanka. Negotiations are ongoing with Cape Verde and Morocco. Currently, the negotiations with Turkey had also been finalised, see Council of the European Union 2011.

12 Directive 2008/115/EC of the European Parliament and Council of 16 December 2008 on common standards and procedures in Member States for returning illegally staying third-country nationals.

13 Notably the UNHCR, the European Council on Refugees and Exiles (ECRE) and human rights advocacy non-governmental organisations.

14 The irreconcilable entrenchment of this clash came to the fore again in 2011 when Italy and Malta resisted the attempts of other EU Member States to impose sanctions on the crumbling Kadhafi regime as it continued the crackdown on anti-regime demonstrations. The argument remained that Kadhafi would open the Libyan borders in retaliation, see www.eubusiness.com/news-eu/libya-politics.8q6/.

15 European Parliament Resolution on Lampedusa, 14 April 2005, available at www.europarl.europa.eu/sides/getDoc.do;jsessionid=8B5BEAAD5A39468ECA77F272A4E6D528.node2?pubRef=-//EP//TEXT+TA+P6-TA-2005-0138+0+DOC+XML+V0//EN.

16 Since late 2007, the European Commission has been invited by the European Council to launch pilot mobility partnerships with a few countries. In June 2008, Cape Verde and Moldova signed partnerships with the EU, Georgia in November 2009, whereas currently Senegal is still negotiating an agreement.

17 EUJUST LEX in Kosovo aims to assist and support the authorities in Kosovo with regard to the rule of law, specifically in the police, judiciary and customs areas, see www.consilium.europa.eu/showPage.aspx?id=1458&lang=en.

18 See Government of the Republic of Moldova Decision No. 1212 from 27.12.2010 on the approval of the National Strategy on Integrated State Border Management for the period 2011–2013, unofficial translation.

19 On Frontex, see Neal (2009), Pollak and Slominski (2009), Léonard (2010) and the chapter in this book by Léonard.

20 See www.frontex.europa.eu/structure/training.

21 See www.frontex.europa.eu/newsroom/news_releases/art40.html.

9 The role of Frontex in European homeland security

Sarah Léonard

As popular unrest spread across the Middle East in 2011 and caused several dictatorial regimes to fall, one of the main concerns of some European governments was that large numbers of asylum-seekers and migrants might try to reach Europe as a result of these momentous events. Following the arrival of about 3,000 irregular migrants and asylum-seekers on the Italian coast in the space of a few days in February 2011, most of whom were from Tunisia, the Italian government requested support from the European Union (EU) to deal with what it saw as an emergency situation. EU support mainly took the form of a joint patrolling operation in the central Mediterranean area, called 'Joint Operation Hermes 2011', which was designed to enhance border surveillance. Led by Italy, it also benefited from staff and equipment contributions from several other EU Member States and was coordinated by Frontex, the EU Agency that supports the coordination of operational cooperation among Member States in the field of border security (Frontex 2011). A few months earlier, Frontex had already hit the headlines when it deployed Rapid Border Intervention Teams (RABITs) in November 2010 in Greece to deal with the arrival of large numbers of asylum-seekers and migrants in the region of Evros at the Greek–Turkish border. Those teams comprised border guards from the 26 other EU Member States and Schengen-associated countries, who aimed to assist their Greek colleagues in various border control-related issues, such as the detection of illegal entries and the interviewing of intercepted migrants and asylum-seekers (Frontex 2010b).

Thus, Frontex, which only started its operations in 2005, has already managed to craft an important role for itself as the EU agency that supports operational cooperation among EU Member States in external border controls. It is important to emphasise that this role has not always been uncontroversial (Léonard 2010). Demonstrations have taken place not only in front of the seat of the Agency in Warsaw, but also in other towns and cities where Frontex training sessions took place, such as in Lübeck in August 2008.[1] Various non-governmental organisations (NGOs) have criticised the activities of Frontex for breaching, in their opinion, the rights of the migrants and asylum-seekers concerned (PRO ASYL 2008;

Amnesty International and European Council on Refugees and Exiles 2010). Given these controversies, it is therefore intriguing that there has been only a limited amount of scholarly work on this EU agency to date. Most of these research papers and journal articles have focused on the activities of Frontex. Focusing on the issue of border management in the EU, Jorry (2007) has examined the extent to which Frontex is likely to contribute to the implementation of the concept of 'integrated border management' (IBM) and can be seen as a major step towards the development of an EU common policy on external borders. Carrera (2007) has also analysed the role played by Frontex in the implementation of the EU Border Management Strategy, with a specific focus on the joint operations coordinated by the agency in the Canary Islands. Pollak and Slominski (2009) have analysed the activities of Frontex through the lens of an experimentalist governance approach in order to question the extent to which Frontex has acquired organisational autonomy and has been accountable. In addition, Neal (2009) has examined the origins of Frontex from a security studies angle, focusing in particular on whether the establishment of Frontex resulted from attempts to securitize asylum and migration in the EU, while Léonard (2010) has examined the ways in which Frontex has contributed to the securitization of migration in the EU through the deployment of various practices.

In contrast with this focus on the activities of Frontex and their consequences, relatively little consideration has been given to institutional issues, and in particular the question of why it was decided to establish an agency to deal with the coordination of EU Member States' activities in the field of external border controls. Indeed, it would have been possible to increase cooperation on external border controls without necessarily establishing a new, separate body for that purpose; for example, through the development of new working groups in the Council. As shown by other contributions in this book, the development of EU cooperation to tackle a specific security issue does not always entail the establishment of an independent agency, as demonstrated by the examples of counter-terrorism and emergency and crisis management.

It is therefore intriguing that it was decided to establish an agency in the case of external borders, whereas this was not the case for other homeland security issues. For this reason, this chapter examines why EU Member States decided to create Frontex in order to support increased cooperation in the field of migration controls by drawing upon the vast literature on EU agencies. It is structured into three main sections. First, it examines the rationales for setting up EU agencies in general. Second, drawing upon these insights, it analyses the policy debates leading to the choice of an 'agency' institutional set-up and the creation of Frontex. In the next section, which also builds on the existing scholarship on agencies in the EU, the chapter analyses the various control mechanisms over Frontex that have been established, before drawing some conclusions.

Explaining the choice of an 'agency' institutional model

In the area of external borders management, the main aim of the EU is to develop an integrated management of the borders, with a view to ensuring a high and uniform level of control of persons and surveillance at the external borders. More precisely, within Title IV of the Treaty establishing the European Community (TEC), as it was before the entry into force of the Lisbon Treaty in 2009, Article 62(2)(a) foresaw the adoption by the European Council of measures establishing 'standards and procedures to be followed by Member States in carrying out checks on persons at such borders', whereas Article 66 concerned the adoption of measures by the Council to ensure cooperation among Member States, as well as between Member States and the Commission, in the policy areas covered by Title IV. As explained by Pawlak and Kurowska in the previous chapter, 'IBM' covers all the activities of the public authorities of the Member States relating to border control and surveillance, including border checks, the analysis of risks at the borders and the planning of the personnel and facilities required.[2]

Among various models for developing such cooperation on external borders management, Member States chose to establish a European agency. According to Majone (2006: 191), 'agency' is 'an omnibus label to describe a variety of organisations which perform functions of a governmental nature, and which generally exist outside of the normal departmental framework of government'. They are specialised bodies staffed with experts, which generally deal with matters of a scientific or technical nature (Mair 2005). Within the EU, an increasing number of agencies have been created over the last few decades, in three agency-creation waves in the 1970s, 1990s and 2000s, respectively (Majone 2006: 191). Interestingly, the EU does not have a formal definition of agencies. A first basic distinction used to be made between Community agencies on the one hand and second- and third-pillar agencies, which operate under the authority of the Council, on the other hand (Groenleer 2006: 161). According to the website of the EU, a 'Community agency is a body governed by European public law; it is distinct from the Community institutions (Council, Parliament, Commission, etc.) and has its own legal personality' (European Union n.d.). In addition, within the category of Community agencies, one can distinguish between regulatory agencies and executive agencies. The former perform a variety of roles, set out in their own legal basis, whereas the latter execute more narrowly defined tasks supporting the management of Community programmes (European Commission 2008e). Following this typology, Frontex can be identified as a Community agency of the 'regulatory' type.[3]

Rationales for setting up agencies

The setting-up of agencies is often understood with reference to the classic 'principal-agent model', which was initially developed in the United States (US) to account for the delegation of executive functions to federal agencies (Magnette 2005: 5). In such a framework, the 'principals' are understood as 'those institutions [...] that use their authority to establish non-majoritarian institutions through a public act of delegation', whereas 'agents' 'are those who govern by exercising delegated powers' (Curtin 2005: 92).

The rationales for delegation, or, in other words, the creation of agencies, have received much attention in the academic literature. In general, scholars have identified six main reasons for which delegating some functions to a given agency may be seen as advantageous by policy-makers. First, agencies are seen as being able to provide policy expertise to policy-makers, as they are staffed with professionals characterised by a high level of expertise (Everson 1995). Second, it is considered that agencies contribute to enhancing the efficiency of decision-making, as they deal with technical and scientific matters, thereby allowing principals to focus on less technical tasks (Everson 1995; Groenleer 2006; Magnette 2005: 9). Third, agencies, which are insulated from political pressures, are seen as being more capable of pursuing long-term policy objectives than governments, which generally feel the need to be more responsive to political pressures and public opinion (Majone 2006: 193). This claim is based on the following assumptions. First, policy continuity is necessary to ensure policy credibility. Second, policy continuity is best ensured by the delegation of powers to agencies, as those are best able to preserve policy continuity despite possible changes in parliamentary majorities. Third, agencies are often presented as giving more visibility to EU policies (Dehousse 2008), especially compared to other institutional arrangements such as the comitology system, thereby increasing their legitimacy and that of the EU in general. In that respect, delegation to agencies often has a strong element of symbolism (Wilks 2002: 148). Fourth, it is considered that agencies can foster cooperation among Member States through information-sharing and coordination activities (Magnette 2005: 9). Finally, agencies are generally seen as being able to ensure a greater involvement of stakeholders; for example, from the industry or consumer groups, in the EU policy-making process. This involvement can take the form of representation in the Management Board of agencies.

However, several scholars have emphasised that these rationales, although they evidently play an important role in political debates, are not able to fully account for the creation of agencies. The delegation process in the EU is not as neat and simple as suggested by the classic 'principal-agent' model. Dehousse (2008) argues that it is important to recognise that in the EU there are multiple principals, rather than one single clearly defined principal, and that each of them has its own interests. As a result, the analysis of the process of agency creation needs to take into account the political struggles among policy-makers in order to fully account for the delegation of functions in the EU. Evidence for this claim is provided by the case of the six new European agencies created between 1990 and 1994 (Kelemen 2002; Groenleer 2006). On the one hand, the completion of the single market project had increased the workload of the European Commission to the point of overstretch. This required additional financial and staff resources. On the other hand, an increase in the size of the Commission was not an option favoured by all Member States in the European Council. The compromise between these two positions was the creation of agencies to which tasks could be delegated. The Commission itself played an important role in this delegation process, as it proposed the establishment of these agencies and had a significant influence on their functions, powers and structure (Dehousse 2008: 793). The creation of the agencies allowed the regulatory capacity of the EU to increase in a manner more acceptable to the Council than a direct expansion of the Commission would have been. Such a solution did not play into the hands of the Eurosceptics bemoaning the ever-increasing 'Eurocracy' in Brussels (Kelemen 2002: 100). Moreover, this institutional design was approved by Member States since it ensured their representation in the Management Board of each of these agencies (Groenleer 2006: 164).

Although it is important to recognise the *sui generis* character of each case of agency creation in the EU, it is also possible to make some general observations concerning the role of each institution of the so-called 'institutional triangle' (European Commission, Council of the EU and European Parliament) in the delegation process based on past examples. First of all, Member States in the Council can block the creation of European agencies, as has been the case with the plans for a European telecom agency (Kelemen 2002: 110). Unsurprisingly, it appears that they do not favour the delegation of tasks to European agencies that would question the very existence of national bureaucracies in a given policy area. In cases where they are willing to delegate some tasks, then they are likely to privilege the setting up of a relatively weak agency, which they can control through its Management Board and which is limited to the coordination of the activities of national bureaucracies in a specific policy area (Magnette 2005). As far as the Commission is concerned, it is likely to resist the delegation of tasks to an agency in policy areas where it has acquired large competences. Given its key role as agenda-setter and legislation initiator, the Commission occupies a strong position in the agency-creation process. This has been evidenced by its refusal to submit a proposal for an independent European Cartel Office, which would diminish its powers in the competition policy field (Kelemen 2002: 111). Finally, the European Parliament, which is generally involved in the creation of first-pillar agencies through the co-decision procedure,[4] tends to emphasise issues such as transparency and accountability in the institutional design of agencies. Having examined the various rationales for setting up agencies, as well as the general positions of the main EU institutions regarding the establishment of agencies, it is now possible to analyse the process leading to the creation of Frontex.

The creation of Frontex

The establishment of Frontex came as a response to the perceived need for an increase in cooperation among EU Member States with regard to external border controls. This was prompted by three main factors. First, migration has generally become an increasingly contentious issue in Europe since the 1990s, which has led European states to examine ways of reinforcing border controls to restrict the access of migrants and asylum-seekers to their territory (Collinson 1993; Joly 1996; Bigo 1998; Uçarer 2001; Guild 2003, 2004; Huysmans 2006; Baldaccini and Guild 2007; Chebel d'Appollonia and Reich 2008). Second, as the date of the enlargement of the EU to ten new Member States in 2004 drew closer, there were specific concerns that these new Member States would not be able to control the new external borders of the EU effectively. There were increasing calls for strengthening cooperation among EU Member States on border controls as a way to alleviate the lack of border control capabilities of the future EU Member States and their difficulties to meet the Schengen/EU border control standards (Monar 2006c: 75). In addition, the terrorist attacks on 11 September 2001 led to the identification of a wide range of measures aiming to reinforce homeland security, including the tightening-up of external border controls (Monar 2005: 147; Mitsilegas 2007: 362). This was particularly visible in the Hague Programme adopted in 2004:

> The management of migration flows [...] should be strengthened by establishing a continuum of security measures that effectively links visa application procedures and entry and exit procedures at external border crossings. Such measures are also of importance for the prevention and control of crime, in particular terrorism.
>
> (European Council 2004a: 18)

These three factors explain the identification of the need for increased cooperation on external border controls among EU Member States. However, such cooperation could have taken other institutional forms than that of an agency. How and why, then, was it decided to create an agency? Answering this question requires the examination of the political debates and the policy process that led to the creation of Frontex.

An ambitious vision: the concept of a 'European Corps of Border Guards'

Initially, cooperation on external border controls among EU Member States developed outside the EU framework, within the Schengen Group following the signing of the Schengen Agreement of 14 June 1985 (Monar 2006c: 74–75). The Schengen *acquis* was integrated into the EU legal framework by the Amsterdam Treaty, which came into force in 1999 (Peers and Rogers 2006: 169; Kaunert 2005). Article 62(2)(a), within Title IV of the TEC, which governs visas, asylum, immigration and other policies related to free movement of persons, gave the European Community the power to adopt measures concerning the 'standards and procedures to be followed by Member States in carrying out checks on persons' at the external borders. It is important to emphasise that this article, like others in Title IV, was characterised by peculiar rules of decision-making. Indeed, the communitarisation of asylum and migration matters had only been partial, as a transition period of five years was in place until 1 May 2004. During that time, the Commission and the Member States were sharing the right of initiative. In addition, decisions had to be taken unanimously in the Council, whereas the European Parliament was only consulted on legislative proposals, rather than being fully involved in the policy-making process through the co-decision procedure (Kaunert 2005; Peers 2006).

During the early part of 2001, Germany and Italy presented a joint initiative aiming to establish a 'European Border Police' to the European Council. This was followed by the launch of a feasibility study regarding the creation of a European Border Guard, organised by a group led by Italy and comprising, in addition to this country, Belgium, France, Germany and Spain. These countries were in favour of setting up such a body in order to share the burden of external border controls and increase the efficiency of such controls, notably through the development of technical expertise on the matter. This initiative received financial support from the European Commission based on the Odysseus programme (Monar 2005: 147). However, it is important to note that some Member States were not enthusiastic about this idea. In particular, the British government favoured increased cooperation on external border controls, but was reluctant to see any centralisation in that policy area. This lack of complete agreement among EU Member States was reflected in the carefully worded Conclusions of the Laeken European Council on 14–15 December 2001. The EU Heads of State and Government agreed on pursuing four objectives: (1) strengthening and standardising European border controls; (2) assisting candidate states in organising controls at Europe's future external borders, through the development of operational cooperation; (3) facilitating crisis management with regard to border control; and (4) preventing illegal immigration and other forms of cross-border crime. Nevertheless, their lack of agreement on the precise institutional form that their reinforced cooperation should take was evident in the vagueness of the call for the Council and the European Commission to elaborate 'arrangements for cooperation between services responsible for external border control and to examine the conditions in which a mechanism or common services to control external borders could be created' (Presidency of the Council of the European Union 2001: 12). Thus, terms such as 'European Border Guard' or 'European Border Police' were not mentioned in the official mandate, although they were used by the media and some governments.

The results of the Italy-led feasibility study were unveiled in May 2002. Those have often been criticised for their lack of precision and clarity, as the study failed to adopt a clear position regarding the establishment of a European Border Police. Actually, this degree of confusion only reflected the lack of consensus amongst the Member States involved in the study. The main idea put forward by this feasibility study was that the border guard authorities of the EU Member States should cooperate through a 'polycentric' network, which would be based on a common training curriculum, common risk assessment and various ad hoc centres specialising in different issues relating to border controls (Monar 2006c: 77). Following its Laeken mandate, the European Commission also tabled a Communication in May 2002 entitled 'Towards Integrated Management of the External Borders of the Member States of the European Union'. Based on an analysis of the challenges and the current situation with regard to the management of external borders, the Commission made several proposals to move towards a 'European Corps of Border Guards'. Those focused on 'five mutually interdependent components: (1) a common corpus of legislation; (2) a common coordination and operational cooperation mechanism; (3) common integrated risk analysis; (4) staff trained in the European dimension and inter-operational equipment; and (5) burden-sharing between Member States in the run-up to a European Corps of Border Guards' (European Commission 2002b: 12).

A first attempt at institutionalisation: the establishment of the External Borders Practitioners Common Unit

Acknowledging that a European Corps of Border Guards could not be established in the short term, the European Commission suggested that the 'common coordination and operational cooperation mechanism' could involve at first the establishment of an External Borders Practitioners Common Unit, as well as the gradual development of a 'permanent process of exchange and processing of data and information' between the authorities of the Member States. The Commission argued that this common unit 'should most probably develop from the Strategic Committee for Immigration, Frontiers and Asylum (SCIFA) working group meeting in its formation of those responsible for the Member States services ensuring controls at the external borders' (European Commission 2002b: 14). According to the European Commission, this common unit 'should play a full multidisciplinary and horizontal role' to gather managers and practitioners carrying out the full range of tasks concerning external borders security, that is, 'the police, judicial and customs authorities and EUROPOL' (European Commission 2002b: 14). It would play four main roles:

- acting as a 'head' of the common policy on management of external borders to carry out common integrated risk analysis;
- acting as 'leader' coordinating and controlling operational projects on the ground, in particular in crisis situations;
- acting as manager and strategist to ensure greater convergence between the national policies in the field of personnel and equipment;
- exercising a form of power of inspection, in particular in the event of crisis or if risk analysis demands it.

(European Commission 2002b: 14)

In addition, the Commission expressed the view that, in the long term, the national services of the Member States should be supported by a European Corps of Border Guards. The proposal of the Commission was generally well received as it contained at least some points with which each Member State could agree. Nevertheless, some still opposed the idea that increased cooperation efforts could ultimately lead to the establishment of a European Corps of Border Guards. This proposal was followed in June 2002 by a Council 'Action Plan for the Management of the External Borders of the Member States of the European Union' (Council of the European Union 2002a). This document emphasised the issue of operational cooperation and coordination and endorsed the establishment of a common unit in the framework of the SCIFA. The idea of establishing a 'European Corps of Border Guards' was also mentioned, but more cautiously than it had been in the Commission proposal. The Action Plan concluded that '[based] on the experiences of this gradual development, further institutional steps could be considered, if appropriate [...]. Such steps could include a possible decision on the setting up of a European Corps of Border Guards, composed of joint teams, which would have the function of supporting the national services of the Member States, but not replacing them' (Council of the European Union: p. 27). This was in line with the generally more pragmatic approach of the Council. A few days later, this Action Plan was endorsed by the Seville European Council, which took place in an atmosphere of intense politicisation of asylum and migration matters (Ludlow 2002). The Heads of State and Government 'applauded' the approval of the Action Plan and 'urged the introduction without delay' of the External Borders Practitioners Common Unit within the framework of the Council (European Council 2002: 9).

The Common Unit was subsequently created under SCIFA+ (i.e. SCIFA and the heads of national border guards) and took the lead in coordinating various operations and pilot projects relating to border controls from 2002 onwards (Mitsilegas 2007: 365). Those aimed to improve operational standards and coordination. Among them, one can mention the 'International Airports Plan' led by Italy, and joint operations at the maritime borders such as 'Operation Ulysses' under Spanish leadership and 'Operation Triton' led by Greece. Ad hoc centres were also created, including the Centre for Land Borders (Germany), the Risk Analysis Centre (Finland) and the Centre of Excellence at Dover for developing new surveillance and border control technologies (UK) (Council of the European Union 2003a).

The limits of pragmatism: challenges to the External Borders Practitioners Common Unit

Soon after their establishment, the effectiveness of the SCIFA+ arrangements began to be challenged by both the European Commission and some EU Member States. The European Commission argued that experience had shown the structural limits of the SCIFA+ institutional arrangements. In its 'Communication on the Development of a Common Policy on Illegal Immigration, Smuggling and Trafficking of Human Beings, External Borders and the Return of Illegal Residents' tabled on 3 June 2003, the Commission called for the establishment of a body which could pursue border management activities on a more systematic and permanent basis (European Commission 2003a). It suggested leaving strategic coordination issues with the Common Unit, while entrusting operational tasks to a new permanent Community structure, which would be in charge of the daily management and coordination tasks in the area of external border controls. On the same day, the Presidency of the Council released a 'Report on the Implementation of Programmes, Ad hoc Centres, Pilot Projects and Joint Operations', which also highlighted several problems stemming from the institutional arrangements under SCIFA+. The report argued that the various activities approved by SCIFA+ had been hampered by serious deficiencies concerning planning, preparation, evaluation, operational coordination, the treatment of difficulties arising during the implementation of projects and the commitment of the participating countries (Council of the European Union 2003a). In addition, the Presidency report emphasised the lack of a suitable legal basis for conducting common operations and establishing ad hoc centres of cooperation (Council of the European Union 2003a: 8, 33). These various activities were indeed, from a legal point of view, the products of intergovernmental cooperation. The TEC had not given the Council 'the competence to engage in such coordinating activities, but merely [...] the power to adopt legislation for that purpose' (Rijpma 2009: 9).

In response to the Commission Communication and the Presidency report, the Council adopted its 'Conclusions on Effective Management of the External Borders of the EU Member States' on 5 June 2003 (Council of the European Union 2003c). They notably called for the Practitioners Common Unit (PCU) to develop operational cooperation distinctly from SCIFA+, after being reinforced as a Council Working Party by experts seconded from the Member States. These Council Conclusions were in turn endorsed by the Thessaloniki European Council on 19–20 June 2003, which asked the Commission 'to examine in due course [...] the necessity of creating new institutional mechanisms, including the possible creation of a Community operational structure' in order to enhance operational cooperation in the management of EU external borders (European Council 2003a: 4).

A new attempt at institutionalisation: towards the establishment of an agency

The European Commission, which had showed its preference for such a Community structure in the previous years, rapidly seized this opportunity. It responded to this request by tabling a proposal for a Council Regulation establishing a European Agency for the Management of Operational Cooperation at the External Borders in November 2003 (European Commission 2003b). The main objective of this Agency, according to the proposal of the European Commission, was to better coordinate operational cooperation among Member States in order to increase the effectiveness of the implementation of Community policy on the management of the external borders. The Commission justified the choice of establishing an agency by highlighting 'the clear need for creating an independent, specialised Community operational structure' (European Commission 2003b: 7). It further argued that

> the Agency will be in a better position than even the Commission itself to accumulate the highly technical know-how on control and surveillance of the external borders that will be necessary [...]. Moreover, the establishment of an Agency is expected to lead to increased visibility for the management of external borders in the public and cost-savings with regard to the operational cooperation [...].
>
> (European Commission 2003b: 7)

The Commission argued that the Agency should have the following functions: (1) coordinating the operational cooperation between Member States on control and surveillance of the external borders; (2) assisting Member States in training national border guards; (3) conducting risk assessments; (4) following up on the development of research concerning external borders control and surveillance; (5) assisting Member States in circumstances requiring increased assistance at the external borders; and (6) coordinating operational cooperation between Member States on the removal of illegal third country residents (European Commission 2003b: 19).

The European Council rapidly reached a political agreement on the Draft Regulation, despite the requirement for unanimity. It agreed with the tasks allocated to Frontex by the European Commission. However, and this was the main point of contention between the Commission and the Council, it disagreed with the composition of the Management Board of the Agency (Council of the European Union 2003b), which led to an amendment of this provision in the final text of the Regulation, as will be later explained. Involved in the decision-making process only through the consultation procedure, the European Parliament proposed several amendments aiming to strengthen the 'communitarian' dimension of Frontex, as will be shown below, but those were ignored by the Council.

Two looming deadlines arguably facilitated and accelerated the attainment of an agreement among Member States. First of all, the 'big bang' enlargement of the EU was due to take place on 1 May 2004. This event had generated fears of uncontrolled migration flows from the East, notably in the media (Lavenex 1999). There was therefore some public pressure on EU Member States to demonstrate that they were taking measures to strengthen controls at the external borders of the EU and to support the future Member States in developing their border control regimes. The second factor that facilitated the swift conclusion of the negotiations in the European Council was of an institutional nature, as it concerned the move to co-decision on external borders matters. As explained earlier, with regard to measures concerning the crossing of external borders (among others), Article 67 TEC provided for a transitional period of five years, during which exceptional decision-making rules applied. While the European Commission shared the right of initiative with the Member States, the European Parliament was only consulted on the legislative proposals. In addition, the Council had to take decisions according to the unanimity rule. On the basis of Article 68(2) TEC, the Council decided that measures concerning the crossing of the external borders of the Member States should be adopted according to the co-decision procedure as of 1 January 2005. This meant that the Commission proposal had to be swiftly adopted if the Council wanted to avoid the active involvement of the European Parliament in the adoption of the Regulation, which would have been allowed by the application of the co-decision procedure. At the time of the discussions of the draft Regulation, the European Parliament was only associated with the decision-making procedure through the consultation procedure, which meant that its opinion could be ignored.

Thus, it is evident that the establishment of an agency in order to increase operational cooperation on external border management was only one option among several possible options. Various models for increased cooperation were considered and explored by the European Commission and the Member States. Following initial discussions that largely focused on the ambitious and rather vague – and also unacceptable for some – idea of a 'European Border Police' (or 'European Border Guard'), a pragmatic and more modest solution was adopted, in the form of the External Borders Practitioners Common Unit. However, such an institutional arrangement rapidly gave rise to criticisms. This led to a proposal by the European Commission for the establishment of a European agency, citing some of the classic justifications for agency creation. In particular, it emphasised the policy expertise and technical know-how that such an agency would be able to develop. It also argued that the establishment of Frontex would increase the visibility of EU action in the field of border controls, which was significant given the importance of migration issues on the political agenda of many European governments. These arguments convinced the Member States that an agency should be created to deal with operational cooperation in external border controls. In the Conclusions on the main elements of the Commission proposal on the establishment of Frontex, the Council noted that 'the creation of an Agency is the most appropriate way to organise and develop the indispensable coordination of operational cooperation at the external borders' (Council of the European Union 2003b: 3).

Although Frontex does not embody the same high degree of cooperation on external border controls than a European Corps of Border Guards, it is nevertheless remarkable to observe such a significant development of operational cooperation in that homeland security sector over a short period of time. As some states were initially reluctant to go beyond merely intergovernmental cooperation on external border controls, it was initially attempted to enhance cooperation through the work of SCIFA+. However, it was rapidly claimed by several actors, including the European Commission and the Greek Presidency, that this institutional model hampered successful cooperation among EU Member States and that it was necessary to adopt a more centralised model of governance through the creation of a Community structure. The European Commission then proposed the establishment of an agency to fulfil these tasks.

Thus, as observed by Dehousse, one should not underestimate the role played by the European Commission in the establishment of (now former) pillar I agencies such as Frontex (Dehousse 2008: 793). In line with the literature on European agencies, it appears that the Commission was not reluctant to propose the establishment of an agency which would be given tasks that were until then generally fulfilled by Member States, rather than by the Commission itself. Also in line with the literature, the analysis has demonstrated that Member States were able to agree relatively swiftly on the creation of an agency that they would be able to control through its Management Board and other mechanisms (see below) and which would be limited to the coordination of operational cooperation at the external borders. In that respect, many documents on Frontex emphasise that 'the responsibility for the control and surveillance of external borders lies with the Member States' and that the role of the agency is strictly limited to the coordination of Member States' actions. Finally, it is important to note that Member States' positions were particularly unchallenged in the negotiations regarding Frontex, as the European Parliament was only consulted on the draft Council Regulation. The lack of involvement of the European Parliament also meant that issues such as transparency and accountability received relatively less attention in the debates leading to the adoption of the Council Regulation.

The controls over Frontex

Having examined why EU Member States decided to establish an agency to increase cooperation in external border management and which tasks they decided to give to this agency, it is now necessary to examine another important issue in any case of agency creation; that is, the controls exercised over the agency activities. Indeed, as argued by Tallberg, '[every] decision to delegate essentially involves two choices – what powers to delegate and what institutional control mechanisms to craft' (Tallberg 2002: 28).

Such control tools (Everson *et al.* 1999: 13) are seen as necessary by principals, because it is generally considered that agents are likely to develop their own interests over time and may attempt to pursue their own policy (Magnette 2005: 11). This phenomenon is commonly referred to as 'drift'. According to Kelemen (2002), one can distinguish between 'bureaucratic drifts' and 'political drifts'. The former refer to cases where an agency develops a political agenda differing from that of its political principals, whereas the latter concern cases where 'future holders of public authority direct a bureaucratic agency to pursue objectives different from those of the political coalition that originally delegated authority to the agency' (Kelemen 2002: 96). In that respect, Dehousse (2008: 796) argues that principals mainly fear a specific variant of political drift, that 'in which agencies are somewhat "captured" by one of their institutional rivals in the leadership contest'. As a consequence, principals aim to design control mechanisms that will minimise the risk of bureaucratic and political drifts in the future.

This article is based on a broad definition of 'control', understood as encompassing *ex ante, simultaneous* and *ex post* control mechanisms (also referred to as 'accountability' mechanisms) (Busuioc 2009). Ex ante control mechanisms refer to decisions made during the negotiations leading to the creation of an agency, with regard to the boundaries of its competencies and activities. For an example, if an agency has only limited powers, such as gathering or exchanging information, or has a tightly specified mandate, then it will, by definition, be significantly controlled in its activities. These issues have already been discussed in the previous section analysing the debates on the creation of Frontex. The remainder of this section therefore focuses on the various simultaneous and ex post control mechanisms considered during the negotiations leading to the establishment of Frontex, such as work programmes and reports of activities, budgetary control, hearings, the role of the Management Board, reviews of activities and access to documents.

Management Board

One of the main mechanisms of control on the activities of an agency is the establishment of a Management Board. Frontex has such a Management Board, to which the Executive Director is accountable. The Management Board of Frontex is composed of one representative of each Member State and two representatives of the European Commission, who are 'appointed on the basis of their degree of high-level relevant experience and expertise in the field of operational cooperation on border management' (Council Regulation EC 2007/2004, Article 21). Each member of the Management Board has one vote, whereas the Executive Director has no vote, but can take part in the deliberations of the Board. Originally, the Commission had proposed that the Management Board be composed of 12 members and two representatives of the Commission. However, the Council considered that each Member State should have a representative in the Management Board of the agency (Council of the European Union 2003b: 5). In addition, during the consultation procedure, the European Parliament had proposed several amendments concerning the composition of the Management Board, but those were not taken into account by the Council. First of all, with regard to the composition of the Board, the European Parliament was of the opinion that the Council and the Commission should each appoint six members of the Board, bringing the total number of members to 12. This was an attempt to reinforce the role of the Commission in the Management Board, thereby strengthening the Community character of the Agency, but it was not accepted by the Council (European Parliament 2004: 18). The European Parliament had also suggested that the Management Board be chaired by a representative of the European Commission, but again, this amendment was rejected by the Council.

The Management Board of Frontex fulfils several functions (Council Regulation EC 2007/2004, Article 20), the first of which is to appoint the Executive Director of the Agency on the basis of a proposal from the European Commission. In addition, the Management Board exercises disciplinary authority over the Executive Director. Moreover, it is responsible for adopting the general report of Frontex activities from the previous year, as well as the work programme of Frontex for the coming year after receiving the opinion of the Commission. The European Parliament would have preferred some of these tasks to be entrusted to the European Commission. During the consultation procedure, it had suggested that the Commission itself should appoint the Executive Director of the Management Board and should have the power to dismiss them, but this amendment was not taken into account by the Council (European Parliament 2004: 20).

Thus, the Management Board has been tasked with several important functions regarding the control of the activities of Frontex. Given that it has a strong intergovernmental character, this means that control of the work of the agency is to a large extent in the hands of the Member States, which have been considered the main stakeholders. It appears that, to date, they have generally been satisfied with the ways in which the Management Board has operated as a control mechanism of the activities of Frontex (UK House of Lords 2008a). However, this has not been the opinion of pro-migrant and pro-human rights groups, which, in contrast, have expressed a certain level of dissatisfaction with the use of a Management Board as an accountability mechanism. According to the British Immigration Law Practitioners' Association (ILPA), '[a] Management Board is a weak method of scrutiny and for accountability at the best of times, but is particularly weak in the context of Frontex' (UK House of Lords 2008a: 109). The ILPA has also criticised the fact that the Management Board only comprises representatives of the EU Member States and the European Commission.

Work programmes and reports of activities

Another common way of controlling agencies is to require them to produce work programmes and reports of activities. In that respect, the Executive Director of Frontex is responsible for preparing, every year, the draft programme and the activity report, which will then be submitted to the Management Board (Council Regulation EC 2007/2004, Article 25). The Management Board is responsible for their adoption (Council Regulation EC 2007/2004, Article 20). Both reports are subsequently forwarded to the European Parliament, the Council and the Commission, as well as to the European Economic and Social Committee and the Court of Auditors in the case of the activity report only (Council Regulation EC 2007/2004, Article 20). The European Parliament wanted this control mechanism to be reinforced by suggesting, during the consultation procedure, that the annual report on the Agency's activities should also be presented by the Executive Director to the European Parliament (European Parliament 2004: 22). However, this amendment was not included in the final text of the Regulation.

Budgetary control

One of the most powerful ways of controlling an agency is to adopt measures relative to its budget. For the European Parliament, which was sidelined during the negotiations of the Draft Regulation establishing Frontex
and whose amendments to the legislative text were ignored, budgetary
control is the main instrument at its disposal to exercise some control over
Frontex activities. According to Article 29 of the European Council Regulation establishing Frontex, the budget of the agency has four different
strands: (1) a Community subsidy, (2) a contribution from the countries
associated with the implementation, application and development of the
Schengen *acquis*, (3) fees charged for the services provided, and (4) any
voluntary contribution from the Member States. When consulted on the
Commission proposal, the European Parliament had suggested adding a
fifth source of income, namely a contribution from the host Member State
(European Parliament 2004: 23), but this amendment was rejected by the
Council. In practice, the Community subsidy is by far the most important
income strand for Frontex, which gives the European Parliament a substantial amount of leverage on the agency. It made use of it in October
2007, for example, when the Budget Committee of the European Parlia-
ment voted in favour of an increase of €30 million for the 2008 budget of
Frontex, but at the same time voted to put in reserve up to 30 per cent of
the Agency's administrative budget (EPP-ED Group 2007; UK House of
Lords 2008a).[5] In addition to the control by the budgetary authority, the
Court of Auditors also gives its observations on the accounts of the Agency
(Council Regulation EC 2007/2004, Article 30).

Hearings

In general, the activities of agencies can also be controlled through hearings. On the basis of Article 25 of Council Regulation EC 2007/2004, both
the European Parliament and the Council 'may' invite the Executive
Director of Frontex to report on the activities of the Agency. During the
consultation procedure, the European Parliament had expressed the
opinion that this provision should be rephrased as to read 'The European
Parliament [...] or the Council *shall* invite the Executive Director of the
Agency to report on the carrying out of his/her tasks'. From the European
Parliament's point of view, this amendment aimed to convey the idea that
'Parliament should exercise political scrutiny as of right, and not simply as
an option' (European Parliament 2004: 20). This amendment did not find
its way into the final version of the Regulation. However, in practice, this
has not prevented the European Parliament from managing to convey the
importance, if not the necessity, of attending hearings to Frontex representatives, thanks to its budgetary powers.[6]

Reviews of activities

Another way of controlling agencies is to review their activities and make subsequent organisational changes. Article 33 of the European Council Regulation EC 2007/2004 stipulates that an independent external evaluation of Frontex is to be commissioned within three years from the date at which it took up its responsibilities, and every five years thereafter. This disposition is rather vague as to the exact content of this evaluation, as it merely indicates that the evaluation should examine the effectiveness of the Agency, its impact and its working practices, and that it should include the views of 'stakeholders at both the European and national level'. When consulted on the European Commission proposal, the European Parliament had expressed its preference for a closer control of the activities of the Agency, through the commissioning of the first independent external evaluation within two years of Frontex taking up its activities, and every two years thereafter. With regard to the content of the evaluation, the European Parliament had suggested that it should give particular attention to the following issues: the respect for fundamental rights, the need and feasibility of setting up a European Border Guard and the added value of the agency (European Parliament 2004: 24). The European Parliament had also suggested the insertion of an amendment to the effect that, like the Council, it would also receive the documents relating to the evaluation of the Agency. However, these proposals were not included in the final text of the Regulation. In practice, a first external evaluation of Frontex was conducted by COWI, which published its final report in January 2009 (COWI 2009).

Access to documents

Requiring agencies to give access to their documents is also another mechanism aiming to control their activities. Article 28 of Council Regulation EC 2007/2004 stipulates that Frontex is subject to Regulation EC 1049/2001, which concerns access to EU documents that have not been publicly released. During the consultation procedure, the European Parliament had asked for Regulation EC 45/2001 to apply to the processing of personal data by the Agency (European Parliament 2004: 23), but this amendment was not taken into account by the Council.

Thus, this section has demonstrated that several control mechanisms have been put in place to avoid any unwanted 'drifts' in the activities of Frontex. When it was consulted on the Commission proposal, the European Parliament put forward several amendments aiming to reinforce its own control powers and those of the European Commission over the agency. However, in a context where the European Parliament was weak because of the consultation procedure, they were not accepted by the Council and were not included in the Council Regulation in the end. As a result, the various mechanisms of control over Frontex are firmly in the hands of the main stakeholders (i.e. the Member States), with the important exception of budgetary control, where the European Parliament can play (and has already played) a crucial role.

Conclusion

Drawing upon insights from the literature on European agencies, this chapter has shed light on the role of Frontex in European homeland security by focusing on its institutional nature as an *agency*. It has analysed the process that led to the creation of Frontex, identifying and examining the various institutional configurations for increasing cooperation on external borders management that were considered and, in some cases, even implemented on a temporary basis. It has also discussed the various justifications given by the European Commission and the European Council for establishing Frontex, while showing how the creation of Frontex can also be understood as the product of power struggles within the EU. Finally, it has examined the various control mechanisms designed to avoid possible 'drifts' in the activities of the Agency.

In addition to shedding light on the origins of Frontex, this analysis has also strengthened our understanding of the activities of Frontex since it became operational. In particular, it has demonstrated the lack of influence of the European Parliament, whose proposed amendments – aiming to increase its control over the agency – were all rejected. This explains why the European Parliament has made a significant use of the budget control instrument to date, as it is the only significant control mechanism over Frontex that it has at its disposal. The isolation of the European Parliament – the traditional human rights champion in the EU – in the negotiations also contributes to explaining the relative low priority originally given to human rights issues in the activities of the Agency (see Léonard 2010). Following the adoption of a new Frontex Regulation at the end of September 2011, it remains to be seen how the balance between security and human rights will evolve in the activities of this new actor in European homeland security.

Notes

This contribution is based on an article previously published in the *Journal of Contemporary European Research* (volume 5, issue 3).

1 More detailed information on these events, including pictures, is available at www.Frontexplode.eu/action/ (accessed on 1 June 2010).
2 This concept has influenced the development of the Area of Freedom, Security and Justice (AFSJ) since the adoption of the Tampere Programme in 1999 and was precisely defined by the European Council in 2006. The Council Conclusions on Integrated Border Management outlined the five main dimensions of

IBM: (1) border control, which includes border checks, border surveillance and relevant risk analysis and crime intelligence; (2) the detection and investigation of cross-border crime; (3) the 'four-tier access control mode' (which includes activities in third countries, cooperation with neighbouring third countries, controls at the external border sites, and inland border control activities inside the Schengen area); (4) inter-agency cooperation for border management and international cooperation; and (5) coordination and coherence of the activities of the Member States and institutions, as well as other bodies of the European Community and the EU.

3 This is the typology recently proposed by the European Commission in its Communication 'European Agencies – The Way Forward' of March 2008. Other typologies have been suggested, but discussing those is beyond the scope of this chapter.

4 It is important to note that, in the case of Frontex, the European Parliament was not involved in the creation of the agency through the co-decision procedure, but only through the consultation procedure.

5 This decision was justified at the time on the grounds that the agency had to improve both its accountability and its effectiveness.

6 According to the Members of the European Parliament (MEPs) Moreno Sanchez and Deprez, '[at] the beginning [Frontex] did not come [to the European Parliament], but now they do [...] because they understand that they have to present their programme to the committee in the Parliament' (UK House of Lords 2008a: 28).

10 Conclusion

European homeland security after Lisbon and Stockholm

Christian Kaunert, Sarah Léonard and
Patryk Pawlak

This book has highlighted an interesting paradox. On the one hand, 'homeland security' is a term conspicuous by its absence in European political debates. It remains controversial given its association with some of the actions taken by the United States (US) administration in the wake of 9/11. On the other hand, there have been significant policy developments in the European Union (EU) in recent years that suggest the influence of homeland security ideas, notably through policy transfer from the US to the EU, despite the fact that this label has not been explicitly used. Thus, although 'homeland security' is not part of the EU's security rhetoric, it is appropriate for researchers to use this concept to analyse various developments in EU security in recent years. This book has also argued that using such a concept is actually beneficial. It has the advantage of highlighting certain trends, which may not be identified otherwise, for example, if one continues to draw upon the more traditional dichotomy – in the EU context – of 'internal security' versus 'external security' or the distinction between the Common Foreign and Security Policy (CFSP) on the one hand and Justice and Home Affairs (JHA) on the other hand. Finally, this book has shown that, although homeland security ideas have implicitly underpinned EU policy developments to a significant extent in recent years, this has not led to the adoption of any overarching strategy for European homeland security, not even under a different label. As also demonstrated by Schroeder in Chapter 3, European homeland security has seen a plethora of policy initiatives, which have led to the adoption of partially overlapping strategies, including the European Security Strategy (ESS) and the Internal Security Strategy (ISS).

The gradual development of European homeland security

This book has documented the absence of explicit efforts to mobilise European societies towards the protection of a 'homeland'. However, another concept has become increasingly important in European debates, namely the 'Area of Freedom, Security and Justice' (AFSJ). Article 3 of the Treaty on European Union (TEU) states that '[the] Union shall offer its citizens an area of freedom, security and justice without internal frontiers, in which the free movement of persons is ensured in conjunction with appropriate measures with respect to external border controls, asylum, immigration and the prevention and combating of crime'. Nonetheless, despite the lack of political efforts to construct a 'European homeland' in public debates, this book has shown that EU policies have amounted to an expression of a political process attempting to construct an area for a political community, that is, the AFSJ, which would be safe from security threats. This threat perception has arguably influenced the negotiations of the Lisbon Treaty, which contains a solidarity clause as discussed below.

This book has further reflected upon the development of European homeland security after the entry into force of the Lisbon Treaty and the adoption of the Stockholm Programme. EU institutional actors, especially the European Commission, have played a crucial role in shaping policy developments in this particular way (Kaunert 2007, 2009, 2010c; Kaunert and Della Giovanna 2010). Member States traditionally called for national solutions to such issues. However, since 9/11, European institutions have managed to channel this process towards developing a 'European' – rather than a 'national' – solution. Nonetheless, as shown by the various contributions in this book, homeland security in Europe still lacks a strategic vision. In contrast, as emphasised particularly by Schroeder's chapter, there is no lack of 'strategies' in the sense of programmatic documents, from the ESS of 2003 to the ISS of 2010 through the Information Management Strategy (IMS) for EU internal security of 2009. Yet, how strategic is the development of EU policies if several security aspects are addressed separately, rather than in the framework of a more general 'homeland security' policy? In that respect, broader questions about the political community, which security policies seek to protect, and the overall direction of the European integration process also need to be asked. The EU does not easily fit within accepted categories of political organisation, since it is less than a 'federation', but more than a mere 'regime'. In a process akin to national political community-building (Linklater 1998), European integration is also building a political community, although it is still under construction. Despite the messiness inherent to strategies such as 'variable geometry' with various 'opt-outs' and 'opt-ins' (e.g. UK, Ireland and Denmark) and intergovernmental agreements, such as the Schengen and Prüm Conventions, attempts at constructing a political community are at the heart of European integration. Equally, political communities often establish themselves against security threats.

The ESS of 2003, which is entitled 'A Secure Europe in a Better World', can be seen as such an attempt at political community-building. It emphasises that

> Europe has never been so prosperous, so secure nor so free. The violence of the first half of the 20th Century has given way to a period of

peace and stability unprecedented in European history. The creation of the European Union has been central to this development.

(European Council 2003b: 1)

The causality of the argument made in the first paragraph of the ESS is clear – Europe has had security problems in the past and the EU has been the solution to these security problems. Thanks to European integration, Europe today is prosperous and free. One could, of course, cite alternative explanations, from the US military presence in western Europe, the Soviet threat, and the role of the North Atlantic Treaty Organization (NATO), which the document also acknowledges. Yet, it is quite clear that the document aims to construct a clear role for the EU in security policy developments in Europe. The ESS also sets out the key parameters for the future of the European political community: there are many security threats facing Europe in the future, and no single country alone is able to tackle these challenges. Indeed, globally, 'since 1990, almost four million people have died in wars, 90% of them civilians. Over 18 million people worldwide have left their homes as a result of conflict' (European Council 2003b: 2). The ESS then identifies five key threats, namely terrorism, the proliferation of weapons of mass destruction, regional conflicts, state failure and organised crime. Two out of these five security challenges – terrorism and organised crime – have been traditionally seen as internal security threats, which implies a strong emphasis on internal security threats within the ESS. The terrorist attacks on 11 September 2001 are identified as a defining moment – for European integration and the EU's role in tackling security threats. As suggested elsewhere (Kaunert 2007, 2010c), the European Commission was significant in constructing a role for the EU into this emerging 'War on Terror' led by the US. The EU supported the US – the ESS points to the significant importance of the European Arrest Warrant (EAW) in this process (European Council 2003b: 6). In line with this reasoning, the normative purpose of JHA policy changed from being 'a flanking measure of the Single Market' to constituting an 'Area of Freedom, Security and Justice' (AFSJ) (Kaunert 2005, 2010c), which has also been termed a 'European Public Order' in line with the phrase used during the Convention on the Future of Europe.

The Lisbon Treaty, which entered into force on 1 December 2009, amends two separate bodies of treaties, namely the TEU and the Treaty on the Functioning of the European Union (TFEU). Article 3(2) TEU elevates the 'AFSJ' to the status of objective of the EU and even lists it as the second EU objective, before the Internal Market (Article 3(3) TEU), as it lays down that:

[the] Union shall offer its citizens an area of freedom, security and justice without internal frontiers, in which the free movement of persons is ensured in conjunction with appropriate measures with

respect to external border controls, asylum, immigration, and the prevention and combating of crime.

The EU legal competences in the AFSJ are also now clarified, as Article 4(2j) TFEU identifies this policy area as one of shared competences. Furthermore, the Lisbon Treaty creates a simplified decision-making procedure. First, the pillar structure is formally abolished, which results in the advanced, but incomplete, communitarisation of the areas of criminal justice, policing and terrorism, albeit with drawbacks in the form of 'emergency brakes' and 'accelerators'. Second, decisions in the AFSJ are to be taken according to the 'ordinary legislative procedure' outlined in Article 294 TFEU. This notably entails qualified majority voting (QMV) in the European Council and gives the European Parliament joint decision-making power. In addition, the Commission is given the exclusive power to propose legislation, with the exception of criminal justice and policing legislation, where the latter power is shared with a quarter of the Member States.

Third, the disappearance of the pillar structure leads to a commonality of legal instruments between titles that were formerly pillar I and pillar III. In the Lisbon Treaty, this is achieved under the name of 'ordinary legislative procedure'. In addition, the Lisbon Treaty retains the traditional Community instruments; that is, regulations, directives, decisions and so on, while some legal instruments previously used in the AFSJ, such as framework decisions, common positions, and conventions are abolished. Judicial control is expanded by applying the normal court rules on the jurisdiction of the General Court (previously known as the European Court of Justice (ECJ)) to all AFSJ matters in all Member States, including the possibility for all national courts or tribunals to send questions to the General Court. Fourth, the legal status of the Charter of Fundamental Rights of the EU is clarified for the majority of Member States. By virtue of the first subparagraph of Article 6(1) TEU, the Charter has the same legal value as the treaties. This article provides a cross-reference to the Charter of Fundamental Rights, which renders the Charter directly legally binding on the European institutions, Union bodies, offices and agencies, as well as Member States when they implement Union law (except those that have exceptions to various degrees, such as the UK, Poland, and in principle, soon the Czech Republic and Ireland). This has the following significant implications: (1) EU institutions and other EU agencies and bodies can be held to account on the basis of the fundamental rights contained in the Charter; and (2) Member States can be held to account on the basis of the same rights, generally when implementing EU legislation, but possibly also when adopting national legislation with an EU dimension (depending on the interpretation of the Courts). This will put EU actors and Member States under a clear legal obligation to ensure that fundamental rights are respected and will thus strengthen the 'freedom' dimension of the AFSJ.

Furthermore, these institutional changes may have very strong implications for the role of EU institutions in the AFSJ. The Lisbon Treaty evidently provides for a potential reshaping of the inter-institutional balance in this policy area. In general, the supranational institutions have been greatly strengthened. This implies an even stronger role for the European Commission, as its role as an initiator of legislation has been reinforced. Even more importantly, the European Parliament has been given the role of co-legislator in the area, which has the potential to greatly influence the future balance of power between the different EU institutions. Nonetheless, while the supranational dimension of the EU institutional structure has been strengthened in the AFSJ, the role of the European Council as a strategic decision-making institution in this policy area has also been reinforced. Finally, one of the most significant innovations of the Lisbon Treaty has been the introduction of a solidarity clause for homeland security matters modelled on NATO's mutual defence clause. Article 222 of the TFEU stipulates that, in the case of a terrorist attack or a 'natural or manmade disaster', the Union 'shall mobilise all the instruments at its disposal, including the military resources made available by the Member States'. It also states that the European Council is to regularly assess the threats faced by the Union in order to be able to take effective decisions. Although some have pointed out that this legal provision leaves several questions unanswered (Myrdal and Rhinard 2010), it is undeniable that the introduction of a solidarity clause is symbolically very important for the development of the European homeland security policy area. Overall, it can also be concluded that, with the various changes that it has introduced, the Lisbon Treaty represents a significant advance in European integration for homeland security matters.

Since the negotiation of the Lisbon Treaty, EU Member States have adopted a European Union Information Management Strategy (EU IMS) for EU internal security, which aims 'to support, streamline and facilitate the management of information necessary to the competent authorities to ensure the EU internal security' (Council of the European Union 2009d: 3). In addition, in 2010, they adopted the ISS, which defines internal security as 'a wide and comprehensive concept which straddles multiple sectors in order to address these major threats and others which have a direct impact on the lives, safety, and well-being of citizens, including natural and man-made disasters such as forest fires, earthquakes, floods and storms' (European Council 2010b: 8). The major objective of the ISS is to 'to help drive Europe forward, bringing together existing activities and setting out the principles and guidelines for future action. It is designed to prevent crimes and increase the capacity to provide a timely and appropriate response to natural and man-made disasters through the effective development and management of adequate instruments' (European Council 2010b: 9). These initiatives were notably informed by the work of the so-called 'Future Group', which was established by the German

Presidency in January 2007 (The Future Group 2008). It was co-chaired by the Interior Minister of the country in charge of the Presidency and the Vice-President of the European Commission (first Franco Frattini, and subsequently Jacques Barrot) and attended by the Interior Ministers of Germany, Portugal, Slovenia, France, the Czech Republic and Sweden, as well as Britain as a 'common law observer'. The report of the Future Group appears to have been influenced by homeland security ideas (Bunyan 2008: 3) and is phrased in terms of 'European Home Affairs'. Thus, although the term 'homeland security' is not explicitly used, 'European homeland security' – both as an objective to be attained and a policy area – is increasingly in the making through the development of numerous policy initiatives and the negotiation and adoption of various security strategies with differing scopes.

The chapters in this book have provided important empirical and theoretical evidence for this suggestion. Chapter 2 by Pawlak has highlighted the benefits of examining EU internal security through the lenses of 'homeland security', while acknowledging the problems and challenges inherent to addressing security threats, such as terrorism, in the same ways as the US has done. His chapter has also illustrated how similar threat scenarios on both sides of the Atlantic have, to a significant extent, played out differently. Schroeder in Chapter 3 has strengthened this argument by emphasising the incremental development of various EU security strategies. In contrast with the comprehensive top-down overhaul of US security thinking after the 9/11 attacks, the EU did not radically depart from established security concepts and procedures. Enabled by a strategic void at the heart of the European security project, actors in the EU institutions have developed broader and more encompassing security strategies with sometimes overlapping and at other times conflicting strategic aims, including counter-terrorism, human security, common defence, crime-fighting and stability.

In Chapter 4, Bossong has emphasised how the evolution of counter-terrorism has become a focal issue for the EU, as each serious attack has also been seen as an opportunity for expanding integration in security matters more generally. Chapter 5 by Argomaniz has added to these findings by highlighting the ways in which the EU counter-terrorism policy has been profoundly affected by a proliferation of bureaucratic actors with competing competences. His analysis highlights the significant policy coordination problems to which this institutional proliferation has led. In Chapter 6, MacKenzie has emphasised the existence of another trend adding to the complexity of EU homeland security, namely the increasing importance of cooperation with external actors, in particular the US, to tackle traditionally internal security threats, such as terrorism.

Finally, the book has also demonstrated the broad and comprehensive nature of homeland security in the EU. It cannot be reduced to counter-terrorism, although it is one of its key components, but also encompasses policies such as civilian crisis management and border policies. In that respect, Wendling's contribution has focused on explaining the evolution of EU emergency and crisis management structures. It has highlighted another layer of complexity in the analysis of European homeland security, namely the gap that can develop, for a variety of reasons, between legal arrangements and how they are implemented in practice. Chapters 8 and 9 have focused on the EU external borders policy. Pawlak and Kurowska in Chapter 8 have highlighted the extreme complexity of this policy, which, like the EU counter-terrorism policy, has been characterised by a very large number of actors with competing interests and a growing number of initiatives. In Chapter 9, Léonard has focused on the origins of one of these actors, namely the External Borders Agency Frontex, which has been identified in the Stockholm Programme as one of the most important actors for European homeland security in the future.

The absence of an overarching strategy for European homeland security

Over time, the EU has adopted various strategies concerning homeland security matters, which has led to the development of an increasingly complex web of partially overlapping programmatic documents. In this conclusion, only the strategies with a broad scope will be considered, although one should bear in mind that others have also been adopted, notably in the field of counter-terrorism. As explained before, the first significant security strategy adopted by the EU was the ESS in 2003 (European Council 2003b). The publication of 'A Secure Europe in a Better World' can be interpreted as an attempt at political community-building in Europe against a common external threat. The document clearly aims to construct a role for the EU in security matters by identifying five main threats. As previously mentioned, two out of these five security challenges, that is, terrorism and organised crime, have been traditionally seen as internal security threats. The ESS emphasises that the EU has responded to the threat of terrorism with instruments, such as the EAW, as well as steps against counter-terrorist financing and mutual legal assistance with the US. Equally, the EU stands against nuclear proliferation and is committed to multilateral treaty regimes and verification procedures against nuclear proliferation. The ESS further cites the EU's assistance for failed states in order to help deal with regional conflicts. Significantly, however, the document then explains how global criminal and terrorist activities have become a threat to European countries and citizens. Consequently, the 'first line of defence will often be abroad. [...] This implies we should be ready to act before the crisis occurs' (European Council 2003b: 7). 'Each [threat] requires a mixture of instruments. [...] Dealing with terrorism may require a mixture of intelligence, police, judicial, military, and other means. [...] The European Union is particularly well equipped to respond to such multi-faceted situations' (European Council 2003b: 7). The ESS highlights that these security challenges have important policy implications for the EU. In order to successfully tackle them, the following is required: more capabilities, including military capabilities, pooled use of assets, diplomatic capabilities and threat assessments; more coherence among the different instruments and capabilities, including better coordination between external action and JHA policies; and working with partners. The conclusion of the ESS depicts an ambitious EU:

> This is a world of new dangers but also of new opportunities. The European Union has the potential to make a major contribution, both in dealing with the threats and in helping realise the opportunities. An active European Union would make an impact on a global scale. In doing so, it would contribute to an effective multilateral system leading to a fairer, safer and more united world.
>
> (European Council 2003b: 14)

However, despite the EU's insistence on bringing external action closer together with JHA matters, the European Council approved a separate ISS on 25 February 2010, which led to the publication of a European Commission Communication on concrete actions resulting from the ISS in November 2010 (European Commission 2010a). Like the ESS, the ISS can also be seen as an attempt at building an EU political community. It recalls how the EU, its institutions and Member States have promoted freedom and security, as well as guaranteeing human rights, the rule of law and solidarity. It also emphasises the removal of internal border controls as a significant event for Europe, resulting in the opening up of European societies. The ISS is threefold: it identifies common threats and challenges, sets out the EU's common internal security policy and defines a European Security Model (European Council 2010b). The following threats are identified as common threats: (1) terrorism, in any form; (2) serious and organised crime; (3) cybercrime; (4) cross-border crime; (5) violence itself, (6) natural and man-made disasters; and (7) common phenomena, such as road traffic accidents. A comparison of the ISS with the ESS demonstrates that, far from bringing external action closer to internal security, these two Strategies are largely underpinned by a very traditional understanding of security; that is, there are internal threats and external security threats, which should be dealt with in separate frameworks. In this way, arguably, the ISS even goes against some of the logic of the ESS. The ISS provides for the following five responses to the internal security challenges identified: analysis of future situations and scenarios (threat anticipation); adequate response (planning, programming and handling); effectiveness in the field (agencies); tools of mutual recognition, information-sharing and joint investigations; and evaluation mechanisms. This analysis leads to the following strategic guidelines for action: (1) a wide and comprehensive approach to internal security; (2) ensuring the effective democratic and judicial supervision of security activities; (3) prevention and anticipation; (4) development of a comprehensive model for information exchange; (5) operational cooperation; (6) judicial cooperation in criminal matters; (7) integrated border management; (8) commitment to innovation and training; (9) external dimension of internal security/cooperation with third countries; and (10) flexibility to adapt to future challenges (European Council 2010b).

On the basis of the ISS, the European Commission identified the following 'five strategic objectives for internal security' in its communication of November 2010: (1) serious and organised crime; (2) terrorism; (3) cybercrime; (4) border security; and (5) natural and man-made disasters (European Commission 2010a). In this context, with regard to border security, a new programme has also been suggested – Eurosur, in the field of border surveillance, which is meant to 'work closely' with Frontex. This programme is controversial as it appears to blur the boundaries between asylum-seekers and irregular migrants on the one hand and traffickers and organised crime gangs on the other hand. As explained by Pawlak and Kurowska elsewhere in this book, Eurosur is envisaged to be a 'system of systems' of enhanced border surveillance with the aim of reducing the number of irregular immigrants crossing the Mediterranean and entering the EU. Other changes that are envisaged are the setting-up of a new cyber-crime centre at Europol, as well as the establishment of a European crisis management system aiming to coordinate risk assessment on natural disasters, as well as linking it to nuclear risk monitoring and terrorism.

Both the ESS and the ISS in themselves appear to be coherent documents. Some may criticise them for constructing an environment with heightened security risks in the EU, but, to a large extent, they actually represent a mere amalgamation of commonly accepted security threats without necessarily creating new ones. However, there are two points that are worth further consideration: do the two strategies add up? And how far do they construct a European political community against these security threats? On the first point, it needs to be emphasised that the ESS does make a good attempt at bringing internal and external security threats together in one more or less coherent framework. The five main threats identified are coherent and can be derived from empirical evidence. However, the ISS goes against the spirit of the ESS to some extent. While the ISS is very good at outlining a multitude of potential security threats, it appears more like an amalgamation of threats than a strategic clustering of prioritised threats. A clear hierarchy of threats is lacking. As a consequence, the Action Plan drawn up by the European Commission looks more like a summary of actions planned than a strategy for planned actions.

On the second point, it can be argued that the EU is increasingly successful at creating a political community around these security threats. In the European Parliament, a political community is certainly in the making in response to security threats. For example, the Stockholm Programme provoked strong criticism from southern European states. Maltese centre-right Member of European Parliament (MEP) Simon Busuttil commented that 'the axis on security seems to have been watered down in the text', a point which was reinforced by a number of Italian MEPs. British Liberal MEP Diana Wallis observed that '[we]'re beginning to see where the fracture lines in the house are'. She also declared that 'security is the main sticking point. Do we want to go further in terms of underlining security? Who knows what the final outcome will be in terms of immigration and migration? That could be difficult' (EurActiv 2009). The same political fault lines exist within the European Council. After it approved the Stockholm Programme, the real political battles began to emerge. When the European Commission outlined its vision for the Stockholm Programme on 10 June 2009, Commission President José Manuel Barroso suggested:

> In future, EU action must aim above all at delivering the best possible service to the citizen in an area of freedom, security and justice more tangible for the citizens. We want to promote citizens' rights, make their daily lives easier and provide protection, and this calls for effective and responsible European action in these areas. In this context, I consider immigration policy particularly important. This is the vision the Commission is presenting to the Council and Parliament for debate, with a view to the adoption of the new Stockholm Programme by the European Council in December 2009.
>
> (European Commission 2009b: 1)

Vice-Commission President Jacques Barrot expressed similar views:

> Freedom, security and justice are core values which constitute key components of the European model of society. We have made substantial progress in creating an area of freedom, security and justice in recent years. The priority now must be to put the citizen at the heart of this project in order to demonstrate the added value of the European Union in areas that have such a bearing on people's daily lives.
>
> (European Commission 2009b: 1)

The fact that the Charter of Fundamental Rights has now become legally binding for the European institutions, EU bodies, offices and agencies, as well as Member States (with few exceptions) when they implement Union law, as explained earlier, is an important development. This puts EU actors and Member States under a clear legal obligation to ensure that fundamental rights are respected, which strengthens the 'freedom' dimension of the AFSJ, as the Charter proclaims various civil, political, economic and social rights, as well as rights attached to European citizenship.

As shown in this book, it is therefore important to emphasise that the development of European homeland security should not be only seen in a negative light. It is true that such a concept can be explicitly or implicitly used to push forward controversial reforms, as has been highlighted elsewhere in this book. However, thinking in terms of 'homeland security' also has the positive consequence that it draws attention to the question of whom is being secured and the fact that members of a political community have rights, which should be balanced against the requirements of addressing security threats.

References

Abrahamsen, R. and Williams, M.C. (2010) *Security Beyond the State: Security Privatization and International Politics*, Cambridge: Cambridge University Press.

Aldrich, R. (2009) 'US–European intelligence co-operation on counter-terrorism: low politics and compulsion', *British Journal of Politics and International Relations*, 11(1): 122–139.

Alegre, S. and Leaf, M. (2004) 'Mutual recognition in European judicial cooperation: a step too far too soon? Case study – the European Arrest Warrant', *European Law Journal*, 10: 200–217.

Ameyugo, G. (2010) 'EUROSUR: the pilot'. Paper presented at the Conference on Surveillance Technology for Border Control, Warsaw, 24 May 2010.

Amnesty International and European Council on Refugees and Exiles (2010) 'Briefing on the Commission proposal for a Regulation amending Council Regulation (EC)2007/2004 establishing a European Agency for the Management of Operational Cooperation at the External Borders of the Member States of the European Union (FRONTEX), Brussels: Amnesty International/ ECRE.

Archik, K. (2010) 'US-EU co-operation against terrorism', *CRS Report for Congress*. Available online at: www.fas.org/sgp/crs/row/RS22030.pdf (accessed 1 November 2010).

Argomaniz, J. (2009) 'When the EU is the "norm-taker": the Passenger Name Records Agreement and the EU's internalization of US border security norms', *Journal of European Integration*, 31(1): 119–136.

—— (2011) *The EU and Counter-terrorism*, London: Routledge.

Arteaga, F. (2010) *The EU's Internal Security Strategy*, Madrid: Real Instituto Elcano.

Australian Minister for Foreign Affairs (2010) 'Australia and the EU sign Passenger Name Record (PNR) Agreement'. Available online at: www.foreignminister.gov. au/releases/2008/fa-s080701.html (accessed 14 December 2010).

Bailes, A.J.K. (2004) 'EU and US Strategic Concepts: a mirror for partnership and difference?', *The International Spectator*, XXXIX(1): 19–33.

—— (2005) 'The European Security Strategy: an evolutionary history', *SIPRI Policy Paper No. 10*, Stockholm: SIPRI.

Baldaccini, A. and Guild, E. (eds) (2007) *Terrorism and the Foreigner: A Decade of Tension around the Rule of Law in Europe*, Leiden: Martinus Nijhoff.

Ball, N. (2004) 'Reforming security sector governance', *Conflict, Security and Development*, 4(3): 509–527.

Balzacq, T. (2008) 'The external dimension of EU Justice and Home Affairs: tools, processes, outcomes', *CEPS Working Document No. 303*, Brussels: Centre for European Studies.

Balzacq, T. (ed.) (2009) *The External Dimension of EU Justice and Home Affairs: Governance, Neighbours, Security*, Basingstoke: Palgrave Macmillan.

BBC News (2000) 'The scandal of the Erika', 16 August 2000.

—— (2002) 'Stricken oil tanker sinks', 19 November 2002.

—— (2005) 'The Hamburg connection', 19 August 2005.

—— (2006) 'Swollen Danube reaches Ukraine', 18 April 2006.

—— (2009) 'Wildfires break out across Greece', 22 August 2009.

—— (2010) 'Bomb was designed to explode on cargo plane – UK PM', 30 October 2010.

Belgian Presidency of the Council of the European Union (2010) 'The European Interior Ministers approve a European security plan to be put in place by 2014', Brussels: Belgian Presidency of the Council of the European Union, Brussels: Council of the European Union, 15 July 2010.

Berenskoetter, F. and Giegerich, B. (2006) 'What War on Terror are we talking about? A response to Alistair Shepherd', *International Politics*, 43: 93–104.

Bet-El, I. (2006) 'Wanted: a strategic vision', *European Voice*, 7 December 2006.

Bezes, P. (2005) 'The steering state model: the emergence of a new organisational form in the French public administration', *Sociologie du Travail*, 47: 431–450.

Bigo, D. (1998) 'Europe passoire et Europe forteresse: la sécurisation/humanitarisation de l'immigration' in A. Rea (ed.) *Immigration et racisme en Europe*, Bruxelles: Complexe.

—— (2000) 'When two become one: internal and external securitizations in Europe', in M. Kelstrup and M.C. Williams (eds) *International Relations Theory and the Politics of European Integration: Power, Security and Community*, London: Routledge.

Bigo, D. and Walker, R.B.J. (2006) 'Liberté et sécurité en Europe: enjeux contemporains', *Cultures & Conflits*, 61: 103–136.

Biscop, S. (2004) 'The European Security Strategy: implementing a distinctive approach to security', *Paper No. 82*, Brussels: Royal Defence College.

Boin, R.A. and Ekengren, M. (2009) 'Preparing for the world risk society: towards a new security paradigm for the European Union', *Journal of Contingencies and Crisis Management*, 17(4): 285–294.

Block, L. (2007) 'Europe's emerging counter-terrorism elite: the ATLAS network', *Terrorism Monitor*, 5: 10–12.

Bossong, R. (2008) 'The Action Plan on Combating Terrorism: a flawed instrument of EU security governance', *Journal of Common Market Studies*, 46: 27–48.

Brouwer, E. (2009) 'Towards a European PNR system? Questions on the added value and the protection of fundamental rights', *Briefing Paper*, Brussels: European Parliament.

Brunsson, N. (1985) *The Irrational Organization*, Chichester: John Wiley and Sons.

—— (2002) *The Organization of Hypocrisy: Talk, Decision and Actions in Organizations*, 2nd edn, Abstrakt Forlag, Liber: Copenhagen Business School Press.

Bullock, J. *et al.* (2006) *Introduction to Homeland Security*, Burlington: Elsevier Butterworth-Heinemann.

Bundesverfassungsgericht (2009) *2 BvE 2/08, 30 Juni 2009, Absatz-Nr. (1–421)*. Available online at: www.bverfg.de/entscheidungen/es20090630_2bve000208en. html (accessed 15 January 2010).

Bunyan, T. (2008) 'Statewatch: the shape of things to come – EU Future Report', London: Statewatch. Available online at: www.statewatch.org/analyses/the-shape-of-things-to-come.pdf (accessed 5 February 2011).

Bures, O. (2006) 'EU counterterrorism policy: a paper tiger?', *Terrorism and Political Violence*, 18(1): 57–78.

—— (2008) 'Europol's fledgling counterterrorism role', *Terrorism and Political Violence*, 20: 498–517.

—— (2011) *EU Counterterrorism Policy: A Paper Tiger?* Farnham: Ashgate.

Busuioc, M. (2009) 'Accountability, control and independence: the case of European agencies', *Research Paper (Europe Award 2009)*, The Hague: Montesquieu Institute. Available online at: www.montesquieu-institute.eu (accessed 15 October 2009).

Cameron, F. (2007) 'Transatlantic relations and terrorism', in D. Spence (ed.) *The European Union and Terrorism*, London: John Harper.

Carrera, S. (2007) 'The EU Border Management Strategy, FRONTEX and the challenges of irregular immigration in the Canary Islands', *CEPS Working Document No. 261*, Brussels: Centre for European Studies.

Carrera, S. and Geyer, F. (2007) 'Terrorism, borders and migration: the Commission's 2008 policy strategy in the Area of Freedom, Security and Justice', *CEPS Policy Brief No. 131*, Brussels: Centre for European Studies.

Cassarino, J.-P. (2010) 'Readmission policy in the European Union', Study Report commissioned by the European Parliament, DG for Internal Policies, Policy Department C: Citizens' Rights and Constitutional Affairs, Brussels: European Parliament.

Chebel d'Appollonia, A. and Reich, S. (eds) (2008) *Immigration, Integration, and Security: America and Europe in Comparative Perspective*, Pittsburgh, PA: University of Pittsburgh Press.

Christiansen, T. (2001) 'Intra-institutional politics and inter-institutional relations in the EU: towards coherent governance?', *Journal of European Public Policy*, 8(5): 747–769.

Collantes Celador, G. (2005) 'Police reform: peacebuilding through 'democratic policing?', *International Peacekeeping*, 12(3): 364–376.

Collinson, S. (1993) *Beyond Borders: West European Migration Policy towards the 21st Century*, London: Royal Institute of International Affairs.

Comfort, L. (2002) 'Managing intergovernmental responses to terrorism and other extreme events', *Publius*, 32(4): 29–49.

Congress of the United States of America (2001a) 'Aviation and Transportation Security Act', Public Law 107–71, 19 November 2001.

—— (2001b) 'Uniting and Strengthening America by Providing Appropriate Tools Required to Intercept and Obstruct Terrorism (PATRIOT Act)', Public law 107–56, 26 October 2001.

—— (2002) 'Enhanced Border Security and Visa Entry Reform Act', Public Law 107–173, 14 May 2002.

—— (2004) 'Intelligence Reform and Terrorist Prevention Act of 2004', Public Law 108–458, Washington, 17 December 2004.

Coolsaet, R. (2010) 'EU counterterrorism strategy: value added or chimera?', *International Affairs*, 86: 857–873.

Council of Europe (2010a) 'Readmission agreements: a mechanism for returning irregular migrants', *Doc. No. 12168*, Strasbourg: Council of Europe.

—— (2010b) 'Council of Europe Report to the Italian Government on the visit to Italy carried out by the European Committee for the Prevention of Torture and Inhuman or Degrading Treatment or Punishment (CPT) from 27 to 31 July 2009', Strasbourg: Council of Europe.

Council of the European Union (1995) 'The Euro-Mediterranean Partnership: Barcelona Declaration adopted at the Euro-Mediterranean Conference', Brussels: Council of the European Union.

—— (1999) 'Analysis of the Institute Concerning Readmission Agreements', Brussels: Council of the European Union.

—— (2001) 'Special meeting of the General Affairs Council, 12 September 2001', 11795/01 (Presse 318). Brussels: Council of the European Union.

—— (2002a) 'Plan for the Management of the External Borders of the Member States of the European Union', 10019/02, Brussels: Council of the European Union.

—— (2002b) '5th Euro-Mediterranean Conference of Ministers for Foreign Affairs: Valencia Action Plan', Brussels: Council of the European Union.

—— (2003a) 'Report on the Implementation of Programmes, Ad hoc Centres, Pilot Projects and Joint Operations', 10058/03, Brussels: Council of the European Union.

—— (2003b) 'Council Conclusions on the Main Elements of the Commission Proposal for a Council Regulation Establishing a European Agency for the Management of Operational Cooperation at the External Borders of the Member States of the European Union', 15446/03, Brussels: Council of the European Union.

—— (2003c) 'Effective Management of the External Borders of the EU Member States', 10274/03, Brussels: Council of the European Union.

—— (2003d) 'Draft Joint Declaration by the Council and the Commission on the Use of the Community Civil Protection Mechanism in Crisis Management referred to in Title V of the Treaty of the European Union', Brussels: Council of the European Union.

—— (2003e) 'Joint Declaration by the Council and the Commission on the Use of the Community Civil Protection Mechanism in Crisis Management referred to in Title V of the Treaty of the European Union', Brussels: Council of the European Union.

—— (2004a) 'Declaration on Combating Terrorism', 7906/04, Brussels: Council of the European Union.

—— (2004b) 'Working Structures in the Council in Terrorism Matters: Options Paper', 9791/04, Brussels: Council of the European Union.

—— (2005a) 'EU Concept for ESDP Support to Security Sector Reform (SSR)', 12566/4/05, Brussels: Council of the European Union.

—— (2005b) 'The European Union Counter-Terrorism Strategy', 14469/4/05, Brussels: Council of the European Union.

—— (2005c) 'A Strategy for the External Dimension of JHA: Global Freedom, Security and Justice', 15446/05, Brussels: Council of the European Union.

—— (2005d) 'Implementation of the Strategy and Action Plan to Combat Terrorism', 15704/05, Brussels: Council of the European Union.

—— (2005e) 'Final Report on the Evaluation of National Anti-Terrorist Arrangements: Improving National Machinery and Capability for the Fight against Terrorism', 12168/3/05, Brussels: Council of the European Union.

—— (2005f) 'JHA Council Declaration on the EU Response to the London Bombings', 11158/1/05 REV 1, Brussels: Council of the European Union.

—— (2005g) 'The European Union Strategy for Combating Radicalisation and Recruitment to Terrorism', 14781/05, Brussels: Council of the European Union.

—— (2005h) 'Report by the Friends of the Presidency on the Technical Modalities to Implement the Principle of Availability', 13558/05, Brussels: Council of the European Union.

—— (2006a) 'Action Oriented Paper on Improving Cooperation, on Organized Crime, Corruption, Illegal Immigration and Counter-Terrorism, between the EU, Western Balkans and Relevant ENP Countries', 9272/06, Brussels: Council of the European Union.

—— (2006b) 'Vienna Declaration on Security Partnership', Brussels: Council of the European Union.

—— (2006c) 'Council of the European Union, Justice and Home Affairs, 2768th Council Meeting, 4–5 December 2006', 15801/06, Brussels: Council of the European Union.

—— (2006d) 'Conclusions of the First High Level Political Dialogue on Counter-Terrorism, between the Council, the Commission, and the European Parliament', 15448/07, Brussels: Council of the European Union.

—— (2007a) 'Fight against Terrorist Financing – Six-monthly Report', 11948/2/07 REV 2, Brussels: Council of the European Union.

—— (2007b) 'Council Conclusions on Cooperation to Combat Terrorist Use of the Internet ("Check the Web")', 8457/3/07 REV 3, Brussels: Council of the European Union.

—— (2007c) 'Implementation of the EU Counter-terrorism Strategy: Discussion Paper', 15448/07, Brussels: Council of the European Union.

—— (2007d) 'Security and Development – Conclusions of the Council and the Representatives of the Governments of the Member States meeting within the Council', 15097/07, Brussels: Council of the European Union.

—— (2009a) 'EU/US Agreements on Extradition and on Mutual Legal Assistance', 14826/09, Brussels: Council of the European Union.

—— (2009b) 'EU CBRN Action Plan and Council Conclusions', 17705/09, Brussels: Council of the European Union.

—— (2009c) 'Proposal for a Council Framework Decision on the Use of Passenger Name Record (PNR) for Law Enforcement Purposes', 5618/09, Brussels: Council of the European Union.

—— (2009d) 'Council Conclusions on an Information Management Strategy for EU Internal Security, 2979th Justice and Home Affairs Council Meeting, Brussels, 30 November 2009', Brussels: Council of the European Union.

—— (2010a) 'EU Action Plan on Combating Terrorism', 15893/10, Brussels: Council of the European Union.

—— (2010b) 'EU Counter-Terrorism Strategy: Discussion Paper', 15894/1/10, Brussels: Council of the European Union.

—— (2010c) 'Towards a Comprehensive Approach: The Operational Implications – EUMS Paper for the EUMC', Brussels: Council of the European Union.

—— (2010d) 'Further Direction of SIS II', 10833/10, Brussels: Council of the European Union.

—— (2010e) 'Draft Internal Security Strategy for the European Union: "Towards a European Security Model"', 5842/2/10, Brussels: Council of the European Union.

—— (2011) 'Council Conclusions on EU-Turkey Readmission Agreement and Related Issues, 3071st Justice and Home Affairs Council Meeting, Brussels, 24–25 February 2011', Brussels: Council of the European Union.

Court of First Instance (2005) 'Judgment of the Court of First Instance of 21 September 2005 – Case T-306/01 *Yusuf and Al Barakaat International Foundation* v. *Council and Commission*', OJ C 281/17, 12 November 2005.

COWI (2009) 'FRONTEX: External evaluation of the European Agency for the Management of Operational Coordination at the External Borders of the Member States of the European Union', final report, Kongens Lyngby: COWI A/S. Available online at: www.frontex.europa.eu/specific_documents/other/ (accessed 1 June 2010).

Crenshaw, M. (2005) 'Counterterrorism in retrospect: chronicle of a war foretold', *Foreign Affairs*, 84(4): 187–93.

Crozier, M. and Friedberg, E. (1977) *L'acteur et le système*, Paris: Seuil.

Curtin, D. (2005) 'Delegation to non-majoritarian agencies and emerging practices of public accountability', in D. Geradin, R. Muñoz and N. Petit (eds) *Regulation through Agencies in the EU: A New Paradigm of European Governance*, Cheltenham: Edward Elgar.

Deflem, M. (2004) 'Social control and the policing of terrorism: foundations for a sociology of counter-terrorism', *The American Sociologist*, 35: 75–92.

—— (2006) 'Europol and the policing of international terrorism: counter-terrorism in a global perspective', *Justice Quarterly*, 23(3): 336–359.

De Hert, P. and Bellanova, R. (2009) 'Data protection in the Area of Freedom, Security and Justice: a system still to be fully developed?', *Briefing Paper* PE 410.692, Brussels: European Parliament.

De Hert, P., Papakonstantinou, V. and Riehle, C. (2008) 'Data protection in the third pillar: cautious pessimism', in M. Mike (ed.) *Crime, Rights and the EU: The Future of Police and Judicial Cooperation*, London.

Dehousse, R. (2008) 'Delegation of powers in the European Union: the need for a multi-principles model', *West European Politics*, 31(4): 789–805.

DeLeon, P. (1999) The stages approach to the policy process: what has it done? Where is it going?, in P.A. Sabatier (ed.) *Theories of the Policy Process*, Boulder, CO: Westview.

den Boer, M. (2003) 'The EU counter-terrorism wave: window of opportunity or profound policy transformation?', in M. van Leeuwen (ed.) *Confronting Terrorism: European Experiences, Threat Perceptions and Policies*, The Hague: Kluwer Law International.

den Boer, M. and Wallace, W. (2000) 'Justice and Home Affairs: integration through incrementalism?', in H. Wallace and W. Wallace (eds) *Policymaking in the European Union*, Oxford: Oxford University Press.

de Vries, G. (2008) 'The nexus between EU crisis management and counter-terrorism', in S. Blockmans (ed.) *The European Union and Crisis Management: Policy and Legal Aspects*, The Hague: TCM Asser Press.

Di Federico, A. (2010) 'GMES pre-operational services for borders surveillance'. Paper presented at the the conference on Surveillance Technology for Border Control, Warsaw, 24 May 2010.

Di Maggio, P. (1988) 'Interest and agency in institutional theory', in L.G. Zucker (ed.) *Institutional Patterns and Organizations: Culture and Environment*, Cambridge, MA: Ballinger.

Dittrich, M. (2007) 'Radicalisation and recruitment: the EU response', in D. Spence (ed.) *The European Union and Terrorism*, London: John Harper.

Donnelly, B. (2008) 'Justice and Home Affairs in the Lisbon Treaty: a constitutionalising clarification?', *EIPAScope 2008/1*, Maastricht: EIPA.

Dubois, D. (2002) 'The attacks of 11 September: EU-US cooperation against terrorism in the field of Justice and Home Affairs', *European Foreign Affairs Review*, 7(3): 317–355.

Duke, S. (2004) 'The European Security Strategy in a comparative framework: does it make for secure alliances in a better world?', *European Foreign Affairs Review*, 9(4): 459–481.

EPP-ED Group (2007) 'EP Committee votes to double Frontex budget', 3 October 2007. Available online at: www.eppgroup.eu/Press/ (accessed 5 February 2008).

Eriksson, J. and Rhinard, M. (2009) 'The internal-external security nexus: notes on an emerging research agenda', *Cooperation and Conflict*, 44(3): 243–267.

EurActiv (2007) 'Belgian appointed new EU counter-terrorism co-ordinator', 19 September 2007.

—— (2009) 'Parliament split on "progressive" Swedish immigration programme', 12 October 2009.

—— (2010) 'EU to launch anti-terror finance tracking plan', 25 March 2010.

Eurojust (2007) 'Eurojust 2006 Annual Report', The Hague: Eurojust.

—— (2009) 'Eurojust News – Issue 1', The Hague: Eurojust.

European Commission (2002a) 'A wider Europe – a proximity policy as the key to stability', Speech by Romano Prodi, President of the European Commission, SPEECH/02/619, Sixth ECSA–World Conference 'Peace, Security and Stability International Dialogue and the Role of the EU', Brussels: European Commission.

—— (2002b) 'Communication from the Commission to the Council and the European Parliament: Towards Integrated Management of the External Borders of the Member States of the European Union', COM (2002) 233 final, Brussels: European Commission.

—— (2002c) 'Communication from the Commission to the Council and the European Parliament on a Community Return Policy on Illegal Residents', COM (2002) 504 final, Brussels: European Commission.

—— (2003a) 'Communication to the European Parliament and the Council on the Development of a Common Policy on Illegal Immigration, Smuggling and Trafficking of Human Beings, External Borders and the Return of Illegal Residents', COM (2003) 323 final, Brussels: European Commission.

—— (2003b) 'Proposal for a Council Regulation Establishing a European Agency for the Management of Operational Cooperation at the External Borders', COM (2003) 687 final, Brussels: European Commission.

—— (2003c) 'Communication from the Commission on Governance and Development', COM(2003) 615 final, Brussels: European Commission.

—— (2003d) 'Communication from the Commission: Wider Europe – Neighbourhood: A New Framework for Relations with our Eastern and Southern Neighbours', COM(2003) 104 final, Brussels: European Commission.

—— (2004a) 'Communication from the Commission: European Neighbourhood Policy – Strategy Paper', COM(2004) 373 final, Brussels: European Commission.

—— (2004b) 'Research for a Secure Europe: Report of the Group of Personalities in the field of Security Research', Brussels: European Commission.

—— (2004c) 'Communication from the Commission to the Council and the European Parliament: Critical Infrastructure Protection in the Fight against Terrorism', COM(2004) 702 final, Brussels: European Commission.

—— (2005a) 'Communication from the Commission to the European Parliament and the Council Concerning Terrorist Recruitment: Addressing the Factors Contributing to Violent Radicalisation', COM(2005) 313 final, Brussels: European Commission.

—— (2005b) 'Communication from the Commission: A Strategy on the External Dimension of the Area of Freedom, Security and Justice', COM (2005) 491 final, Brussels: European Commission.

—— (2005c) 'Proposal for a Council Decision on the Conclusion of an Agreement between the European Community and the Government of Canada on the processing of Advance Passenger Information (API)/Passenger Name Record (PNR) Data', COM (2005) 200, Brussels: European Commission.

—— (2006a) 'Communication from the Commission on Strengthening the European Neighbourhood Policy', COM(2006) 726 final, Brussels: European Commission.

—— (2006b) 'Communication from the Commission to the Council and the European Parliament: Strategy for Africa – An EU Regional Political Partnership for Peace, Security and Development in the Horn of Africa', COM(2006) 601 final, Brussels: European Commission.

—— (2006c) 'A Concept for European Community Support for Security Sector Reform', COM(2006) 253 final, Brussels: European Commission.

—— (2007a) 'Communication from the Commission to the European Parliament, the Council, the European Economic and Social Committee and the Committee of the Regions of 16 May 2007 on Circular Migration and Mobility Partnerships between the European Union and Third Countries', COM(2007) 248, Brussels: European Commission.

—— (2007b) 'Communication from the Commission to the European Parliament and the Council: Stepping Up the Fight against Terrorism', COM(2007) 649 final, Brussels: European Commission.

—— (2008a) 'Commission Communication – Preparing the Next Steps in Border Management in the European Union', COM(2008) 69 final, Brussels: European Commission.

—— (2008b) 'Commission Staff Working Document: Summary of the Impact Assessment "Preparing the Next Steps in Border Management in the European Union"', SEC(2008) 154, Brussels: European Commission.

—— (2008c) 'Communication of 13 February 2008 from the Commission to the European Parliament, the Council, the European Economic and Social Committee and the Committee of the Regions: Examining the Creation of a European Border Surveillance System (EUROSUR)', COM(2008) 68 final, Brussels: European Commission.

—— (2008d) 'Communication from the Commission to the European Parliament, the Council, the European Economic and Social Committee and the Committee of the Regions of 17 June 2008 – A Common Immigration Policy for Europe: Principles, Actions and Tools', COM(2008) 359, Brussels: European Commission.

—— (2008e) 'Communication from the Commission to the European Parliament and the Council: European Agencies – The Way Forward', COM(2008) 135, Brussels: European Commission.

—— (2009a) 'Towards a More Secure Society and Increased Industrial Competitiveness: Security Research Projects under the 7th Framework Programme for Research', Brussels: European Commission.

—— (2009b) 'European Commission outlines its vision for the area of freedom, security and justice in the next five years', IP/09/894, Brussels: European Commission.

—— (2010a) 'Communication from the Commission to the European Parliament and the Council: The EU Internal Security Strategy in Action – Five Steps towards a More Secure Europe', COM(2010) 673 final, Brussels: European Commission.

—— (2010b) 'Commission Staff Working Document: Impact Assessment Accompanying the Proposal for a Regulation of the European Parliament and of the Council Amending Council Regulation (EC) No 2007/2004 establishing a European Agency for the Management of Operational Cooperation at the External Borders of the Member States of the European Union (FRONTEX)', SEC(2010) 149, Brussels: European Commission.

—— (2010c) 'Turkey 2010 Progress Report', SEC(2010) 1327, Brussels: European Commission.

—— (2010d) 'Communication from the Commission to the European Parliament and the Council: Towards a Stronger European Disaster Response – The Role of Civil Protection and Humanitarian Assistance', COM(2010) 600 final, Brussels: European Commission.

—— (2011a) 'Proposal for a Directive of the European Parliament and of the Council on the use of Passenger Name Record Data for the Prevention, Detection, Investigation and Prosecution of Terrorist Offences and Serious Crime', COM(2011) 32 final, Brussels: European Commission.

—— (2011b) 'Communication from the Commission to the European Parliament and the Council: Evaluation of EU Readmission Agreements', COM(2011) 76 final, Brussels: European Commission.

European Community (2004) 'Agreement between the European Community and the United States of America on Intensifying and Broadening the Agreement on Customs Co-operation and Mutual Assistance in Customs Matters to Include Co-operation on Container Security and Related Matters', OJ L304/34.

—— (2006) 'Agreement between the European Community and the Government of Canada on the Processing of Advance Passenger Information and Passenger Name Record Data', OJ L82/15.

European Council (1999a) 'Presidency Conclusions of the Tampere European Council, 15–16 October 1999', 200/1/99, Brussels: European Council.

—— (1999b) 'Presidency Conclusions of the Helsinki European Council, 10–11 December 1999', 00300/1/99, Brussels: European Council.

—— (2000) 'Presidency Conclusions of the Feira European Council, 19–20 June 2000', 200/1/00, Brussels: European Council.

—— (2001a) 'Presidency Conclusions of the Göteborg European Council, 15–16 June 2001 – EU Programme for the Prevention of Violent Conflicts', SN 200/1/01 REV 1, Brussels: European Council.

—— (2001b) 'Conclusions and Plan of Action of the Extraordinary Meeting of the

European Council Meeting on September 21', SN140/01, Brussels: European Council.

—— (2001c) 'Presidency Conclusions of the Laeken European Council, 14–15 December 2001', SN 300/1/01 Rev 1, Brussels: European Council.

—— (2002) 'Presidency Conclusions of the Seville European Council, 21–22 June 2002', SN 200/02, Brussels: European Council.

—— (2003a) 'Presidency Conclusions of the Thessaloniki European Council, 19–20 June 2003', Brussels: European Council.

—— (2003b) 'European Security Strategy: A Secure Europe in a Better World', Brussels: European Council.

—— (2004a) 'Presidency Conclusions of the Brussels European Council, 4–5 November 2004', D/04/5, Brussels: European Council.

—— (2004b) 'The Hague Programme: Strengthening Freedom, Security and Justice in the European Union', 16054/04, Brussels: European Council.

—— (2005) 'Emergency and Crisis Coordination Arrangements', Brussels: European Council.

—— (2008) 'Report on the Implementation of the European Security Strategy: Providing Security in a Changing World', S407/08, Brussels: European Council.

—— (2010a) 'The Stockholm Programme – An Open and Secure Europe Serving and Protecting Citizens', Brussels: European Council.

—— (2010b) 'Internal Security Strategy for the European Union: Towards a European Security Model', Luxembourg: Publications Office of the European Union.

European Court of Human Rights (2008a) 'Case of *Liberty and others* v. *the United Kingdom*', 1 October 2008.

—— (2008b) 'Case of S. and *Marper* v. *the United Kingdom*', 4 December 2008.

European Data Protection Supervisor (2007) 'Opinion of the European Data Protection Supervisor on the draft Proposal for a Council Framework Decision on the use of Passenger Name Record (PNR) data for law enforcement purposes', Brussels: European Data Protection Supervisor.

—— (2008) 'Preliminary Comments of the European Data Protection Supervisor on: Communication from the Commission to the European Parliament, the Council, the European Economic and Social Committee and the Committee of the Regions, "Preparing the next steps in border management in the European Union", COM(2008) 69 final; Communication from the Commission to the European Parliament, the Council, the European Economic and Social Committee and the Committee of the Regions, "Examining the creation of a European Border Surveillance System (EUROSUR)", COM(2008) 68 final; Communication from the Commission to the European Parliament, the Council, the European Economic and Social Committee and the Committee of the Regions, "Report on the evaluation and future development of the FRONTEX Agency", COM(2008) 67 final', Brussels: European Data Protection Supervisor.

—— (2009) 'Opinion of the European Data Protection Supervisor: on the proposal for a Regulation of the European Parliament and of the Council establishing an Agency for the operational management of large-scale IT systems in the area of freedom, security and justice; and on the proposal for a Council Decision conferring upon the Agency established by Regulation XX tasks regarding the operational management of SIS II and VIS in application of Title VI of the EU Treaty', Brussels: European Data Protection Supervisor.

European Parliament (2004) 'Report on the Proposal for a Council Regulation Establishing a European Agency for the Management of Operational Cooperation at the External Borders (COM (2003) 687 – C5–0613/2003–2003/0273 (CNS))', A5–0093/2004.

—— (2007a) 'European Parliament Resolution of 12 July 2007 on the PNR Agreement with the United States of America', P6_TA-PROV(2007)0347.

—— (2007b) 'European Parliament Resolution on SWIFT, the PNR Agreement and the transatlantic dialogue on these issues', P6_TA(2007)0039.

—— (2008) 'European Parliament Recommendation of 22 October 2008 to the Council concerning the conclusion of the Agreement between the European Union and Australia on the processing and transfer of European Union-sourced passenger name record (PNR) data by air carriers to the Australian customs service', P6_TA(2008)0512.

—— (2009) 'European Parliament Resolution of 17 September 2009 on the envisaged international agreement to make available to the United States Treasury Department financial payment messaging data to prevent and combat terrorism and terrorist financing', P7_TA(2009)0016.

—— (2010a) 'EU external strategy on passenger name record (PNR) – European Parliament Resolution of 11 November 2010 on the global approach to transfers of passenger name record (PNR) data to third countries, and on the recommendations from the Commission to the Council to authorise the opening of negotiations between the European Union and Australia, Canada and the United States', P7_TA-PROV(2010)0397.

—— (2010b) 'European Parliament Resolution of 5 May 2010 on the launch of negotiations for Passenger Name Record (PNR) Agreements with the United States, Australia and Canada', P7_TA(2010)0144.

European Security Research and Innovation Forum (2009) 'ESRIF Final Report', Brussels: European Commission.

European Union (n.d.) 'Agencies of the European Union: Community Agencies'. Online. Available at: http://europa.eu/agencies/community_agencies/index_en.htm (accessed 12 March 2009).

—— (2000) 'Council Regulation (EC) No 2725/2000 of 11 December 2000 Concerning the Establishment of "Eurodac" for the Comparison of Fingerprints for the Effective Application of the Dublin Convention', OJ L 316: 1–10.

—— (2001) 'Council Decision of 23 October 2001 establishing a Community Mechanism to Facilitate Reinforced Cooperation in Civil Protection Assistance Interventions (2001/792/EC, Euratom)', OJ L 297: 7–11.

—— (2004) 'Council Directive 2004/82/EC of 29 April 2004 on the Obligation of Carriers to Communicate Passenger Data', OJ L 261: 24–27.

—— (2005) 'Council Decision 2005/671/JHA of 20 September 2005 on the Exchange of Information and Cooperation concerning Terrorist Offences', OJ L 253: 22–24.

—— (2006a) 'Directive 2006/24/EC of the European Parliament and of the Council of 15 March 2006 on the Retention of Data Generated or Processed in Connection with the Provision of Publicly Available Electronic Communications Services or of Public Communications Networks and Amending Directive 2002/58/EC', OJ L 105: 54–63.

—— (2006b) 'Joint Press Release: First EU Emergency and Crisis Coordination Arrangement Exercise (CCA EX06)'. Available online at: www.consilium.europa.

eu/ueDocs/cms_Data/docs/pressData/en/misc/91480.pdf (accessed 15 December 2010).

—— (2007) 'Joint Press Release: Second EU Emergency and Crisis Coordination. Arrangements Exercise (CCA EX07)'. Available online at: www.consilium. europa.eu/ueDocs/cms_Data/docs/pressData/en/misc/95958.pdf (accessed 15 December 2010).

—— (2008) 'Regulation (EC) No 300/2008 of the European Parliament and of the Council of 11 March 2008 on Common Rules in the Field of Civil Aviation Security and Repealing Regulation (EC) No 2320/2002', OJ L 97: 72–84.

—— (2010a) 'Agreement between the EU and Canada on Passenger Name Record Data'. Available online at: http://ec.europa.eu/home-affairs/policies/police/police_pnr_canada_en.htm (accessed 13 December 2010).

—— (2010b) 'EU-US SWIFT Agreement'. Available online at: www.statewatch.org/news/2010/jun/eu-usa-draft-swift-agreement-com-final-2.pdf (accessed 17 November 2010).

Europol (2007) 'Europol 2006 Annual Report', The Hague: Europol.

—— (2009) 'Europol 2008 Annual Report', The Hague: Europol.

—— (2011) 'EU Terrorism Situation and Trend Report', The Hague: Europol.

Everson, M. (1995) 'Independent agencies: hierarchy beaters?', *European Law Journal*, 1(2): 180–204.

Everson, M., Majone, G., Metcalfe, L. and Schout, A. (1999) *The Role of Specialised Agencies in Decentralising EU Governance: Report Presented to the Commission*. Available online at: www.ec.europa.eu/governance/areas/group6/contribution_en.pdf (accessed 20 February 2008).

Fritzon, Å. and Ljungkvist, K. (2007) 'Protecting Europe's critical infrastructures: problems and prospects', *Journal of Contingencies and Crisis Management*, 15: 30–41.

Frontex (2007a) 'Frontex 2006 Annual Report', Warsaw: Frontex.

—— (2007b) 'BIOPASS: Study on automated biometric border crossing systems for registered passengers at four European airports', Warsaw: Frontex.

—— (2010a) 'Frontex General Report 2009', Warsaw: Frontex.

—— (2010b) 'Frontex to deploy 175 specialist border personnel to Greece', 29 October 2010. Available online at: www.frontex.europa.eu/newsroom/news_releases/art81.html (accessed 20 February 2011).

—— (2011) 'Hermes 2011 running', 22 February 2011. Available online at: www.frontex.europa.eu/newsroom/news_releases/art96.html (accessed 28 February 2011).

Fuster, G.G., De Hert, P. and Gutwirth, S. (2008) 'SWIFT and the vulnerability of transatlantic data transfers', *International Review of Law, Computers, and Technology*, 22(1): 191–202.

Gammeltoft-Hansen, T. (2009) *Access to Asylum: International Refugee Law and the Offshoring and Outsourcing of Migration Control*, Aarhus: Aarhus University Press.

General Accountability Office (2009a) 'Despite progress, DHS continues to be challenged in managing its multi-billion dollar annual investment in large-scale information technology systems', Statement of Randolph C. Hite, Director Information Technology Architecture and Systems Issues, testimony before the Subcommittee on Government Management, Organization, and Procurement, House Committee on Oversight and Government Reform, GAO-09–1002T.

—— (2009b) 'Key US-VISIT components at varying stages of completion, but integrated and reliable schedule needed', Report to Congressional Requesters, GAO-10–13, November 2009.

General Accountability Office (2010) 'DHS needs to reconsider its proposed investment in key technology program', Report to Congressional Requesters, GAO-10–340, May 2010.

General Court (2010) 'Judgment of the General Court of 30 September 2010, Case T-85/09 *Kadi v. Commission*', OJ C 317, 20 November 2010.

Geyer, F. (2008) 'Taking stock: databases and systems of information exchange in the Area of Freedom, Security and Justice', *CHALLENGE Research Paper No. 9*, Brussels: Centre for European Policy Studies.

Gourlay, C. (2006) 'Civil–civil co-ordination in EU crisis management', in A. Nowak (ed.) *Civilian Crisis Management: The EU Way, Chaillot Paper No. 90*, Paris: European Union Institute for Security Studies.

Gowan, R. (2005) 'The battlegroups: a concept in search of a strategy?', in S. Biscop (ed.) *E Pluribus Unum? Military Integration in the European Union, Egmont Paper No. 7*, Brussels: Royal Institute for International Relations.

Gray, C.S. (1999) *Modern Strategy*, Oxford: Oxford University Press.

Greenwood, R., Oliver, C., Sahlin, K. and Suddaby, R. (2008) 'Introduction', in R. Greenwood, C. Oliver, K. Sahlin and R. Suddaby (eds) (2008) *The SAGE Handbook of Organizational Institutionalism*, London: Sage Publications.

Grevi, G. (2009) 'ESDP Institutions', in G. Grevi, D. Helly and D. Keohane (eds) *European Security and Defence Policy: The First Ten Years (1999–2009)*, Paris: European Union Institute for Security Studies.

Groenleer, M. (2006) 'The European Commission and agencies', in D. Spence (ed.) *The European Commission*, 3rd edn, London: John Harper.

Guardian (2010) 'Hungary toxic sludge spill an "ecological catastrophe" says government', 5 October 2010.

Guild, E. (2003) 'International terrorism and EU immigration, asylum and border policy: the unexpected victims of 11 September 2001', *European Foreign Affairs Review*, 8(3): 331–46.

—— (2004) 'Seeking asylum: storm clouds between international commitments and EU legislative measures', *European Law Review*, 29(2): 198–218.

—— (2008) 'The uses and abuses of counter-terrorism policies in Europe: the case of the "terrorist lists"', *Journal of Common Market Studies*, 46(1): 173–193.

Guild, E. and Brouwer, E. (2006) 'The political life of data: the ECJ decision on the PNR Agreement between the EU and the US', *CEPS Policy Brief No. 109*, Brussels: Centre for European Policy Studies.

Guild, E. and Geyer, F. (eds) (2008) *Security versus Justice? Police and Judicial Cooperation in the European Union*, Aldershot: Ashgate.

Guild, E., Carrera, S. and Geyer, F. (2008) 'The Commission's new border package: does it take us one step closer to a "cyber-fortress Europe"?' *CEPS Policy Brief No. 154*, Brussels: Centre for European Policy Studies.

Haas, E. (1958) *The Uniting of Europe: Political, Social, and Economic Forces 1950–57*, Palo Alto, CA: Stanford University Press.

Haas, P.M. (1992) 'Introduction: epistemic communities and international policy coordination, *International Organization*, 46(1): 1–35.

Hailbronner, K., Papakonstantinou, V. and Kau, M. (2008) 'The Agreement on Passenger-Data Transfer (PNR) and the EU–US co-operation in data communication', *International Migration*, 46(2): 187–197.

Hansen, A. (2006) 'Against all odds – the evolution of planning for ESDP operations: civilian crisis management from EUPM onwards', *Studie 10/06*, Berlin: Zentrum für Internationale Friedenseinsätze.

Hayes, B. (2009) *NeoConOpticon: The EU Security-Industrial Complex*, Amsterdam: The Transnational Institute.

Hill, C. (2004) 'Renationalizing or regrouping? EU foreign policy since September 11', *Journal of Common Market Studies*, 42: 143–163.

Hobbing, P. (2005) 'Integrated Border Management at the EU level', *CEPS Working Document No. 227*, Brussels: Centre for European Policy Studies.

—— (2008) 'Tracing Terrorists: The EU-Canada Agreement in PNR Matters', Brussels: Centre for European Studies.

Hobbing, P. and Koslowski, R. (2009) 'The tools called to support the "delivery" of freedom, security and justice: a comparison of border security systems in the EU and in the US', Brussels: European Parliament.

Hoffman, B. (2006) *Inside Terrorism*, 2nd edn, New York, NY: Columbia University Press.

Howorth, J. (2005) 'From Security to defence: the evolution of the CFSP', in C. Hill and M. Smith (eds.) *International Relations and the European Union*, Oxford: Oxford University Press.

Hsu, S.S. (2009) 'Agencies clash on military's border role', *The Washington Post*, 28 June 2009.

Huysmans, J. (2006) *The Politics of Insecurity: Fear, Migration and Asylum in the European Union*, London: Routledge.

Joint Research Centre (2005) 'Research Strategy Paper "Emerging technologies in the context of "security"', issued in the framework of Science and Technology Foresight, Brussels: European Commission.

Joly, D. (1996) *Haven or Hell? Asylum Policies and Refuges in Europe*. Basingstoke: Macmillan.

Jordan, A. and Schout, A. (2006) *The Coordination of the European Union: Exploring the Capacities of Networked Governance*, Oxford: Oxford University Press.

Jorry, H. (2007) 'Construction of a European model for managing operational cooperation at the EU's external borders: is the Frontex Agency a decisive step forward?', *CHALLENGE Research Paper No. 6*, Brussels: Centre for European Policy Studies.

Kaldor, M., Martin, M. and Selchow, S. (2007) 'Human security: a new strategic narrative for Europe', *International Affairs*, 83(2): 273–288.

Kaunert, C. (2005) 'The Area of Freedom, Security and Justice: the construction of a "European public order", *European Security*, 14(4): 459–483.

—— (2007) '"Without the power of purse or sword": The European Arrest Warrant and the role of the Commission', *Journal of European Integration*, 29(4): 387–404.

Kaunert, C. (2009) 'Liberty versus security? EU asylum policy and the European Commission, *Journal of Contemporary European Research*, 5(2): 148–70.

—— (2010a) 'The external dimension of EU counterterrorism relations: competences, interests, and institutions', *Terrorism and Political Violence*, 22(1): 41–61.

—— (2010b) 'Europol and EU counterterrorism: international security actorness in the external dimension', *Studies in Conflict & Terrorism* 33(7): 652–671.

—— (2010c) *European Internal Security: Towards Supranational Governance in the Area of Freedom, Security and Justice?* Manchester: Manchester University Press.

Kaunert, C. and Della Giovanna, M. (2010) 'Post 9/11 EU counter-terrorist financing cooperation: differentiating supranational policy entrepreneurship by the Commission and the Council Secretariat', *European Security*, 19(2): 275–295.

Kaunert, C. and Léonard, S. (eds) (2010) *After the Stockholm Programme: An Area of Freedom, Security and Justice in the European Union?*, Special Issue of *European Security*, 19(2): 143–149.

Keck, M.E. and Sikkink, K. (1998) *Activists beyond Borders: Advocacy Networks in International Politics*, Ithaca, NY and London: Cornell University Press.

Kelemen, R.D. (2002) 'The politics of "Eurocratic" structure and the new European agencies', *West European Politics*, 25(4): 93–118.

Kennedy, P. (ed.) (1991) *Grand Strategies in War and Peace*, New Haven, CT: Yale University Press.

Keohane, D. (2005) *The EU and Counter-Terrorism*, London: Centre for European Reform.

—— (2006) 'Implementing the EU's Counter-terrorism Strategy: intelligence, emergencies and foreign policy', in D. Mahncke and J. Monar (eds) *International Terrorism: A European Response to a Global Threat?*, Brussels: P.I.E Peter Lang.

—— (2008) 'The absent friend: EU foreign policy and counter-terrorism', *Journal of Common Market Studies*, 46: 125–146.

Khol, R. (2006) 'Civil-military co-ordination in EU crisis management', in A. Nowak (ed.) *Civilian Crisis Management: The EU Way, Chaillot Paper No. 90*, Paris: European Union Institute for Security Studies.

Kirchner, E. and Sperling, J. (2002) 'The new security threats in Europe: theory and evidence', *European Foreign Affairs Review*, 7(4): 423–452.

Klingebiel, S. (ed.) (2006) *New Interfaces between Security and Development: Changing Concepts and Approaches*, Bonn: German Development Institute/DIE.

Koslowski, R. (2004a) 'International cooperation on electronic advanced passenger information transfer and passport biometrics'. Paper presented at the International Studies Association Convention, Montreal, 17–20 March 2004.

—— (2004b) *International Cooperation to Create Smart Borders*, Washington, DC: Woodrow Wilson International Center for Scholars.

Kratochwil, F. (2011) 'Of maps, law and politics: an inquiry into the changing meaning of territoriality', *DIIS Working Paper 2011/03*, Copenhagen: Danish Institute of International Studies.

Kurowska, X. (2008) 'The role of ESDP missions', in M. Merlingen and R. Ostrauskaite (eds) *European Security and Defence Policy: An Implementation Perspective*, London: Routledge.

Kurowska, X. and Kratochwil, F. (2012) 'The social constructivist sensibility and Common Security and Defence Policy research', in X. Kurowska and F. Breuer (eds) *Explaining the EU's Common Security and Defence Policy: Theory in Action*, Basingstoke: Palgrave Macmillan.

Kurowska, X. and Pawlak, P. (eds) (2009a) *The Politics of European Security Policies: Actors, Dynamics and Contentious Outcomes*, Special Issue of *Perspectives on European Politics and Society*, 10(4): 474–485.

Kurowska, X. and Pawlak, P. (2009b) 'The politics of European security policies: actors, dynamics and contentious outcomes', *Perspectives on European Politics and Society*, 10(4): 474–485.

Kurowska, X. and Seitz, T. (2011) 'The EU's role in international crisis management: innovative model or emulated script?', in E. Gross and A. Juncos (eds) *EU*

Conflict Prevention and Crisis Management: Roles, Institutions and Policies, New York and London: Routledge.

Kurowska, X. and Tallis, B. (2009) 'EU Border Assistance Mission to Moldova and Ukraine: beyond border monitoring?', *European Foreign Affairs Review*, 14(1): 47–64.

Ladenburger, C. (2008) 'Police and criminal law in the Treaty of Lisbon: a new dimension for the Community method', *European Constitutional Law Review*, 4: 20–40.

Laitinen, I. (2008) 'Shaping European security', *ASD Focus* 02 (Summer): 8.

Lavenex, S. (1999) *Safe Third Countries: Extending the EU Asylum and Immigration Policies to Central and Eastern Europe*, Budapest: Central European University Press.

Lavenex, S. and Wichmann, N. (2009) 'The external governance of EU internal security', *Journal of European Integration*, 31(1): 83–102.

Léonard, S. (2010) 'EU border security and migration into the European Union: FRONTEX and securitization through practices', *European Security*, 19(2): 231–254.

Liddell Hart, B. (1991) *Strategy*, 2nd revised edn, New York, NY: Meridian.

Linklater, A. (1998) *The Transformation of Political Community: Ethical Foundations of the Post-Westphalian Era*, Cambridge: Polity.

Ludlow, P. (2002) *The Seville Council*, Brussels: EuroComment.

Lugna, L. (2006) 'Institutional framework of the European Union counter-terrorism policy setting', *Baltic Security & Defence Review*, 8: 101–127.

Magnette, P. (2005) 'The politics of regulation in the European Union', in D. Geradin, R. Muñoz and N. Petit (eds) *Regulation through Agencies in the EU: A New Paradigm of European Governance*, Cheltenham: Edward Elgar.

Mair, P. (2005) 'Popular Democracy and the European Union Polity', *European Governance (EUROGOV) Paper C-05-03*. Available online at: www.connex-network. org/eurogov/pdf/egp-connex-C-05-03.pdf (accessed 5 June 2009).

Majone, G. (2006) 'Managing europeanisation: the European agencies', in J. Peterson and M. Shackleton (eds) *The Institutions of the European Union*, 2nd edn, Oxford: Oxford University Press.

Manners, I. (2006) 'European Union "normative power" and the security challenge', *European Security*, 15: 405–421.

Marenin, O. (2010) 'Challenges for Integrated Border Management in the European Union', *Occasional Paper No. 17*, Geneva: Geneva Centre for the Democratic Control of Armed Forces.

Martin, G. (2006) *Understanding Terrorism: Challenges, Perspectives, and Issues*, Thousand Oaks, CA: Sage Publications.

Matlary, J.H. (2006) 'When soft power turns hard: is an EU strategic culture possible?', *Security Dialogue*, 37(1): 105–121.

Mégie, A. (2004) 'Le 11 septembre: élément accélérateur de la coopération judiciaire européenne?', in P.K. Manning, C. Murphy and J.-P. Brodeur (eds) *Reconstruire la sécurité après le 11 septembre: la lutte antiterroriste entre affichage politique et mobilisation policière*, La Plaine Saint-Denis: Institut National des Hautes Etudes de Sécurité.

Menon, A. (2009) 'Empowering paradise? The ESDP at ten', *International Affairs*, 85(2): 227–246.

Meyer, J.W. and Rowan, B. (1977) 'Institutionalized organizations: formal structures as myth and ceremony', *American Journal of Sociology*, 83: 340–363.

Missiroli, A. (2006) 'Disasters past and present: new challenges for the EU', *Journal of European Integration*, 28(5): 423–436.

Mitsilegas, V. (2007) 'Border security in the European Union: towards centralised controls and maximum surveillance', in A. Baldaccini, E. Guild and H. Toner (eds) *Whose Freedom, Security and Justice? EU Immigration and Asylum Law and Policy*, Oxford: Hart.

Mitsilegas, V., Monar, J. and Rees, W. (2003) *The European Union and Internal Security: Guardian of the People?*, Basingstoke: Palgrave Macmillan.

Monar, J. (2005) 'The European Union's "integrated management" of external borders', in J. DeBardeleben (ed.) *Soft or Hard Borders? Managing the Divide in an Enlarged Europe*, Aldershot: Ashgate.

—— (2006a) 'Cooperation in the Justice and Home Affairs domain: characteristics, constraints and progress', *Journal of European Integration*, 28(5): 495–509.

—— (2006b) 'Conclusions: International terrorism – a "European response" to a global threat?', in D. Mahncke and J. Monar (eds) *International Terrorism: A European Response to a Global Threat?*, Brussels: P.I.E Peter Lang.

—— (2006c) 'The external shield of the Area of Freedom, Security and Justice: progress and deficits of the integrated management of external EU borders', in J.W. de Zwaan and F.A.N.J. Goudappel (eds) *Freedom, Security and Justice in the European Union: Implementation of the Hague Programme*, The Hague: T.M.C. Asser Press.

—— (2007) 'Common threat and common response? The European Union's counter-terrorism strategy and its problems', *Government and Opposition*, 42: 292–313.

—— (2010a) 'The EU's externalisation of internal security objectives: perspectives after Lisbon and Stockholm', *The International Spectator*, 45(2): 23–39.

—— (2010b) 'The rejection of the EU-US SWIFT Interim Agreement by the European Parliament: a historic view and its implications', *European Foreign Affairs Review*, 15(2): 143–151.

Moravcsik, A. (1998) *The Choice for Europe: Social Purpose & State Power from Messina to Maastricht*, Ithaca, NY: Cornell University Press.

—— (1999) 'A new statecraft? Supranational entrepreneurs and international cooperation', *International Organization*, 53(2): 267–306.

Mueller, J. (2005) 'Simplicity and spook: terrorism and the dynamics of threat exaggeration', *International Studies Perspectives*, 6: 208–234.

Müller-Wille, B. (2008) 'The effect of international terrorism on EU intelligence co-operation', *Journal of Common Market Studies*, 46(1): 49–73.

Myrdal, S. and Rhinard, M. (2010) 'The European Union's solidarity clause: empty letter or effective tool? An analysis of Article 222 of the Treaty on the Functioning of the European Union', *UI Occasional Paper No. 2*, Stockholm: Swedish Institute of International Affairs.

Naylor, R.T. (2006) *Satanic Purses: Money, Myth, and Misfortune in the War on Terror*, Montreal and Kingston: McGill-Queen's University Press.

Neal, A.W. (2009) 'Securitization and risk at the EU border: the origins of FRONTEX', *Journal of Common Market Studies*, 47(2): 333–356.

Nowak, A. (2006) 'Civilian crisis management within ESDP', in A. Nowak (ed.) *Civilian Crisis Management: the EU Way, Chaillot Paper No. 90*, Paris: European Union Institute for Security Studies.

Number 10 (2011) 'PM's Speech at Munich Security Conference', 5 February

2011. Online. Available online at: www.number10.gov.uk (accessed 10 February 2011).

Nuttall S. (2001) '"Consistency" and the CFSP: a categorization and its consequences', *Working Paper 2013*, London: London School of Economics and Political Science, European Foreign Policy Unit.

—— (2005) 'Coherence and Consistency', in C. Hill and M. Smith (eds.) *International Relations and the European Union*, Oxford: Oxford University Press.

Occhipinti, J. (2010) 'Partner or pushover? EU relations with the US on internal security', in D. Hamilton (ed.) *Shoulder to Shoulder: Forging a Strategic US–EU Partnership*, Washington DC: Johns Hopkins University Centre for Transatlantic Relations.

O'Neill, M. (2008) 'A critical analysis of the EU legal provisions on terrorism', *Terrorism and Political Violence*, 20(1): 26–48.

Pawlak, P. (2007) 'From hierarchy to networks: transatlantic governance of homeland security', *Journal of Global Change and Governance* 1(1): 1–22.

—— (2009a) 'Transatlantic networks and transatlantic homeland security cooperation', *Perspectives on European Politics and Society*, 10(4): 560–581.

—— (2009b) 'The external dimension of the Area of Freedom, Security and Justice: hijacker or hostage of cross-pillarization?, *Journal of European Integration*, 31(1): 25–44.

—— (2009c) *Made in the USA? The Influence of the US on the EU's Data Protection Regime*, Brussels: Centre for European Policy Studies.

—— (2010a) 'Made in the USA? The impact of transatlantic norms on the European Union's data protection regime', in M.B. Salter (ed.) *Mapping Transatlantic Security Relations: The EU, Canada and the War on Terror*, London: Routledge.

—— (2010b) 'Transatlantic homeland security cooperation: the art of balancing internal security objectives with foreign policy concerns', in M. Cebeci (ed.) *Issues in European Union and U.S. Foreign Policy*, Lanham: Lexington.

—— (2010c) 'Transatlantic homeland security cooperation: the promise of new modes of governance in international affairs', *Journal of Transatlantic Studies* 8(2): 142–160.

Peers, S. (2009) 'The "third pillar acquis" after the Treaty of Lisbon enters into force', *Statewatch Report*, London: Statewatch.

Peers, S. and Rogers, N. (eds) (2006) *EU Immigration and Asylum Law: Text and Commentary*, Leiden: Martinus Nijhoff.

Poincignon, Y. (2004) 'Aviation civile et terrorisme: naissance et enjeux d'une politique européenne de sûreté des transports aériens', *Cultures & Conflits*, 56: 83–119.

Pollak, J. and Slominski, P. (2009) 'Experimentalist but not accountable governance? The role of FRONTEX in managing the EU's external borders', *West European Politics* 32(5): 904–924.

Présidence de la République Française (2008) *White Paper on Defence and National Security*, Paris: Présidence de la République Française.

Presidency of the Council of the European Union (2001) 'Presidency Conclusions of the European Council Meeting in Laeken, 14 and 14 December 2001', SN 300/1/01 REV 1, Brussels: Presidency of the Council of the European Union.

PRO ASYL (2008) 'Petition to the European Parliament: Year by year thousands die at Europe's borders. Stop the deathtrap at the EU borders', Frankfurt: PRO ASYL, 10 December 2008. Available online at: www.proasyl.de/fileadmin/

proasyl/fm_redakteure/Kampagnen/Stoppt_das_Sterben/Petition_engl..pdf (accessed 1 June 2010).

Quille, G. (2004) 'The European Security Strategy: a framework for EU security interests?', *International Peacekeeping*, 11(3): 422–438.

Rees, W. (2006) *Transatlantic Counter-terrorism Co-operation: The New Imperative*, London: Routledge.

—— (2008) 'Inside out: the external face of EU internal security policy', *Journal of European Integration*, 30(1): 97–111.

Relyea, H. (2002a) 'Homeland security: the concept and the Presidential Coordination Office – first assessment', *Presidential Studies Quarterly*, 32(2): 397–411.

—— (2002b) 'Homeland security and information', *Government Information Quarterly*, 19: 213–223.

Rhinard, M. (2009) 'European cooperation on future crises: toward a public good?', *Review of Policy Research*, 26: 439–455.

Rijpma, J.J. (2009) 'EU border management after the Lisbon Treaty'. Ppaper presented at the Jean Monnet Seminar, Advanced Issues of European Law, 7th Session on 'Boundaries of EU Law after the Lisbon Treaty', 19–26 April 2009, IUC Dubrovnik. Available online at: www.pravo.hr/_download/repository/Jorrit_Rijpma.doc (accessed 5 July 2009).

Rhinard, M. (2009) 'European cooperation on future crises: toward a public good?', *Review of Policy Research*, 26: 439–455.

Rosati, J.A. (2004) *The Politics of United States Foreign Policy*, Belmont, CA: Wadsworth/Thomson Learning.

Schmitt, B. (2005) 'European Capabilities Action Plan (ECAP)'. Factsheet, updated May 2005, Paris: EU Institute for Security Studies.

Schroeder, U.C. (2009) 'Strategy by stealth: the development of EU Internal and External Security Strategies', *Perspectives on European Politics and Society*, 10(4): 486–505.

Seiffarth, O. (2010) 'The development of the European Border Surveillance System (EUROSUR)'. Paper presented at the conference on Surveillance Technology for Border Control, Warsaw, 24 May 2010.

Seiple, C. (2002) 'The new protracted conflict: homeland security concepts and strategy', *Orbis*, 46(2): 259–273.

Selznick, P. (1948) 'Foundations of the theory of organization', *American Sociological Review*, 13(1): 25–35.

Serrano, J. (2010a) 'Seahorse'. Paper presented at the conference on Surveillance Technology for Border Control, Warsaw, 24 May 2010.

—— (2010b) 'SIVE', presented at the Conference on Surveillance Technology for Border Control, Warsaw, 24 May 2010.

Smith, A.D. (1981) 'States and homelands: the social and geopolitical implications of national territory', *Millennium: Journal of International Studies*, 10(3): 187–202.

Spanish Presidency of the Council of the European Union (2010) 'The JHA in Toledo focuses on Internal Security Strategy and the fight against terrorism', Brussels: Council of the European Union, 18 January 2010.

Spence, D. (2007) 'Introduction: international terrorism – the quest for a coherent EU response', in D. Spence (ed.) *The European Union and Terrorism*, London: John Harper.

Stevens, A. and Stevens, H. (2001) *Brussels Bureaucrats? The Administration of the European Union*, Basingstoke: Palgrave Macmillan.

Strachan, H. (2005) 'The lost meaning of strategy', *Survival*, 47(3): 33–54.

Study Group on Europe's Security Capabilities (2004) 'A human security doctrine for Europe: the Barcelona Report of the Study Group on Europe's Security Capabilities'. Available online at: www.consilium.europa.eu/uedocs/cms_data/docs/pressdata/solana/040915capbar.pdf (accessed on 2 January 2011).

SWIFT (2010) 'Company information'. Available online at: www.swift.com/about_swift/company_information/index.page?lang=en (accessed 21 December 2010).

Tallberg, J. (2002) 'Delegation to supranational institutions: why, how, and with what consequences?', *West European Politics*, 25(1): 23–46.

The Future Group (2008) 'Freedom, Security, Privacy – European Home Affairs in an Open World: Report of the Informal High Level Advisory Group on the Future of European Home Affairs Policy ("The Future Group")', June 2008. Available online at: www.statewatch.org/news/2008/jul/eu-futures-jha-report.pdf (accessed 5 February 2011).

The White House (2001a) 'Address by President George W. Bush to a joint session of Congress and to the American people', 20 September 2001, Washington, DC: Office of the Press Secretary.

—— (2001b) 'Homeland Security Presidential Directive-2: Combating Terrorism through Immigration Policies', 29 November 2001, Washington, DC: The White House.

—— (2002a) 'National Strategy for Homeland Security', Washington, DC: Office for Homeland Security.

—— (2002b) 'Smart borders for the 21st century', 25 January 2002, Washington, DC: Office of the Press Secretary.

—— (2002c) 'US–Canada Action Plan for creating a secure and smart border', 12 December 2001, Washington, DC: Office of Homeland Security.

—— (2002d) 'Smart border: 22 Point Agreement – US–Mexico Border Partnership Action Plan, 21 March 2002, Washington, DC: Office of the Press Secretary.

—— (2002e) 'President of the United States George W. Bush: The Department of Homeland Security', June 2002, Washington, DC: The White House.

—— (2002f) 'The National Security Strategy of the United States of America', September 2002, Washington, DC: The White House.

—— (2010) 'National Security Strategy', May 2010, Washington, DC: The White House.

Toje, A. (2005) 'The 2003 European Union Security Strategy: a critical appraisal', *European Foreign Affairs Review*, 10: 117–133.

Trauner, F. and Krause, I. (2008) 'EC Visa Facilitation and Readmission Agreements: implementing a new EU security approach in the neighbourhood', *CEPS Working Document No. 290*, Brussels: Centre for European Studies.

Uçarer, E.M. (2001) 'Managing asylum and European integration: expanding spheres of exclusion?', *International Studies Perspectives*, 2(3): 288–304.

UK Cabinet Office (2008) 'The National Security Strategy of the United Kingdom: Security in an Interdependent World', *Cm 7291*, London: UK Cabinet Office.

UK Department for Transport Aviation Directorate (2007) 'Memorandum by Department for Transport Aviation Directorate'. London: Department for Transport Aviation Directorate. Online. Available online at: www.publications.parliament.uk/pa/ld200607/ldselect/ldeucom/108/108we03.htm (accessed 27 December 2010).

UK House of Lords (2003) 'EU/US Agreements on Extradition and Mutual Legal

Assistance', *European Union Committee 38th Report of Session 2002–03*, HL Paper 153, London: HMSO.

—— (2004) 'Judicial cooperation in the EU: the role of Eurojust', *European Union Committee 23rd Report of Session 2003–04*, HL Paper 138, London: HMSO.

—— (2005) 'After Madrid: the EU's response to terrorism', *European Union Committee 5th Report of Session 2004–05*, HL Paper 53, London: HMSO.

—— (2008a) 'FRONTEX: the EU External Borders Agency', *European Union Committee 9th Report of Session 2007–08*, HL Paper 60, London: HMSO.

—— (2008b) 'The Treaty of Lisbon: an impact assessment', *European Union Committee 10th Report of Session 2007–08*, HL Paper 62, London: HMSO.

—— (2008c) 'The Passenger Name Record (PNR) Framework Decision', *European Union Committee 15th Report of Session 2007–08*, HL Paper 106, Session 2007–2008, London: HMSO.

—— (2008d) 'EUROPOL: coordinating the fight against serious and organised crime', *European Union Committee 29th Report of Session 2007–08*, HL Paper 183, London: HMSO.

—— (2008e) 'Adapting the EU's approach to today's security challenges – the Review of the 2003 European Security Strategy', *European Union Committee 31st Report of Session 2007–08*, HL Paper 190, London: HMSO.

US 9/11 Commission (2004) 'The 9/11 Commission Report', Washington, DC: US 9/11 Commission.

US Bureau of Customs and Border Protection (2008) 'Container Security Initiative'. Available online at: www.cbp.gov/xp/cgov/newsroom/fact_sheets/trade_security/csi.xml (accessed 14 December 2010).

US Department of Homeland Security (2002) 'Fact sheet: border security – securing America's borders', 25 January 2002. Available online at: www.dhs.gov/xnews/releases/press_release_0052.shtm (accessed 16 January 2011).

—— (2007) 'Remarks by Secretary Michael Chertoff to the Johns Hopkins University Paul H. Nitze School of Advanced International Studies', Washington, DC, 3 May 2007.

—— (2008) 'Brief documentary history of the Department of Homeland Security 2001–2008', Washington, DC: US Department of Homeland Security, History Office.

US Homeland Security Council (2007) 'The National Homeland Security Strategy', Washington, DC: Office of the President of the United States.

Van Buuren, J. (2009) *Secret Truth: The EU Joint Situation Centre*, Amsterdam: Eurowatch.

Vennesson, P. and Büger, C. (2009) 'Coping with insecurity in fragile situations'. Paper presented at the conference on Moving towards the European Report on Development 2009 organized by the European Report on Development, Florence, Italy, 21–23 June 2009, Florence: European Report on Development.

Verbruggen, F. (2004) 'Bull's eye? Two remarkable EU framework decisions in the fight against terrorism', in P.K. Manning, C. Murphy and J.-P. Brodeur (eds) *Legal Instruments in the Fight Against International Terrorism: A Transatlantic Dialogue*, Leiden: Martinus Nijhoff.

Wendling, C. (2010) 'L'approche globale dans la gestion civilo-militaire des crises: analyse critique et prospective du concept', *Cahier de l'IRSEM No. 6*, Paris: Institut de recherche stratégique de l'école militaire.

Wennerholm, P., Brattberg, E. and Rhinard, M. (2010) 'The EU as a counter-terrorism actor abroad: finding the opportunities, overcoming constraints', *European Policy Centre Issue Paper No. 60*, Brussels: European Policy Centre.

Wilks, S. with Bartle, I. (2002) 'The unanticipated consequences of creating independent competition agencies', *West European Politics*, 25(1): 148–172.

Wolff, S. (2009) 'The Mediterranean dimension of EU counter-terrorism', *Journal of European Integration*, 31(1): 137–156.

—— (2010) 'EU border management beyond Lisbon: contrasting policies and practice', in R. Zapata-Barrero (ed.) *Shaping the Normative Contours of the European Union: A Migration-border Framework*, Barcelona: CIDOB Foundation.

Wolff, S., Wichmann, N. and Mounier, G. (eds) (2009a) *The External Dimension of Justice and Home Affairs: A Different Security Agenda for the EU?*, Special Issue of *Journal of European Integration*, 31(1): 9–23.

Wolff, S., Wichmann, N. and Mounier, G. (2009b) 'The external dimension of Justice and Home Affairs: a different security agenda for the EU?', *Journal of European Integration*, 31(1): 9–23.

Youngs, R. (2008) 'Fusing security and development: just another Euro-platitude?, *Journal of European Integration*, 30(3): 419–437.

Zapata-Barrero, R. (ed.) (2010) *Shaping the Normative Contours of the European Union: A Migration-border Framework*, Barcelona: CIDOB Foundation.

Zimmermann, D. (2006) 'The European Union and post-9/11 counter-terrorism: a reappraisal', *Studies in Conflict and Terrorism*, 29(2): 123–145.

Index

Page numbers in *italics* denote tables, those in **bold** denote figures.